Site Dance

Site Dance

Choreographers and the Lure of Alternative Spaces

Edited by Melanie Kloetzel and Carolyn Pavlik

University Press of Florida

Gainesville Tallahassee Tampa Boca Raton Pensacola Orlando Miami Jacksonville Ft. Myers Sarasota

18 17 16 15 14   7 6 5 4 3 2

First cloth printing, 2009
First paperback printing, 2010

Library of Congress Cataloging-in-Publication Data
Site dance: choreographers and the lure of alternative spaces/edited by Melanie Kloetzel
and Carolyn Pavlik.
p. cm.
Includes bibliographical references and index.
ISBN 978-0-8130-3400-3 (cloth)
ISBN 978-0-8130-3693-9 (papberback)
1. Choreographers—United States—Interviews. 2. Choreography. 3. Dance—Stage-setting
and scenery. I. Kloetzel, Melanie. II. Pavlik, Carolyn.
GV1785.A1S58 2009
792.8'20929–dc22   2009022469

The University Press of Florida is the scholarly publishing agency for the State University System
of Florida, comprising Florida A&M University, Florida Atlantic University, Florida Gulf Coast
University, Florida International University, Florida State University, New College of Florida,
University of Central Florida, University of Florida, University of North Florida, University
of South Florida, and University of West Florida.

University Press of Florida
15 Northwest 15th Street
Gainesville, FL 32611–2079
http://www.upf.com

Contents

Illustrations

Foreword

Site Dance has given me the great pleasure of visiting with old friends and new, in the world of site-specific dance. When I started Dancing in the Streets in 1984, I hadn't a clue of the power of the medium nor of the inner strength of the artists who defy all reasonable odds to make it happen. What is odd to me is that (to my knowledge) there are no books that attempt to capture either the theory or the practice of this extraordinarily effective "field." It is strange, too—more than 30 years after Trisha Brown walked down the side of a building and Meredith Monk performed in a parking lot—how little government or private support is available for this utterly transforming genre of performance.

At a retreat Dancing in the Streets organized for site artists in the early 1990s, artist Ann Carlson commented that, like the visual art world, practitioners of site-specific performance need to create a critical language of their own. Without such a vocabulary, there would be no critical discourse, and the artists who make such adventurous work would never be considered seriously. It is therefore with great affection, admiration, and gratitude that I invite you into this very special book by Melanie Kloetzel and Carolyn Pavlik. Finally someone has begun to capture the voices, stories, observations, successes, theories, and working methods of the pioneering artists who have embarked on this integrated civic and artistic adventure. May this be the first of many volumes that puts site-specific dance into the realm of serious art and social critique.

My memory is location-based, and reading these interviews has prompted a flood of recollections, many of which I had the pleasure of experiencing first-hand. Even the logistical nightmares come back as delightful: the overwhelming smell of kerosene from a generator warming the crowd in a Civil War–era warehouse on a freezing November day in Red Hook for Martha Bowers's *On the Waterfront*; the brave audience withstanding post-hurricane winds on the Coney Island boardwalk to watch a struggling tech crew hold together Elizabeth Streb's set for *Rebound* in which dancers hurtled from wall to wall; Sun Ra spinning like a dervish in layers of sparkling polyester on a 104-degree day in Astoria, Queens, calming the overheated, near-rioting crowd. Hundreds and thousands of people from all walks of life have had transforming experiences—from Joanna Haigood's rappelling down a grain terminal in Minneapolis's Powderhorn Park, to the "moving stained glass" created by Stephan Koplowitz and Tony Giovannetti in Grand Central Terminal's Vanderbilt Windows; from the haunting tableaux vivants staged by Ann Carlson in Chelsea and again in Montana; to Meredith Monk's death parade past the abandoned smallpox hospital on Roosevelt Island at the end of *American Archaeology*; or to Sara Pearson and Patrik Widrig's magical water toss on a steaming day at Wave Hill. From our very first production, we knew that if an audience stayed in the rain, we had a success, and it was proved again as a wet throng sat silently along the Delaware River in a rainstorm to watch Eiko & Koma slowly float past. One shouldn't underestimate the superhuman powers of artists when it comes to weather.

These moments of heightened reality are seared in the imagination of their spectators and have indelibly marked the places they have touched. Regardless of the artist, the context, or the location, there are strong commonalities and recurring themes found in each interview and tale. Multiple times one reads about how site-specific performance has changed the artists' (and audiences') perceptions of a place; how both history and physicality affect the way a piece resonates in its space; that rehearsing and performing outside the theater engages all manner of people—from homeless people to CEOs; that the logistical challenges are often more daunting than the artistic ones; that the degree of risk involved in "making" one of these works is perhaps greater than any other single artistic endeavor. Yet these artists are drawn back, like moths to flame, and their diverse audiences continue to be engaged in ways that defy replication in traditional venues.

The Hebrew word for space, *Makom*, is one of the ways of saying God's name. The artists in this volume are shamans, helping us to register beauty and history, using movement to imbue these places with joy, leading us to new realizations within the everyday, and bringing us to transcendent moments in our ordinary lives. *Makom* indeed.

Elise Bernhardt

Preface

Site Dance consists of a collection of artists who seem to relish frustration. Negotiating with government officials, police, community members, and business owners or struggling with potentially dangerous equipment or landscapes, site-specific choreographers venture on arduous artistic quests to create work in some of the most unlikely places. Yet, whether those places are subway terminals or abandoned jails, river barges or rose gardens, they shoulder such challenges with remarkable poise.

When Carolyn Pavlik and I first started researching site-specific dance, we couldn't help wondering at these feats. After all, how is it that Joanna Haigood managed to convince the San Francisco municipal authorities that it would be okay for her dancers to rappel off the side of a city building? What would induce Eiko and Koma Otake to spend long hours in icy cold rivers, streams, and lakes to convey their artistic thoughts on water? Why did Marylee Hardenbergh take on the challenge of not one but seven simultaneous site performances along the Mississippi River? This book offers some insight into how these artists accomplish such tasks. As these site choreographers discuss their artistic journeys, we are reminded of the value of perseverance in the face of daunting obstacles. The details of their performance projects tell us much about artistic determination and the impressive results that can be achieved with such determination.

After 40-odd years of stumbling upon dancers lining the walls of a museum or taking over the staircase at the public library, we feel it is time to investigate the artists behind such exploits. Until now, site-specific choreographers have rarely been asked to talk about their endeavors, and examinations of their performances seldom tiptoe across the pages of dance, theater, and performance studies journals. Enter *Site Dance*, a book that informs us about the process and production of site works over the past four decades. *Site Dance* delves into performances ranging from Meredith Monk's earliest site works in Manhattan museums to Heidi Duckler's more recent forays in a Los Angeles Laundromat; as such, *Site Dance* gives us vital primary source material to inform the scholarly discourse developing around performance and place. As the 16 American artists included in this text contemplate their creative efforts, we discover the different processes that site choreographers employ. We find out what compelled these artists to find a way of working outside the norm, why site dance developed when it did, and what continues to make it relevant in our current cultural framework.

But this is not just a book for scholars and theorists. This is also a book for artists and activists, for community leaders and organizers, and even for the unsuspecting passerby who is lured into the spectacle of site art. Leah Stein's journey among the weeds of an urban parking lot can offer us new possibilities for engaging with place. Jo Kreiter's collaboration with muralists in the Mission District of San Francisco demonstrates the joys of joining artistic disciplines. Martha Bowers's description of her work with immigrant populations in Ireland inspires new avenues for activating community. As a whole, these artists' insights contribute valuable information to those of us who wish to create, participate in, observe, or analyze public art in our communities. Their explanations regarding motivation, inspiration, process, and performance allow us to advance the discussion about the import and impact of dance on site.

In short, this book provides a foundation for an informed conversation about the genre of site-specific dance. Dancers and choreographers are quite familiar with people analyzing their work—critics, producers, granting agencies, and the like—who have little understanding of what they do. As Brenda Dixon Gottschild has pointed out in her examination of the black dancing body in American culture, those from outside an art form or cultural practice who wish to analyze it often make the mistake of "comparing pigs to fish."[1] In other words, people have a tendency to judge one form based on the standards of another. This tendency presents itself when ballet or modern dance critics attempt to evaluate site-specific dance. Assuming that site work can be examined for the same technical and performance goals as modern dance works for the stage, many critics dismiss the often very different interests of the site choreographer. They ignore the context of the work and focus solely on choreographic details as if surrounded by the blank slate of the theater space.

Site Dance forbids such indifference to place. As choreographers with hands-on expertise discuss their connections to varied sites, they envelop us in the elation as well as the tribulation of place. They take us to the green expanses of urban parks, to stunning mountainsides, and to the filthy coal chutes of a defunct factory. They send us swinging off industrial cranes, prancing through fountains, and scrambling up the sheer sides of a billboard. We may find ourselves reflecting on painful present circumstances, while also catching a glimpse of a far distant past; we may laugh at the impish behavior of children at play, while questioning the presumptions about appropriate public behaviors.

It is for love of these experiences that we have created this book. Carolyn and I do not approach this material lightly. We too have explored the ditches, risked the heights, and cavorted among the weeds. We became fascinated by site-specific dance early in our careers. After graduating from our respective universities and beginning our choreographic and performance careers, we both found ourselves engaged by choreographers who had an interest in site work. Through the years, in our performances of site work (with Sally Jacques, Leah Stein, and Ann Carlson) as well as in our own choreography of site work (in places as wide-ranging as a bridge over the Gowanus Canal in Brooklyn to an old train depot in Pocatello, Idaho), we have developed a deep appreciation for this genre. Even while breaking out in hives from rolling down grassy slopes or being attacked by fire ants in a dilapidated house, we never veered from our dedication to and belief in this work.

Along the way, we have come across site choreographers from all corners of the nation. Many are included in this book; however, it is impossible to cover all of the extraordinary work that exists on site. Of the 16 choreographers who are included, all have made a long-term commitment to making work outside the confines of the traditional theater space. Yet these 16 artists also demonstrate the remarkable diversity within the field. Some have chosen to specialize in work that adapts to multiple sites, while others believe that connecting to one site over a long period of time is the best way of creating a lasting impact. Some feel no pull toward the traditional theater, while others move readily between stage and site. Some have been making site work for many decades, and some are barely into their second decade. The choreographers come from all parts of the country and represent a spectrum of racial, ethnic, and socioeconomic groups. Yet, for all their diversity, all 16 have embraced site-specific dance as a vital form of expression, and all of them have created site work that has left a significant impression on their chosen sites and communities.

By no means does this collection presume to offer a complete picture of the site-specific dance genre. Luckily for us, site choreographers continue to crop up in a variety of venues across the United States and around the world. But we feel it is time to get an initial portrait of the American artists who have helped define this exciting form. We hope you enjoy this first journey through the site dance gallery.

Note

1. Gottschild, "Some Thoughts on Choreographing History," 170.

Acknowledgments

When creating a collection such as this, the task can seem incredibly daunting. After all, who in their right mind would put 16 independent and determined artistic directors together with two highly persistent artist-editors and expect any end result, much less a successful one? Luckily, we had much help as well as inspiration along the way to make this collection come to fruition. First and foremost, the artists featured in this book have been remarkable in terms of their knowledge, support, and flexibility. We would like, above all, to thank Olive Bieringa, Martha Bowers, Ann Carlson, Heidi Duckler, Merridawn Duckler, Joanna Haigood, Marylee Hardenbergh, Sally Jacques, Jo Kreiter, Stephan Koplowitz, Meredith Monk, Eiko Otake, Sara Pearson, Otto Ramstad, Tamar Rogoff, Leah Stein, and Patrik Widrig for providing their insights with such generosity. Working with them has been an enlightening and exciting experience for both Carolyn and me.

In addition, Elise Bernhardt, the founder of Dancing in the Streets and currently the executive director of the National Foundation for Jewish Culture, has been very helpful and encouraging throughout the process. She gave us excellent insider's information, and we are grateful for her foreword, which grounds this book, as well as for the many years that she dedicated her life to supporting site works around the world. Others were also instrumental in the realization of this book; we would like to thank Aviva Davidson as well as the many supporters, producers, company members, and staff of The House, Collage Dance Theatre, Blue Lapis Light, Eiko & Koma, Dance Theatre Etcetera, and Dancing in the Streets. We are also deeply indebted to the photographers who contributed photos of the pieces discussed; their generosity is humbling and much appreciated.

Owing to the large number of contributors and the subsequent organization that such a collection entails, we also would like to thank the following people for their feedback at critical times: Sharon Friedler, Ann Daly, Jan Cohen-Cruz, Susan Foster, Ann Cooper Albright, Joan Herrington, Andrew Lilley, Greg Nicholl, and Brian Norman. We would like to express our gratitude to the director of UPF, Meredith Morris-Babb, our project editor, Jacqueline Kinghorn Brown, and our copy editor, Elaine Durham Otto, whose guidance has proven invaluable. And, of course, our production crew at UPF were extremely helpful during the entire process.

Finally, we would like to thank Andy and Anne as well as young Eli Pavlik, who, through the years of trials and tribulations that this book entailed, stuck by us and were supportive even in the stickiest of moments.

Introduction

The intersections of nature, culture, history, and ideology form the ground on which we stand—our land, our place, the local. The lure of the local is the pull of place that operates on each of us, exposing our politics and our spiritual legacies. It is the geographical component of the psychological need to belong somewhere, one antidote to a prevailing alienation.

Lucy Lippard, *The Lure of the Local*

Walking down the street, lost in thought about tomorrow's job woes or this weekend's possibilities, you start in surprise. A woman dressed in a stylish business suit is rolling down the sidewalk directly in your path. She pauses, balancing on one hip, just as a crowd of people hurtle past her and into a vacant lot. They disappear behind a clump of weeds and then scramble up a crumbling wall; they leap onto a dirt pile and freeze like children at play. You notice a strange faded mural on the wall of the lot as well as a cluster of wildflowers sprouting from the base of the pile of dirt. Brought back to the awareness of the present, you start to observe other people and their surprised reactions. You hear conversations erupt around you about other remarkable experiences—marriage proposals, street protests, a Mardi Gras festival—that may have happened at this particular spot, a spot that barely registered in your consciousness until just this second. Your busy feet pause in their careless flight, and you find yourself watching and marveling in the moment.

This might be your experience when first witnessing site-specific dance. Unusual movement in a public place will capture your eye, call your attention to the present, and expand your awareness of your surroundings. Is this a new phenomenon? Not exactly. For more than 40 years, such dances have been cropping up on skyscrapers, in alleyways, on trains, and in other unexpected locations across the nation. In basic terms, *site-specific* refers to the fact that these dances take a particular place as both the inspiration and setting for the dance. In other words, instead of dances that are made in a studio and then placed on the blank slate of a theater stage, site-specific dances use alternative spaces from drainage ditches to hotel lobbies to shape and inform the movement, spacing, theme, costuming, music, etc., for a given performance. Such performances and the people who create them are the subject of this book.

Site Dance is the first anthology to examine site-specific dance. Although the genre is not new, site-specific dance and its creators have received minimal treatment in text. *Site Dance* is part of a growing movement to reverse this trend. Through a collection of interviews and essays, this book offers a forum for 16 renowned American site choreographers to discuss their work. It provides first-hand descriptions of site-specific dance from those who have committed themselves to the practice, and it contributes vital theoretical and practical information to scholars, practitioners, and audiences invested in the genre.

As these 16 artists represent themselves in text, we become acquainted with the particulars of creating and producing site dance. We encounter the difficulties of the form as well as the surprising successes. We begin to see the allure of the site-specific practice. Most of all, we gain insight into that crucial question: Why work on site? With theater spaces growing more state-of-the-art by the moment in terms of both architecture and technology, what would possess the site choreographer to turn to the capricious whims of inclement weather, insurance permits, and potentially dangerous surfaces to create their work?

The Site Choreographer

In an era of globalization, local places often get lost in the shuffle. Homogenization surrounds us; we can frequent Wal-Mart in every town across the nation, and our identical TV screens may seem more like home than our kitchens. Yet, while many of us get lost in the latest virtual reality game available from New York to Hong Kong or the next indistinguishable chain store to venture into our neighborhood, the site artist zeroes in on local idiosyncrasies. This is because local places are the touchstone, muse, and medium for site artists. These artists examine our neighborhood haunts at length, taking in all the visual and sensual details of a site. Site choreographers, for example, can be found physically investigating a place. They may conduct extensive research into the historical manifestations of the site; they may interview the current residents about their relationship to the place. Then, after all these efforts and meditations, they create artwork that is relevant to *that* place and *that* community. Through the site choreographer's "reading" of our local places physically, sensually, intellectually, and emotionally, they are able to provide a performative translation of place that heightens our awareness of our surroundings. As they put our local parks, buildings, rivers, or thoroughfares at center stage, we rediscover the issues, people, and places that make our home environments unique.

Yet site artists do not only want us to see where we live; they also want us to engage with it. To cultivate such engagement, the site choreographer encourages, and sometimes even compels, us to experience space in novel ways. Using unusual and/or surprising techniques in their processes and performances, they foster physical exchanges between audience and place. For example, in many site pieces, audience members must constantly reposition themselves in space just to continue watching the performance. In Leah Stein's work *Return*, performed along the Manayunk Canal outside of Philadelphia, audience members had to pick their way along an unfrequented and deteriorating part of the canal to view the performance; to the audience's surprise, they found themselves gazing at decaying stone walls, peering through dark underpasses, and pondering the relations between dancers and weeds in an overgrown lot. These were spaces that audience members would rarely see in their typical route through the gentrifying town of Manayunk. In Heidi Duckler's *Mother Ditch*, which was performed in the Los Angeles River in 1995, audience members from the west side of the river physically crossed to the east side for the performance, a crossing that might rarely be made in their everyday lives due to the assumptions regarding the neighborhoods on the other side. These kinds of crossings are not merely symbolic; they are *physicalized* with the indelible stamp of experience to amplify their import.

In their efforts to guide audience members and performers through sites in unusual ways, site choreographers sensitize us to local contexts. They work to replace indifference with interest. As they enliven our awareness of local places and problems, we may find ourselves inclined, not toward the couch or the nearest McDonald's but rather toward more active commitment to our communities.[1] At times, this engagement with place has its political consequences. Martha Bowers, for instance, has helped spur community members to reclaim an economically depressed waterfront on the piers of Red Hook, New York, through her workshops with neighborhood groups that culminated in a highly visible performance called *On the Waterfront*. Eiko and Koma Otake often get community members involved in cleaning up local waterways before performing their piece *River*, involvement that may stimulate interest in water quality issues. In other words, rather than disregarding the corporate buyout of the historic movie theater or the demolition of the community garden, many site-specific dance projects incite concern over the welfare of our surroundings.

Other site dance projects reside more in the celebratory realm. Some may highlight a restoration or redevelopment project; others may draw attention to the whimsy of a city park. Yet, regardless of their aspirations, a characteristic that links these performances is their ability to connect to community members from outside of the dance world. Due to the fact that the majority of site work resides in public places, rather than in a sequestered theater, site dance boasts a level of accessibility seldom associated with dance performances. For many theatrical productions of dance, ticket prices, a lack of familiarity with dance as a discipline, and/or societal assumptions about a theater-going public tend to curtail attendance by a larger public. But site-specific dance typically exists in spaces that anyone can and will frequent. It may appear beside you on the sidewalk or in the water of a nearby pond; it may materialize over your head on a bank building or on the steps of the local library. As such, the numbers that access site-specific performances can far surpass the typical dance performance, and the audience often boasts a much more diverse public with viewers who may never consider going to a theater.

For this expanded audience, site choreographers present a varied palette. Some site choreographers—similar to avant-garde performing artists who enjoy pushing boundaries—pride themselves on provocation. They question our

Figure 1. Inserting art into the public square. The BodyCartography Project with workshop group on Market Street in San Francisco (2000). Photo by Alex Zaphiris.

distinctions between public and private spaces; they probe our preconceptions about the appropriate venues for art. They make us wonder about our choices in urban planning and development. Other site choreographers place more subtle emphasis on the wonders of the natural environment or the beauty of historic buildings. But they all find common ground in their highlighting of place and the human-place interface.

Due to this highlighting, the questions or quandaries implicated in place are often at the forefront of site choreographers' efforts. Whose history of this place is accurate? What are the possibilities for our interaction with this site in the future? Is our current use and understanding of this place beneficial to the community or the environment as a whole? Yet, even as they address these issues, site choreographers do not provide us with easy answers. Instead, site choreographers may suggest seemingly contradictory or incompatible solutions. This is because site work challenges us to have an active mind when approaching place, not landing on the easiest reaction or quickest estimation. As these artists delve into their sites, discovering the layers of past and present, they may supply audiences with assorted narratives and/or possibilities for an individual site. For example, they might depict an alternative chronicle for a site, rather than trumpeting the dominant interpretation of a place; they might amplify voices that have been ignored or whitewashed out of the official history of the site.[2] After seeing a site performance, an audience member may feel reintroduced to a familiar place. She or he may be surprised to discover that the house next door was on the Underground Railroad route or that the neighborhood was the home of Chinese immigrants during the nineteenth century whom municipal authorities forcibly removed to "clean up" the neighborhood's image.

To some, site choreographers seem notoriously mischievous—inserting their work surreptitiously or even forcefully into the public sphere, engaging in "inappropriate" behavior, bringing art into unusual sites, or offering alternative narratives for place. Some may dismiss site artists as mere pranksters or oddballs. But such terms ignore the site choreographer's effect on communities and places. Due to their efforts to uncover multiple narratives and make art accessible to diverse populations, site choreographers can achieve significant transformations in a community. They may break through lines of class, race, ethnicity, and/or perception. They may cross geographical or socioeconomic boundaries. They may touch on important stories that link unusual groups. And, along the way, they typically absorb community members into the process and performance of art. Sometimes this might mean having community members as performers in the work; other times it might mean taking great pains to involve the community as audience members. For Tamar Rogoff's *Demeter's Daughter*, the majority of her Lower East Side New York neighborhood got involved in the production as performers (ages 6–76), audience members, or on-the-spot entrepreneurs who sold food to audience members visiting from other neighborhoods. As Rogoff's performers retold the story of Demeter and Persephone in terms that the whole neighborhood could comprehend, she succeeded in exposing a diverse population to the possibilities in the artistic process; she also kindled her neighborhood's interest in protecting the community garden and helped form a lasting bond among neighbors who had rarely communicated before the project.

Are such accomplishments a common occurrence for the site choreographer? The essays and interviews that follow allow us to answer such a question. But one thing becomes certain upon reading the descriptions of their work: as site choreographers link site, art, and community through a physical and performative process, they make remarkable strides in enlivening the relationship between people and place.

Attending to Place

When reading the contributions to this volume, it becomes clear that site choreographers' goals and methods are far from identical. At times, the differences between site choreographers make the effort toward classification seem improbable, if not impossible. Certain site choreographers have no difficulty in charging entrance fees, while others are adamantly opposed to any commodification of their work. Some of these artists offer overt political messages; others believe abstraction is the only appropriate way of presenting art. Some believe that bringing outside material to a site (lights, music, etc.) removes the work from the site-specific realm, while others have no difficulty using all the theatrical gadgetry available to create large spectacles.

Yet, with all these differences, one particular commonality rings true about all site-specific choreographers. One main link distinguishes the site choreographer from choreographers of all other dance genres: their interest in *attending to place*.

We use the term *attending* because it references two equally important concepts, attention and tending. Site choreographers, as a group, have an interest in *drawing attention to* place. When Meredith Monk, one of the earliest site choreographers, states in this book that she wants to "bring the space to life so that you would see it in a fresh way," and Jo Kreiter, a site artist whose work has appeared in the last dozen years or so, describes her work as "illuminat[ing] a place in a new way," they are both referring to that interest in expanding public awareness of place. Concerned about public inattentiveness to urban, rural, or natural environments, site choreographers want people to behold their surroundings in an active, animated manner.

But there is another level to the work. While all site choreographers want to draw attention to their chosen sites, they also have an interest in public involvement in place. They would like us to establish a connection to place that inspires *tending to* that place. The concept of tending to place suggests a stewardship component to the site process. Such stewardship may adopt the form of maintaining historical knowledge of a site, minimizing its ecological footprint, transforming the community-site relationship, involving government officials or developers in a dialogue about a site, or just appreciating the current aesthetics of a place for future preservation. But for all these models of tending—whether oriented toward past, present, or future—site choreographers see their work as part of a grander scheme, a scheme where community members participate in making decisions around place.[3]

Finally, we choose the word *attending* to highlight the site choreographer's interest in process. The progressive verb form (*attending* rather than *attend*) implies an active and continuing community-place interaction. Since site choreographers work in the medium of movement, they specialize in action. While they do produce a final performance, their focus tends to be on the process of working with people and place over time.[4] They envision art making and the community-place interaction in the same way: both require a sustained commitment, and both are utterly dynamic and mutable. In the end, the deepest hope for the site choreographer is this: that the community connected to a site embodies the process of attending to place long after the ephemeral movement sequences have left only their ghostly remnants in a site.

A Short History

Site-specific dance as a genre did not spring up overnight. Many cultural and political threads can be detected in its makeup, and the form continuously morphs as site choreographers discover and integrate new ideas. What follows is a brief historical sketch of the genre's past to help contextualize the work discussed in this volume.[5]

The inception of site-specific dance can be found at the intersection of multiple artistic efforts of the 1950s and 1960s. During this era, artists in many genres were rebelling against conventional creative processes as well as testing the

boundaries between art and everyday life. Some of the most influential early attempts to unseat standard performance modes can be found in the hills of North
Carolina at Black Mountain College. It was at this experimental institution that
a number of artists—John Cage, Merce Cunningham, William de Kooning, and
Buckminster Fuller, among others—met in the 1950s to discuss art and collaborate on projects. Inspired by the philosophies and artistic efforts of the 1920s
Dadaists, these artists began to explore new methods and venues for art making
during their summer retreats. In 1952, some of the artists-in-residence, including
Cage, a composer, Cunningham, a choreographer, as well as poet Charles Olson,
visual artist Robert Rauschenberg, and pianist and composer David Tudor, took
this experimentation to a new level when they created *Theatre Piece No. 1*, later
recognized as the progenitor to "Happenings."[6]

Happenings, most famously associated with Allan Kaprow and others in the
New York visual arts world of the late 1950s and early 1960s, were mixed-media
events that attempted to overturn standard theatrical practices. Participants in
the Happenings engaged in loose, typically simultaneous, improvisational structures that included directions regarding spoken word, movement, prop usage,
music, etc.[7] Among the Happenings' many characteristics, two stand out when
tracing the Happenings' connection to site-specific dance. First, the Happenings took place in non-theater spaces. They occurred in lofts, stores, and other
unconventional venues, and their creators were purposeful in their rejection of
the proscenium stage. In part, they adopted these new spaces due to their interest in the second characteristic that links them to site-specific dance: the desire
to alter the audience-performance relationship. Happenings often took place in
tight quarters without a cordoned performance area, so that the line between
audience and performer became blurred.[8] In fact, in later Happenings, people
like Claes Oldenburg, Kaprow, Rauschenberg, and others tried to erase the line
completely as they began to invite audiences to participate directly in the presentation. Kaprow, for instance, brought people—whether artists or passersby—
into active relation with objects and sites and left it up to them to create their
own art. These later endeavors often took place outdoors and served to further
destabilize the line between art and everyday activities.[9]

The Happenings, in addition to minimalist efforts among visual artists, joined
with developments among modern dancers to create the elemental stew for site-
specific dance. From opposite sides of the country, choreographers Merce Cunningham (along with John Cage and Robert Ellis Dunn, a composition teacher
at Cunningham's New York studio) and Anna Halprin stand out as especially
influential to the future of site choreography. After the Black Mountain College

days, Cunningham began to explore in earnest the potential of stripping himself of absolute creative agency. One intriguing tactic he adopted included chance determination to structure his pieces. This tactic, where dice might be thrown or a coin might be tossed to determine the order, spacing, or number of dancers on the stage, served to remove an authorial stamp from the creative product and to undermine the heavily symbolic and expressive choreography of the previous two decades.[10] Taking his dance company on tour, Cunningham often performed these chance dances, sometimes called Events, in unusual settings: cafeterias, museums, plazas, and gymnasiums. Through these chance creations, Cunningham, with Cage and Dunn, helped alter the purview of modern dance both in terms of movement themes and performance venues.[11] Young choreographers who studied with these three men began to view venerated dance vocabulary, choreographic procedures, and traditional venues as limiting; instead, this next generation of choreographers turned to improvisational structures, non-proscenium spaces, and pedestrian movements—walking, hair brushing, sitting, yawning, etc.—to make their artistic statements. This choreographic upheaval, linked to the postmodern dance group known as Judson Dance Theater, spurred the first New York experiments in site-specific dance by artists such as Simone Forti, Steve Paxton, Lucinda Childs, and others.

Another key figure who stimulated this interest in outdoor sites and pedestrian movement was Anna Halprin. A choreographer who settled in the Bay Area in 1945 and founded the San Francisco Dancers' Workshop, Halprin figured heavily in the rise of site-specific dance due to the fact that she taught many of those who would become the originators of the genre. Inspired by her architect husband, Lawrence Halprin, Anna Halprin became fascinated by architectural concepts of structure and design and how they played out both in the physical anatomy of the body and in the body's relation to the environment. Conducting class outdoors at the foot of Mount Tamalpais on a dance deck designed by her husband, Halprin encouraged her students to delve into the "sentient" body's capabilities free from the strictures of older dance vocabularies.[12] For her, the body was an instrument of introspection; it was knowledgeable and expressive in its own right, with a connection to its surroundings that needed to remain open and receptive. In an attempt to access the knowing body and to amplify awareness of internal and external environments, Halprin employed personal and sometimes emotionally charged improvisational exercises to clear her students' bodies of movement habits and preferences. Many of these exercises took place outside on her deck, in the woods, on the beach, or in the city.[13] Her students would perform tasks—carrying driftwood, building structures, etc.—that

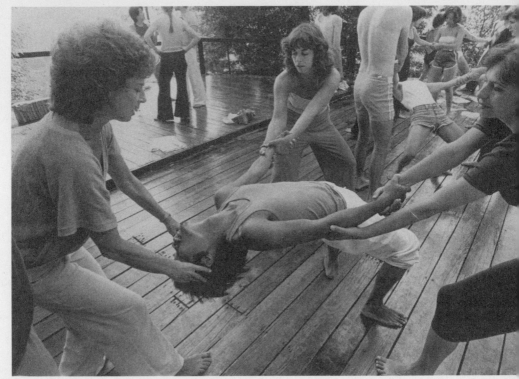

Figure 2. Testing new movements on the Halprin dance deck (1971). Photo by Peter Land.

encouraged them to adapt to the environment at hand. Whether the chosen place was an airport, a hillside, an abandoned building, or scaffolding, Halprin assigned these tasks to stimulate awareness of the environment as a partner in art making and to see the details of the environment as "independent elements related in unpredictable ways."[14] These ideas and the countercultural atmosphere of her workshops helped lead such innovators as Forti, Trisha Brown, and Meredith Monk—all students in Halprin's classes—toward the fundamentals of what would become known as site-specific dance.

The term *site-specific* first appeared in the visual art world in the 1960s and 1970s. It emerged at this moment because a number of sculptors, most famously Robert Smithson, became quite direct about their concerns that artworks must be created for and in collaboration with a particular site. To clarify this idea, these artists moved out of their studios and into remote landscapes to create art. They spent time in their chosen sites understanding the natural processes that already occurred there; then, rather than imposing a separate artistic vision on the site, they would create sculptural work, often large in scale, to draw attention

Figure 3. Dancers under the direction of Halprin experiment in the environment. *Airport Hangar* (1950). Photo by William Heick.

to the site and its processes. The resulting artworks, variously called Earthworks, Land Art, or site-specific art, highlighted the communion possible between art and site.[15]

Just as visual artists were rejecting traditional modes of creation and display, the choreographers of the New York–based Judson Dance Theater, fresh from their studies with Halprin, Cunningham, Cage, and/or Dunn, began abandoning the proscenium theater in favor of "art in context."[16] As early as 1960, Simone Forti created two new works, *See Saw* and *Rollers*, that helped launch this trend. These pieces, billed as Happenings and taking place in a gallery space, used common children's play equipment—a seesaw and two wagons—to break the mold of the traditional dance theater work. The performers used everyday movements; they were no longer framed by a stage space; they focused on the need to adjust to specific equipment; and for *Rollers* they even asked for audience participation.[17] In 1963, another member of Judson Dance Theater, Steve Paxton, took audiences by bus to a New Jersey forest for his piece, *Afternoon*. For this piece, audience members were treated to a forest filled with trees dressed similarly to the dancers, breaking distinctions between natural elements and the dancing body.[18]

Other choreographers in Judson also began embracing outdoor environments, some with an even greater concentration on the chosen site. What might be considered, in retrospect, the first truly site-specific dance, *Street Dance* (1964) by Lucinda Childs, grew out of an assignment in Robert Dunn's choreography class. For *Street Dance*, Childs placed herself and one other performer, James Byars, both dressed in black raincoats, in a very particular area on Broadway between 11th and 12th Streets. Watching from loft windows above and across the street, the audience observed the pair highlighting the details of the site, such as a display window and objects in it, as well as integrating seamlessly with the bustle of the street. During their observation, Childs's taped voice—emanating from a recorder inside the loft—reinforced the audience's perceptions of these details by providing them with exact verbal descriptions of the site's features.[19] Steve Paxton, reflecting back on his experience of *Street Dance* in Sally Banes's *Reinventing Dance in the 1960s,* comments: "By chance another man in a black raincoat walked by, and he stopped for a moment at the window. In the moment when I wondered if she had arranged this or not, my world was illuminated. Nothing changed, except my attitude. People on the street continued to walk. But now, I doubted them. Were they 'real'? Of course they were?! . . . A distant siren went ooooh. The whole city joined the duet Childs made."[20]

Deborah Hay, in *Hill* (1965), a piece performed with Paxton, continued this pattern of underscoring the details of the environment. For *Hill*, Hay and Paxton dressed in grass-colored costumes and performed against the grassy background of a golf course. Drawing from the activities and details of the golf course, Paxton drove around in a golf cart while Hay explored the hillside. Then they wrestled on the soft grass, blending into the background with their environment-inspired costumes.[21] Even Twyla Tharp ventured out into public spaces with large groups of dancers to perform several outdoor works, most notably *Medley* (1969) in New York's Central Park.[22]

These initial efforts in the site-specific realm were followed by two choreographers, Trisha Brown and Meredith Monk, often considered the founders of the genre. As part of the first group of Judson choreographers, Brown witnessed many of the experiments by Childs, Forti, and Paxton, and she felt drawn to such work. In a famous statement, she noted that it was a shame that there were so many spaces left vacant by dancers. "I have in the past felt sorry for ceilings and walls. It's perfectly good space, why doesn't anyone use it?"[23] In her equipment pieces of the late 1960s and early 1970s, Brown attempted to rectify this situation by inhabiting outdoor environments in unusual ways. Attaching herself and/or her dancers to harnesses, Brown created works such as *Man Walking Down the Side of a Building* (1970), where a man attached to a harness and ropes literally walked down the outside wall of a building in Greenwich Village. For such site works, Brown used the present structure and details of a site to inspire her pieces, a point about which she was adamant. As she argues, "I'm not interested in taking a work which was made in a studio and performed in an interior space and placing it outside. I don't like it at all."[24] So, for *Man Walking Down the Side of a Building*, she made sure that the length of the piece would be determined not by any particular artistic agenda but by the height of the building and the length of time it took for the performer to walk from roof to ground. In *Walking on the Wall* (1971), performed in the Whitney Museum, Brown coached her dancers to assume an ordinary posture that made them seem like they were walking on the ground, even though they were sauntering along the gallery walls. Audiences had the sensation that they were watching the performers walk on the ground from above, a strange inversion of perspective.[25] Another seminal site work, *Roof Piece* (1971), employed 12 of Brown's dancers on the rooftops of 8 New York buildings covering 10 city blocks. Through imitative gestures that passed from building to building in one direction over a 15-minute period and then back for another 15 minutes, audiences standing on a ninth rooftop could see the eventual (and inevitable) distortion of movement that occurred when attempting translation over such distances.[26]

Since the late 1960s, Meredith Monk has helped define the site-specific dance genre not only by her initial efforts, but also by her continued ventures into the field. Like Brown, Monk allowed a site's present structure and function to influence her work. But Monk took this a step further as she began using the historical details of her sites as inspiration (a strategy she discusses in her interview in chapter 1). Already by 1967, Monk was experimenting with site work in depth.

Figure 4. *Man Walking Down the Side of a Building* (1970), created by Trisha Brown. Photo by Carol Goodden.

Her first significant site work, *Blueprint* (1967), took place in Woodstock, New York, where, for one part of the work, the audience sat outside and watched a series of activities—flour pouring from the roof, people singing, film clips flickering—as they occurred in the windows, on the roof, and in the doorways of a building.

Monk continued her experimentation on site with the use of the "tour." Instead of a passive audience, Monk required her audiences to explore a site, often with the audience moving more than the performers. In *Tour: Dedicated to Dinosaurs* (1969) at the Smithsonian Natural History Museum, audiences strolled through the museum discovering tableaux that would alter very slowly. In *Juice* (1969), *Needlebrain Lloyd and the Systems Kid* (1970), and *Vessel* (1971), she took this idea of the tour to a new level by moving audiences to completely different sites over a longer period of time. For *Juice*, audiences met first at the Guggenheim Museum, then at the Minor Latham Playhouse, and finally at The House Loft to see the three parts of the performance over the course of a month. Audiences for *Vessel*, which was performed in Monk's New York City loft, the Performing Garage, and a Wooster Street parking lot, traveled by bus from site to site, with the first two parts happening in one evening (audiences chose one of five evenings for viewing these two installments) and the final installment occurring at the end of the week for all five groups of audience members (see chapter 1 for more detail on the *Tours, Juice, Needlebrain Lloyd*, and *Vessel*). This tactic of enforcing audience activity is one that site choreographers still use to ensure their audiences engage proactively with a site.

A more recent site work of Monk's, *American Archaeology #1: Roosevelt Island* (1994), demonstrates her continued interest in excavating sites for their past and present layers.[27] Performed on Roosevelt Island in the middle of New York's East River, *American Archaeology* delved into Roosevelt Island's history as a place for society's outcasts. The piece referenced the multiple past structures of the site—a prison, a poorhouse, and a hospital—yet it did so by layering this past with present visions as well. Audience members observed nearly simultaneous activities including children playing, a horse and rider galloping, people ambling along in period costumes, convicts working, and doctors and patients interacting. The final part of the work included a procession of the whole cast in their costumes of various eras. With the Manhattan skyline in the background, the procession commented on the continuation of an outsider's society through the ages. This image is emblematic of how site choreographers enjoy portraying a place as an accumulation of temporal layers.[28]

By the mid-1970s, organizations in the United States were beginning to spring up to support performance and visual art in the public sphere. Groups such as Creative Time and government efforts like the Comprehensive Employment and Training Act of 1973 (CETA) both served to finance public art. While neither of these efforts was explicitly invested in site-specific dance (a conjunctive term that was not used consciously until the end of the 1970s), both of these support mechanisms offered funds to artists of all types to locate their work outdoors. CETA lasted for nine years, but Creative Time has continued its impact and still commissions work today. One of Creative Time's most famous and long-lasting series, *Art on the Beach*, encouraged artists to create site work at the Battery Park City Landfill between 1978 and 1985. Many well-known New York site choreographers including Eiko & Koma and Tamar Rogoff, both contributors to this volume, participated in this program and thereby furthered their site careers.[29]

A later institution, Dancing in the Streets (DITS), was the first organization to specifically foster and advocate for this new genre of site-specific dance. Started in 1984 by Elise Bernhardt, DITS began to commission site-specific dance in all areas of New York and eventually around the world. To date, DITS has commissioned work by over 400 choreographers in sites from Belarus to Brooklyn. Many of the artists included in this anthology have benefited from DITS's support, and it has been invaluable to the growth of site-specific dance as a genre.[30] In the past 10 years, other organizations have come to the aid of the burgeoning genre, including Bates Dance Festival in Maine, the American Dance Festival in North Carolina, the Wagon Train Project in Nebraska, and the Walker Arts Center in Minnesota.

Today, in part because of these organizations' support, site-specific dance is a thriving field. Evidence of the field's development and impact can be seen in this anthology where artists discuss their many efforts to project art into the public sphere from 1967 to the present. As these choreographers provide insights about their site-specific processes and performances, we can expand on the history of the site-specific dance genre. We can ascertain how the field has changed in the past 40 years and what distinguishes it today. We can discern the impressive depth and diversity of the field and learn about the characteristics that define the genre. Finally, we can discover some possible future trajectories for this varied genre, a genre that grows in both import and dynamism as the years pass by.

Defining Terms

But what exactly do we mean by "site-specific dance"? In this collection, we attempt to characterize a field that has had very little in the way of clear definitions. While site-specific dance has matured as a practice, the form has not seen the same development in theoretical and scholarly terms. This is partly due to a certain hesitancy in the dance world about where site-specific dance should fall. Should it be classified as a genre in its own right, a minor branch of the dance history tree, or a mere fad? If it is a genre, does it link more closely to site-specific theater and visual art or to postmodern dance?

The same uncertainty is not evident in the visual arts world. Site-specific art is an accepted and well-analyzed field, and it is here where debates about what counts as "site-specific" have been bandied about for decades. These debates are often quite vibrant with scholars and practitioners arguing about terms as well as characteristics. Although we can only provide a cursory treatment of such deliberations here, we will attempt to outline some of the main points for purposes of future discussion.

Since critics first started analyzing the works of Robert Smithson and other Land Art sculptors, the site-specific discourse has grown. In the past 10 years it has gotten especially spirited, with many artists and scholars weighing in on the criteria for site-specificity. For example, Lucy R. Lippard, the author of *The Lure of the Local*, draws distinctions between site-specific and place-specific as influenced by topography and human historical threads, respectively.[31] James Meyer, an art historian at Emory University, prefers the distinction between a literal site, where the artwork is determined by the physical traits of the place, and a functional site, where the site acts merely as informational background; the functional site becomes mobile, an allegory for place, even a nonmaterial place.[32] Another dominant figure in this discussion is Miwon Kwon, an art historian at UCLA, who has broken site-specific work into three tiers. The first tier includes art that concentrates on a site's physicality; it stems from the premise that a site's design and sensory evocation produce the performance. In Kwon's second tier, site-specific work begins to delve into the historical layers of a place and starts to interrogate a site's link to social or political ideologies. Similar to Meyer's functional site, work in Kwon's third tier is not constrained by a fixed place, but rather lives in a discursive realm, freed from material reality.[33] Many others in the visual arts realm have joined this discussion, which has allowed for a genuine theorizing of site-specificity.

Like site-specific visual art, site-specific performances have been materializing in atypical venues around the world. But the discussion of these performances has only heated up in the past decade or so. Most of this discussion stems from theater and live art practitioners and scholars in the United Kingdom. Fiona Wilkie, for instance, excited about the site performances she witnessed in the UK, attempted a first survey of site-specific performance in 2002, which has done much to expand our ideas about where site work takes place, why performers practice it, and what kind of terminology is appropriate.[34] Others have deepened the discussion of site-specific work as their analyses of the genre have started to include ideas from psychology, literary criticism, philosophy, and environmental design. For example, Clifford McLucas, a theater director from Wales, designates site-specific performance as a ghost superimposed on a host site; Mike Pearson and Michael Shanks liken site-specific performance to archaeology; and Cathy Turner, of the group Wrights & Sites, plumbs the psychoanalytic theory of D. W. Winnicott to highlight site work's ability to explore "potential space."[35] While we do not have the space to explore these ideas in depth here, it is worth noting that these scholars and practitioners have transformed the discourse around site work and have crafted some intriguing trajectories for future studies.

But placing "site-specific" and "dance" side by side puts a new twist into the theoretical fabric. How will the medium of movement change the site-specific discussion? Will the relation between a dancing body and place alter the outlines of a field delineated by visual art or theater practitioners and scholars? People in the site-specific dance community are only now starting to weigh in on this theoretical dialogue of terms and criteria. Reasons for this sluggishness may vary. First, scholarship on dance as a whole has not been as plentiful or common in part due to the discipline's late arrival (compared to visual art and art history) in the university system. Second, dance researchers, in fleshing out the scholarship on the discipline as a whole, have tended to focus on broad trends in terms of performance, say, modern or postmodern dance, without differentiating performance work outside the theater space as a genre of its own. Finally, scholars or critics sometimes dismiss such performances as too community-centric and therefore too amateurish to warrant serious consideration, a situation bemoaned by many of the choreographers in this collection.

However, with this collection, we are ramping up the conversation. As the choreographers put forth their ideas about what constitutes site-specific dance, we get our first lively dialogue about the characteristics, concerns, and categorization of the genre from the artists directly involved. For example, in his essay, Stephan Koplowitz notes that he sees four main categories for site dance—from dance pieces that get reframed in the move from stage to site, to pieces where nothing is created away from the site. Ann Carlson encourages us to acknowledge the body as the first site of creation in a continually expanding context of site-specificity; Sally Jacques believes that sites in collaboration with the moving body simulate the interdependent relationships of the natural world; and Martha Bowers calls a site-specific act one in which there is "a conscious, performative response to questions concerning locational identity." So starts the discussion from the mouths of the site-specific choreographers themselves. As editors, we hope that this is only the beginning of a much larger discussion on site-specific dance: what it has been, what it is, and what it can become.

One final note about terminology: many of the choreographers in this collection have concerns about categorization, but most use "site-specific dance" and "site dance" interchangeably. For some, this is a decision based on the linguistic ease of the second term, a shorthand if you will. However, some take great pains to differentiate between these two terms based on the notion that site-specific dance is a subset of a larger category of site dance. Although we as editors also have reservations about the accurate usage of these terms, we have chosen to use both terms; for our part, this choice stems not only from the ease of the shorthand "site dance" but also from our interest in instigating dialogue about our collective understanding of these signifiers.

This Site's Design

As we have stressed, all site choreographers have an interest in attending to place. However, for the purposes of clarity and to highlight their distinctive traits, we have grouped the choreographers under four secondary themes. These four themes, which mimic the four sections of the book, are the ones that surface most frequently in the individual choreographer's work, as well as in site-specific dance as a genre. These themes are excavating place, sensing site, revering beauty, and accessing community.

In the first section, "Excavating Place: Memory and Spectacle," we explore the theme of historical influence. While site choreographers rarely dismiss a site's history when they approach a site, certain choreographers tend to place history in a starring role when it comes to the process and performance of their work. While this history may appear in abstract or literal form, a site's past factors heavily into these choreographers' site work. Artists such as the five who make up this section—Meredith Monk, Joanna Haigood, Stephan Koplowitz, Heidi Duckler, and Ann Carlson—delve into the layers of past and present to make work that forefronts a deep temporal understanding of place.

In the second section of the book, "Environmental Dialogues: Sensing Site," we join choreographers who see communicating with place as the main motivator for their site work. Reminiscent of Anna Halprin, these choreographers emphasize the importance of noticing and connecting to our surroundings. With a particular love of overlooked spaces, these artists attempt to lure audiences into a discussion about the present and future of the sites involved. The efforts of Olive Bieringa, Otto Ramstad, Leah Stein, and Marylee Hardenbergh demonstrate the need for a sensual relation to place, one that provides the groundwork for inventive future interactions.

Site choreographers often wax poetic about the beauty of the sites they choose. In part 3, "Revering Beauty: The Essence of Place," we present four choreographers who see beauty, above all, as the main inspiration for their work. These choreographers attempt to enchant audiences and participants alike as they identify beauty as not only site-specific but as a universal trait of place. When Eiko Otake, Sally Jacques, Sara Pearson, and Patrik Widrig perform place, they ignite a love for our surroundings that surpasses the ordinary.

Finally, most site choreographers consider community as they begin a site-specific project. Whether that means they invoke a sense of community among performers and audience members or that they involve local community members as performers in their pieces, the concept of community tends to figure prominently in the site-specific process. In part 4, "Civic Interventions: Accessing Community," three choreographers focus on site-specific dance as a conduit to get to their main objective: creating, serving, and/or supporting community. As Jo Kreiter, Tamar Rogoff, and Martha Bowers detail their interest in communicating with the inhabitants of a site, the site-specific practice shines as a means for building community.

A few additional words about the structure of this text: in the research process for this anthology, we first conducted interviews with each artist or combination of artists. Then, to allow for greater depth, we requested from these artists an essay that addressed either his/her/their creative process or a pressing issue within site work. After conducting the interviews and collecting the initial contributions from each artist, we discovered recurring themes in their words and work, which in turn suggested the sections of this book. We would, however, like to point out that artists are not single-issue beings; they explore a multitude of topics causing much crossover among the four delineated themes. Not only does this bode well for the quality of the work presented, but it also provides for a rich discussion about the characteristics and boundaries of the site-specific dance genre.

In addition, we have included a large number of images to offer some concrete visual access to the site-specific practice. We feel that by providing varied approaches to these artists' work—through visual imagery, interviews, and essays—we can foster a dynamic dialogue about the site choreographers' tactics and objectives; this method resembles the site choreographer's own attempts to present multiple narratives of place.

We would like to reiterate that it is impossible to represent all site work or site choreographers in this text. Due to time constraints on the part of the artists and/or unwieldy length in terms of manuscript, we have landed on 16 dedicated

Figure 5. Sara Pearson and Patrik Widrig's *WaterSkyBoatFly* (1996) in Central Park. Photo by Rebecca Blom.

site artists who cover vast areas in terms of geography and who are at different stages in their careers. We believe that such diversity offers the greatest possibility for understanding the range within the site dance genre and for supporting future analyses of site-specific dance.[36]

In closing, the goal of this book—one akin to the goal of the site artists themselves—is this: To amplify the connection between places, people, and performance. To explore the possibilities that art can bring to the dialogue between humans and their environments. To celebrate the beauty of place, the community spirit, and the deep-seated knowledge of our surroundings that site-specific dance evokes.

As artists who mesh an assortment of roles—activist, installation artist, modern dancer, community organizer, to name a few—site choreographers occupy an intriguing niche, one that needs recognition and appreciation. We have written this collection to serve as the textual foundation for this niche, and we look forward to a continued critical dialogue between site dancers, choreographers, critics, and scholars. As text and movement interweave and overflow into alleyways, alcoves, and avenues, intriguing new sites materialize for us to investigate and perform. Perhaps one will surface in your backyard.

Notes

1. Site performers may, of course, choose locations such as a chain store to stage their performance. By deliberately infusing site work into such locations, site performers can both comment on the homogenized experience of these spaces and perhaps make a statement about the impossibility of absolute homogeneity owing to local flair. Christine Hill, for example, has created a performance piece called *Tourguide?* in New York City that, as she notes, "rang[es] from the 'door to nowhere' on Avenue A to the City's fanciest McDonald's." See www.publicartfund.org/pafweb/realm/99/hill_c_release_f99.html.

2. Kloetzel wrote about this tactic in a paper exploring a work she made in the California Museum of Photography in 2004, "Site Dance: A Deconstruction/Reconstruction of Community and Place." This thesis was inspired by Michel de Certeau's work on memory. As de Certeau notes, "There is no place that is not haunted by many different spirits hidden there in silence, spirits one can 'invoke' or not." I argue that this is precisely what site choreographers do: they invoke spirits or memories that have been quashed or erased, giving voice to the past in all its many forms. De Certeau, *The Practice of Everyday Life*, 108.

3. Rebecca Solnit also toys with the verbs *tending* and *attending* in her analysis of the creative act and its link to women and environment. As she opines, "Works of art call for attendance, for waiting/paying attention to; they push the bodily act of consumption into a mental act of contemplation. . . . The viewer supplies the act of attending that incorporates the artwork into the ongoing conversation." Solnit, *As Eve Said to the Serpent*, 164–66.

4. Brenda Dixon Gottschild, "Some Thoughts on Choreographing History," 168. Gottschild provides an excellent argument for focusing on process over product, a method she feels is modeled by such scholars as Victor Turner; as she notes, we would do well to concentrate on "processual" models over product-oriented tradition, preferring *dancing* to the *dance*.

5. Unfortunately, we cannot create a complete portrait of the genre's past here due to constraints of time and space. However, a fuller treatment of this past is long overdue, and we look forward to future texts that address the history of site-specific dance. In the meantime, the attached bibliography provides a substantial list of resources that explore the site-specific genre in terms of both theory and practice. This bibliography also provides articles, previews, reviews, and Web sites of many of the best known site choreographers in the United States.

6. Stuart Hobbs, *The End of the American Avant-Garde*, 109.

7. Jack Anderson, *Art without Boundaries*, 212–13.

8. Michael Kirby, *Happenings*, 11, 24–25.

9. Sally Banes, "Gulliver's Hamburger: Defamiliarization and the Ordinary in the 1960s Avant-Garde," in *Reinventing Dance in the 1960s*, ed. Banes, 12–13, 16–17.

10. With such intellectual or abstract exercises, Cunningham tried to break the mold set by such luminaries in the dance world as Martha Graham, Doris Humphrey, Helen Tamiris, and others who employed dramatic and/or narrative choreographic strategies to convey emotional and/or psychological messages.

11. For more information about Merce Cunningham and his choreographic strategies, see Susan Foster, *Reading Dancing*, or Roger Copeland, *Merce Cunningham*.

12. Janice Ross, "Anna Halprin and the 1960s: Acting in the Gap between the Personal, the Public, and the Political," in *Reinventing Dance in the 1960s*, ed. Banes, 27.

13. Janice Ross, introduction to *Moving toward Life*, ed. Kaplan, 72–74.

14. Ross, "Anna Halprin and the 1960s," 29.

15. Erika Suderburg, introduction to *Space, Site, Intervention: Situating Installation Art*, ed. Suderburg, 4. The site-specific visual art world has been discussed in depth in many texts. For a general introduction to this field, see Suderburg's book as well as Suzaan Boettger, *Earthworks: Art and the Landscape of the Sixties*; John Beardsley, *Earthworks and Beyond*; Suzanne Lacy, ed., *Mapping the Terrain*; and Nina Felshin, ed., *But Is It Art?*

16. Sally Banes might argue that this was less a pointed rejection of the proscenium stage and more the work of necessity. As she contends, much of the Judson heritage was determined by the fact that these choreographers needed space to perform, and the Judson Church gymnasium was made available to them. But, as she notes, such circumstances can have curious impacts. She states, "The constraints of the physical performance space would affect or directly shape the dances in several future Judson concerts, in fact becoming a hallmark of the innovative spirit of the group." She adds, "One long thread leading from such works was the spate of 'environmental' dances in the late sixties and early seventies." Banes, "Choreographic Methods of the Judson Dance Theater," 356–57.

17. Banes, "Gulliver's Hamburger," 9; Banes, *Terpsichore in Sneakers*, 25–26.

18. Banes, "Gulliver's Hamburger," 12.

19. Banes, *Terpsichore*, 135–36, 146–47. For another excellent description of *Street Dance* and its implications, see Siegel, "Dancing on the Outside," 1–8.

20. Steve Paxton, "PAST*Forward* Choreographers' Statements," in *Reinventing Dance in the 1960s*, ed. Banes, 207.

21. Banes, *Terpsichore*, 116.

22. Deborah Jowitt, "Monk and King: The Sixties Kids," in *Reinventing Dance in the 1960s*, ed. Banes, 130.

23. Effie Stephano, "Moving Structures," 17.

24. Ibid., 20.

25. Banes, *Terpsichore*, 80–82.

26. Details on *Roof Piece* come from Hendel Teicher, ed., *Trisha Brown*, 312, and Marcia Siegel, "Dancing on the Outside," 4–5.

27. In 1994, Monk's work was officially titled *American Archeology #1*; however, in order to remain consistent with the spelling of *archaeology* in the rest of the text, she prefers that we use *American Archaeology #1*.

28. For more information, see chapter 1. In addition, Monk's work has been analyzed in many other texts. In particular, see Deborah Jowitt, *Meredith Monk*; Banes, "The Art of Meredith Monk"; Brooks McNamara, "Vessel."

29. See www.creativetime.org for more information about the *Art on the Beach* series and the history of Creative Time.

30. For more information about DITS, see www.dancinginthestreets.org.

31. Lucy Lippard, *The Lure of the Local*, 274.

32. James Meyer, "The Functional Site; or, The Transformation of Site Specificity," in *Space, Site, Intervention*, ed. Suderburg, 24–25.

33. Miwon Kwon, *One Place after Another*, 11–31.

34. Fiona Wilkie, "Mapping the Terrain."

35. For more detail on these theories, see Nick Kaye, *Site-Specific Art*, 128; Mike Pearson and Michael Shanks, *Theatre/Archaeology*; and Cathy Turner, "Palimpsest or Potential Space?" Also, the bibliography included in this text has many other resources that can help flesh out the theory and practice being debated in the site-specific art and theater realms.

36. We conducted a number of additional interviews for this text; however, not all site choreographers in the United States could fit within one text, and some had difficulty conforming to time and/or financial constraints of the publishing world. We highly regret that we could not include everyone in this text, but would encourage readers to peruse our list of site dance companies' Web sites in the bibliography for further information.

1

Excavating Place

Memory and Spectacle

Figure 6. Jo Kreiter performing in Joanna Haigood's *Cho-Mu* (1993). Photo by Liz Zivic.

In her article, "Looking for the Invisible," Joanna Haigood muses, "What if we really had the capacity of trans-temporal perception? What would it be like to view the intersection of different events separated in time but not in space?" As a group, site-specific choreographers tend to be fascinated by the notion of memory. They want to unearth the memories linked to place, the details of bygone eras. Often they delve into places with rich, storied pasts; at times, they explore sites that had a particular moment of import for a community. Among the site choreographers included in this book, Meredith Monk, Joanna Haigood, Stephan Koplowitz, Heidi Duckler, and Ann Carlson prioritize accessing the memories associated with a site. These choreographers merge art with history or archaeology, uncovering the character of a site over time. In order to access temporal layers or highlight a significant moment in time, these choreographers try a number of approaches: they may do research on a site's historical manifestations; they may interview community members who had connections to a site in the past; they may draw from the site's history for movement threads, evoking through gesture the events of the past; and/or they may use texts or costumes that conjure historical imagery.

Meredith Monk has been intrigued by place memories since the 1960s. As she began her first experiments on site, archaeology played an important role. This became apparent in her earliest site piece, *Blueprint*, created in 1967. For this piece, which took place first in Woodstock, New York, and later in the Judson Memorial Church in New York City, she began to work with the concepts of excavation and layering, both of space and time. But the layers in Monk's work do not always have one-to-one relationships with a site's past. For instance, in *Vessel*, Monk saw the venues she chose as sites with individual histories but also as sites that referenced metaphorical and distant histories, in this case the history of Joan of Arc. Such historical and archaeological references resonate through the majority of her site pieces and became especially apparent in *American Archaeology #1*, performed on Roosevelt Island in New York in 1994. For this piece, audience members explored the site on foot, trammeling across land that historically had been home to those on the fringes of society. As Monk expresses in her succeeding interview, "I wanted to give them the room to go down through the layers of presences and beings that had been there on that island in the past."

For this volume, Monk delves into her initial attraction to nontraditional spaces. Noting her dissatisfaction with frontal stage orientation and her fascination with scale and perspective, Monk helps us understand the staple themes of the field. She explores how site work has changed over the years, remarking on the differences in producing site work in the 1960s versus the 1990s. In her article, "Meredith Monk as Site Pioneer, 1969–71," Monk analyzes her three crucial works that helped launch the site-specific genre, *Juice*, *Needlebrain Lloyd and the Systems Kid*, and *Vessel*. Putting together her own rarely seen archival notes, photos, and manifestos, Monk reveals the thought process behind her earliest ventures into the site-specific realm. This reflection on the watershed years for the genre points to the perceptive as well as imaginative understanding of history and memory that goes into the site-specific process.

Joanna Haigood, a choreographer who began making site work in the 1970s, also creates links between grand narratives and particular sites. In the 1980s and 1990s, after founding Zaccho Dance Theatre in San Francisco, Haigood created pieces in an old military gymnasium, on the Ferry Building in San Francisco, in an industrial canning factory, and along a former trail of the Underground Railroad in Massachusetts. These pieces allowed Haigood to explore narratives from the biological to the historical; *The Keeping of Bees Is Like the Directing of Sunshine* (1987) related the structure of human society to that of bees in a hive, while her 1998 work *Invisible Wings* brought to the fore the slave narrative and the stories of hope found in the history of the Underground Railroad. In the past decade, Haigood has continued connecting historical narratives to individual sites on an ever-grander scale. For *Ghost Architecture* (2003), she created an extensive performance installation at the Yerba Buena Center for the Arts based on an approximation of the architecture and movement that would have occupied the site in years past. In *Departure and Arrival* (2007), Haigood employed aerial work, video projection, and text to turn the San Francisco Airport into a site that commented on the forced travel of the African Diaspora and its links to present-day narratives of immigration.

In chapter 2, Haigood explores site work as a method for bringing to light memories and sensations from diverse peoples and places. As she discusses her tactics of employing personal stories, architectural angles, and psychological sensibilities, she describes her interest in painting an impressionistic, rather than linear, view of her chosen sites. Haigood further contemplates her creative process in her article, "Looking for the Invisible," a reflective look at her efforts to create *Ghost Architecture* at the Yerba Buena Center. Gazing into the Center's past, she mulls over the difficulties of communing with past materials in the present. Her effort to pry open the spatial layers of the place and force them into a fluid dialogue allows for a deeper understanding of how the site choreographer sees places as replete with temporal strata.

While Haigood was investigating sites in the San Francisco area, Stephan Koplowitz was exploring the public spaces of New York City. Since 1987, Koplowitz has been associated with sites that are revered cultural magnets for a community. As he works in spaces such as Grand Central Terminal in New York or the British Museum in London, the past and present sometimes collide in unusual ways. In *Babel Index* (1998) for the British Library, the modern technology of light design made the marble library floor seem like early writing parchment, and for *The Governed Body* (1991), set in the very modern State of Illinois Building, Koplowitz drew on his knowledge of Jeremy Bentham's Panopticon to address current issues of government control. While Koplowitz finds the history of the chosen performance sites important for his work, sometimes the past catches him by surprise; for *Kohle Körper* (1999), a work created in a coal factory in Essen, Germany, Koplowitz alluded to the site's disturbing history more directly than he had expected. As he states, "I didn't go to Germany to make a work about forced labor, death, and the destruction of lives as a result of forced labor. But I ended up making that work; it came out of me." The historical narratives seep into the work as Koplowitz plumbs the architecture and function of place over time.

In his interview, Koplowitz examines how he marries abstract and literal histories by joining light design, sound scores, and movement inspired by a chosen site. From his oblique treatment of evolutionary history in *Genesis Canyon* (1996) at the Natural History Museum in London to his more direct referencing of the Jewish labor camps in *Kohle Körper*, Koplowitz attempts to pull his audiences into a site's history and architecture. To realize his goals, Koplowitz often employs large numbers of dancers to match the grand scale of a site, a strategy that he describes in detail in his interview. In his essay "Still Learning, Doing, and Re-learning: Thoughts on Making and Defining Site-Specific Performance," Koplowitz dives into the task of dividing site work into four categories. He remarks that while all four types of site work function to reveal the beauty of a site, he finds category one, or "site-specific" work, particularly satisfying as it "forces you into another world." Koplowitz provides an in-depth look at one of his site-specific pieces, *Fenestrations* (1987), and, in doing so, comes up with a list of essentials for those interested in creating site work. As scholars explore the site-specific genre in more depth, such an article serves as one example of how site choreographers classify the various efforts in the field.

Heidi Duckler has been making site work since 1988. Her first piece on site, *Laundromatinee*, provided a playful look at the historical role of the Laundromat while also bemoaning its disappearance due to gentrification. Since this first piece, Duckler, with her company Collage Dance Theatre, has continued focusing on how the threads of a site's past weave into its present manifestation. Working mostly in and around Los Angeles, she conjures images of the past through costume choices as well as abstract movement themes. While some sites allow her to explore historical issues or events head on, others force her to be somewhat indirect in her referencing. With such rich sites as the Ambassador Hotel or the Herald Examiner Building, for example, Duckler has found the need to be inventive in the face of restrictions. In the Ambassador Hotel, which became famous as the site of the assassination of Robert Kennedy in 1968, the owners prohibited Duckler from any direct allusion to the shooting; instead, she could only refer to the event through abstract themes and movements. One curious feature of many of Duckler's works: they are often the last public experience of a site. The Ambassador Hotel was torn down soon after her 2003 performance, and her 2004 piece *A Hunger Artist* was a last hurrah for Perino's Restaurant, a fixture on Wilshire Boulevard since the 1950s.

In chapter 4, Duckler discusses her attempts to engage audiences emotionally by shifting their perspectives on past and present memories. Stoking the embers of history, architecture, and interior design, she notes her interest in finding a common language between diverse groups who hold segregated memories. In "Rabbi Pinchas as a Mexican Wrestler: Adventures in Dance," an article by Heidi's sister, Merridawn, the difficult issues of community representation and respect crop up as the Duckler sisters create a site work in the multiethnic neighborhood of Boyle Heights in Los Angeles. In an amusing tale of frustrated inspiration, Merridawn Duckler details the duels between a Jewish past and a Latino present that emerge in Collage Dance Theatre's work *The Entire World Is a Narrow Bridge* (2005). Viewing the past through a performative lens, the Duckler sisters accentuate the site choreographer's ability to define present identity as a product of past layers.

Ann Carlson also relishes how past layers can leak into a present tense. In fact, her persistent interest in past-present collisions has often induced her to cultivate such collisions as a "series" of events rather than as stand-alone occurrences. For example, for her *Night Light* series, she restages historical photos as precisely as she can in their original venues to jar our assumptions about past and present. Carlson has restaged such photographs on the streets of New York, in the mountains of Montana, and in four other sites around the United States. Carlson also enjoys working with people who are closely associated with the sites that she chooses. Her *Real People* series highlights groups who share a profession—nuns, lawyers, basketball players, etc. Crafting and then staging performances by these people in their places of work, she creates yet another collision, this time between the conventions of performance and the quotidian behavior of the workplace.

In her interview in chapter 5, Carlson walks through some of these collisions, paying special attention to her work with the *Night Light* series and then *Geyser Land*. She ponders her own increasing attraction to working outdoors and wonders about the effects of September 11, 2001, on her work. As she continues exploring the *Night Light* series in her essay "Thumbprint," she ponders the impulses that inspire site-specific work, from the idiosyncrasies of her own body to the stuffed wonders of the diorama. Reflecting on the initial performance of *Night Light*, she marvels at the dramatic scale of site work and the precarious nature of realizing one's site-specific vision. Carlson marries her reflections to a fanciful analysis of this anthology as its own site. Fashioning a narrative that could correspond to this book's production, she weaves the voices of past and present into an entertaining tale of creation.

Part of the reason that Monk, Haigood, Koplowitz, Duckler, and Carlson prove adept at bringing the past into the present is that they do not shy away from a grand canvas. Monk, for example, often included multiple sites in her early works, and she did not shrink from mammoth spaces such as the Guggenheim Museum or a whole college campus. Koplowitz sometimes has upwards of 50 performers whom he has gathered from the community; Carlson cleverly handles audiences of over 1,000 for an hour-long performance on a train winding its way through the mountains of Montana. Duckler incorporates entire hotels, from loading dock to lobby, as the set for her work, and Haigood traipses audiences on journeys across the Massachusetts landscape to grasp the distances covered by people following the Underground Railroad. In other words, as a group, these five choreographers embrace the tactic of the spectacle in order to bring the past to life. Using large quantities of performers, extensive multimedia designs, or the impressive experience of choruses, aerial work, and long distances, these choreographers dramatically highlight the rich histories of national and international sites. Their work displays the site dance genre as a vehicle for comprehending place through the ages.

Meredith Monk

Meredith Monk is one of the pioneers of the site-specific performance genre. From her earliest experiences in New York, Monk began pushing the boundaries of postmodern dance and music. In her efforts to use non-traditional performing spaces such as museums, loft spaces, and parking lots by the late 1960s, she set the stage for other choreographers and directors to seek out alternative performing spaces. Monk has had a career that spans four decades, and she is recognized as a visionary artist in the disciplines of music, dance, film, and theater. She has received the MacArthur "Genius" Award, two Guggenheim fellowships, a Brandeis Creative Arts Award, three Obies, two Villager Awards, and two Bessie awards for Sustained Creative Achievement, among others. Kloetzel and Monk spoke in Monk's New York City loft on October 14, 2006.

An Interview with Meredith Monk

MK: What gave you the first inkling to go outside the theater space?

MM: I performed in galleries a lot when I first came to New York and always had an interest in space. In the summer of 1966, I was teaching workshops and I was already getting kind of tired of the frontal orientation of the theater space. So in each workshop I took people to different places in New York, and we explored those spaces. I remember one was Wall Street, one was the Staten Island Ferry, one was a park near the river.

　　　Then, during the summer of 1967, I started thinking about working with a building itself and going beyond the proscenium stage situation. I was up at an artists colony called Group 212 in Woodstock, New York, and I decided to use the outside and the inside of a building as the environment for my piece *Blueprint*. I brought the audience outside, and I had them sit on little benches, quite close to the building, so they were really looking up at the building. There were different activities going on in each of six windows. Some of these activities had to do with sound and music, and some with visuals—shadows, films, red light, etc. There were many different simultaneous layers of activity in that building. There was a certain point where the cast formed a procession that eventually went through the door into the building. The very last image in the piece was of someone up on the roof throwing down 20 pounds of flour from huge bags.

MK: It seems like your process has been heavily influenced by the concept of layering.

MM: Yes, layering is often in my work. I like to explore the layers of texture and skin and surface. I often think more like a visual artist, a painter or a sculptor. I take this sense into the performance experience where I have a dialogue with the three-dimensional space.

For example, I did a version of *Blueprint* in the gallery space at Judson Church in the fall of 1967. The whole piece had an additive structure with each image or tableau building on the previous one. But because the basis was stillness, each action was discrete, altering the visual and aural situation enormously. For this version, we only let 25 people into the space. The audience entered in total darkness, and then at a certain point the lights came on; the first image consisted of me and Alfred North sitting in chairs for about 10 minutes. I had painted the room white. The lights were also white. We were dressed in black clothing and were wearing black blindfolds. After our stillness we began performing very simple activities. Then a third performer, a woman dressed in white, took off our blindfolds and began pouring rocks on the floor from a white pitcher. At the end, the audience heard a piece of music that I wrote with Don Preston, *Candy Bullets and Moon*, from large speakers in the room. The audience then heard the sound of someone knocking on a door, which came from a portable tape recorder that I had hung on my shoulder. Alfred and I got up and started walking toward the door. We opened the door, and it looked like we were going outside, but it was actually a closet. The woman in white went to the window and opened up the black curtains. She invited the audience to look out the window. I had made life-sized dolls of me and Alfred sitting on two chairs with their backs to the audience, so when the audience looked, they thought that it was us out there in the garden. It seemed like another beginning, except the audience would only see the sequence from behind.

MK: Did you use this idea of an additive structure in your later works?

MM: Yes, although it became more episodic as well. For example, in the late 1960s, I started going to sites, particularly museum spaces, and making large epic pieces. I would begin the process by spending time there and listening to what the space had to say to me. In 1969, I was asked to do a piece at the

Smithsonian, and I chose the Museum of Natural History as the site for my piece, *Tour: Dedicated to Dinosaurs*. That space suggested traveling or an expedition to me. For the piece, the audience moved through different areas of the museum. The first part of it was done in the big rotunda with the audience looking up at the various levels. The rotunda of the Museum of Natural History has a mandala-esque spatial structure. So I had large groups of performers on all four sides and on multiple levels. Then I brought the audience into the Whale Room so they were very close to the performers; afterwards they followed me through the little alleyways where there were dioramas. I had performers scattered throughout the space, relating to those images in some way. Finally, I brought the audience into the auditorium where I did a kind of Q&A during which I kept moving while people asked me questions. The thrust of the piece was that it became more intimate as it went along; it started with a large group and ended with just one person.

MK: Did you use the structure of the tour for your other museum works?

MM: Yes, although later I left it up to the audience to decide their own route for the tour. For example, I did a piece called *Tour 2: Barbershop* at the Chicago Museum of Contemporary Art in April 1969. That space suggested to me more simultaneous events, so I created a one-hour piece where the audience could walk around and discover various activities in the different rooms. There was a large space upstairs where I had about 50 people doing a sequence of movements that started way back in the room and moved forward. There was another room where there were five performers doing a series of activities—a song, a movement, and a still—that would repeat. So as an audience member toured the building, he or she would reenter a room and discover a person was upside down or that the performers had progressed forward, etc. Downstairs, I had members of the audience play a little game of placing objects in different configurations. Again, I was working with contrasting large groups with a more intimate relationship between the audience and the performer. I was very interested in these different degrees of scale and perspective of the performer/audience relationship. I was also interested in the irony that the audience moved around while the performers were actually somewhat still.

MK: Was that the first time that you explored contrasting the movement of the audience and performer?

MM: No, actually, I had already used this idea in 1968 for another version of *Blueprint* at my loft on Great Jones Street. Robert Wilson was in that piece. I had him right next to the door with a blindfold on, and he was dressed in white. When you walked in, you had to brush by him. It was like an obstacle

course. One flight down, in sculptor Julius Tobias's loft, I also placed six performers in huge, open-ended, white wooden boxes made by Julius. The piece
lasted an hour with cycles of activity for both upstairs and downstairs going
on simultaneously. The performers were still, but would change configuration
periodically. So the audience would happen upon them in different configurations as they toured the two spaces. It was very much like looking at paintings or sculptures.

MK: It sounds like you enjoy playing with the audience's perspective. What
do you think motivates you to do this?

MM: You know, I don't see three dimensions. I actually only see out of one
eye at a time.

MK: Me, too. That certainly affects how we perceive depth.

MM: Yes, well, I think because of the lack of depth perception, I became fascinated with trying to create depth and trying to come out of the flat world
into three-dimensional space.

MK: Did you feel that other artists at the time were also interested in toying
with perspective, scale, and/or the audience/performer relationship?

MM: When I first came to New York, it was the end of what was called the
Happenings movement. There were a lot of people, like Allan Kaprow, who
were taking people outside and experimenting with different artistic strategies. I would have loved to have seen these experiments. I do remember seeing
the piece Claes Oldenburg did in a swimming pool.

The thing about these visual artists' work was that it was not time-
based. You had to sit there and wait for the next image. It was somewhat
clumsy in the time realm, but it was always worthwhile because their fluid
way of thinking about materials was very inspiring. In those days, many artists in the downtown scene were trying to go past the boundaries of their
own forms.

For me, moving past boundaries seemed very natural. I was a person
with seemingly diverse interests, and experimenting with various artistic
forms was my personal way of weaving my perceptions together. It was kind
of a healing thing for me as a person and soon after led to my realization that
a holistic form could be an antidote to our fragmented culture.

MK: Did these artists have a significant effect on you because they were
working in a site-specific way?

MM: Well, there was no such thing as the term *site-specific* in those days.

MK: When did you first hear that word?

MM: I don't know. I mean, there wasn't anything called "extended vocal
technique" at that time either. We, as artists, were just flailing about in the

unknown and doing work that was necessary to us, and then suddenly it is a whole genre. But in those days it was pretty lonely. And it was hard. I was pushing up against a lot, and I still do. But I was determined. It was life and death for me. Now it is kind of a strange thing that these techniques have become codified. Actually, sometimes I wonder about that because I think that when things get codified or named, then something dies. I feel like art is really about working with the unnamable. So as soon as you name it, something of the mystery gets lost.

MK: When you began working in alternative sites, what did you look for and how did you go about finding it?

MM: It depends. I think each piece was very different. For example, it was so imperative to me to do *Juice* at the Guggenheim. I had gone to a lot of museums in New York looking for a space where I could work with different dimensions and layers. I think the Guggenheim spoke to me due to its vertical organization of space as well as the acoustics. I was already very involved with writing vocal music at that time, and I really wanted sound to be a tactile and immersive element.

For *Vessel*, I looked all over the SoHo area. In those days, SoHo was pretty raw. I walked and walked over those streets trying to find a big open parking lot for the third part of the piece. So I already had a concept for *Vessel*; I needed to have a big, open outdoor place for the idea of a public execution, since I was working with shards of narrative and specifically with the Joan of Arc myth.

The way that I work is sometimes parallel with a space and sometimes in counterpoint. For example, I like to put very magical and mysterious images against very ordinary or funky spaces. I like to bring the space to life so that you would see it in a fresh way. Of course, that was always the idea, that maybe you would go by that parking lot and see it in a new way.

MK: How much do you bring to a site, and how much do you draw from it?

MM: I like to work with what is in a site. It would be the saddest thing in the world for me to go into a space and pretend that it is not there and just do what I would normally do anyway. I love the way space itself speaks, and I want the audience to be able to hear it.

But for some pieces this can be difficult. For example, *American Archaeology*, which was performed on Roosevelt Island in New York, was challenging because the site is quite noisy. It was really hard to direct an audience's focus. One of the ways that I dealt with this was to design the piece so that the audience had to keep scanning. This allowed the audience to experience what was at the site itself. I was not trying to manipulate the audience, but wanted to let them be. I wanted to give them the room to go down through the layers of presences and beings that had been there on that island in the past.

MK: Have you studied archaeology?

MM: I have always been very interested in archaeology. Besides *American Archaeology*, I've used concepts of archaeology in both *Ellis Island* and *Recent Ruins*. Even in *Blueprint* back in 1967, I excavated the downstairs gym of Judson Church. I think that has been a constant metaphor in my site work: excavation or archaeology.

I have also always been interested in history, particularly in how the richness of the present is informed by the past and demonstrates potential for the future. If you don't have that awareness within your present moment, then you are not completely grounded.

MK: It seems like there is at least one figure that represents the child's perspective in many of your works. I wonder if there is any connection between trying to see through the child's eyes and also being interested in site-specific work.

MM: I think the connection for me is that both of them are a means of getting back to a fresh, new, and unbiased way of looking at reality. A child's eyes are not necessarily dependent on what they have learned. They do not always respond based on habituated or learned behavior. And I think that site-specific work also has the potential to open up that kind of vision for people in the audience. As I said earlier, I love the idea that you might never see a space in the same way again. I think it is about art being a means of conveying magic and alertness and now-ness to people. And if they have those moments of being awake, maybe they could apply that to the rest of their lives. Perhaps this will allow them to subvert habitual behavior.

MK: Why is subversion interesting to you?

MM: Well, I think that we are living in a culture that needs to be subverted because the culture is designed to put you to sleep. Our current notion of "entertainment" is about seducing you into numbness. The computer is seducing you to numbness. The television is seducing you to numbness. That is pretty easy politically because as long as everybody is entertained, they don't think about what is happening in the world. That is a good tactic for politicians. A lot of these things started in 1980 when Reagan came to power.

So I think that what we are trying to do as artists, or at least what I am trying to do, is to create an antidote to the numbness. And sometimes that is quite painful for people. Sometimes it is easier to turn on the television than to be in the silence. It feels bracing and maybe uncomfortable to be in the silence. But then, after you get past that initial discomfort, you feel a lot better. In a sense, art allows you to go past the discursive part of your mind. The discursive part of your mind is the part that is narrating your experience. It is very verbal and does not really allow for real direct experience to come in. I think that art has the capacity, particularly site-specific work, to bring back the notion of awe. Not shock and awe, but *awe* and wonder. I am always interested in wonder and the power of the imagination.

MK: Do you feel like your art has a political agenda?

MM: Well, I feel like my work always has a political level. But it is very oblique because I am not a verbal artist. I am not someone like Brecht, who could really articulate a political situation, and I think that I am not necessarily doing work that stimulates that particular part of the mind. I am actually much more interested in experience that is unnamable. Like I said earlier, when you can name something, the mystery of existence and direct experience is gone. So while I am trying to make visible the invisible, I want to acknowledge that the invisible is also very good.

But I think just being an artist in this society is very political. To do work that is poetic, that offers an alternative to the hyperacceleration of our culture. I want to do work that does not manipulate the emotions of the audience but respects the intelligence and autonomy of each member of the audience. In this world of commodification of everything, that aspiration is, by nature, political.

MK: Yes, it is remarkable how similar the artist's role has been in the past few decades in terms of political activism. Have you noticed that the production of site work has also remained similar in the past few decades? Or were there significant differences between producing *Juice* and *Blueprint* in the 1960s and *American Archaeology* in the 1990s?

MM: I think for *American Archaeology* it was much harder to get performers. People just didn't have the same amount of time to be able to work on site pieces because more of their time needed to be spent on survival. People had to have more jobs. When I came to New York, I lived in an apartment by myself for $75 a month. You could never do that now.

I remember with a lot of love that in the late 1960s and early 1970s with pieces like *Vessel* and *Juice*, there was a sense of community that is a little more difficult to put your fingers on now. Everybody that was in *Juice* would get 10 more people involved; whole families and kids got involved. There was a sense of a downtown arts community; everybody was just raring to go in those days.

MK: Are you still attracted to site work, and do you think you might make more site works in the future?

MM: Well, I am working on a new piece with the visual artist Ann Hamilton, and the first incarnation will be in a tower that she has built in Northern California. It feels really nice to look at a space with an eye toward the site-specific again. I like to figure out how a space sounds and how it sings and how the sound and the visual dimension weave together or don't weave together. I am enjoying going back to those thoughts. The stage does get to be really boring.

MK: Do you have any words of advice for young site choreographers?

MM: Well, I would say this for any young artist: try to, as much as possible, sift through everything that is coming in, and try to get down to your inner urgency or what you need to say. Don't worry so much about the outside world.

Personally, I refused to adjust to what was expected of me. Sometimes people love my work; sometimes they hate it. But I just follow my inner road as much as I can or what I am curious about or what I want to learn. I try to put myself into a risky place with every new project.

MK: And in some way that is the beauty of site work.

MM: Yes, every new place represents new possibilities.

○

Meredith Monk as Site Pioneer, 1969–71

By Meredith Monk

Beginning

I started creating site-specific work in the 1960s. At that time, I was questioning the nature of performance. "What was its purpose?" I wondered. "How can performance become something more essential? Can we make it an inherent part of our lives, a template of experience?" I wanted to make art that was useful, experiential, rather than presentational. At that time, theatrical conventions such as the frontal orientation of the proscenium, the one- to three-hour duration, the fact that performances had given times (matinee or evening performances) seemed limiting to me.

Looking back it seems that site-specific work was inevitable in my development as an artist. Site work gave me the ability to create an immersive experience. A proscenium implies a separation between the performance and the audience. Taking people out of the theater and including them in the same space as the performers blurs boundaries and transforms experience, expanding notions of time and space. Working with place opened up my awareness of the world as it was and became a way of affirming my belief in the power of community. Because of the scale of the work, large numbers of people—whole families and groups of friends—were able to perform with us. Art was a natural and organic part of their lives.

By the late 1960s, I had already progressed into exploring sites and altered time structures in workshop situations and through pieces such as *Blueprint*. Some of those early pieces occurred in a single site and acted as a single event. I had also used the idea of moving the audience around one building in my tour pieces such as *Tour: Dedicated to Dinosaurs* (1969), *Tour2: Barbershop* (1969), and *Loft Tour* (1969). By the time I made *Juice*, *Needlebrain Lloyd and the Systems Kid*, and *Vessel*, I was ready to build on the notion of the tour using multiple sites over an extended period. In these three works, five interwoven strands began to appear again and again: multiplicity, the materiality of time, spatial dialogue, framing, and music.

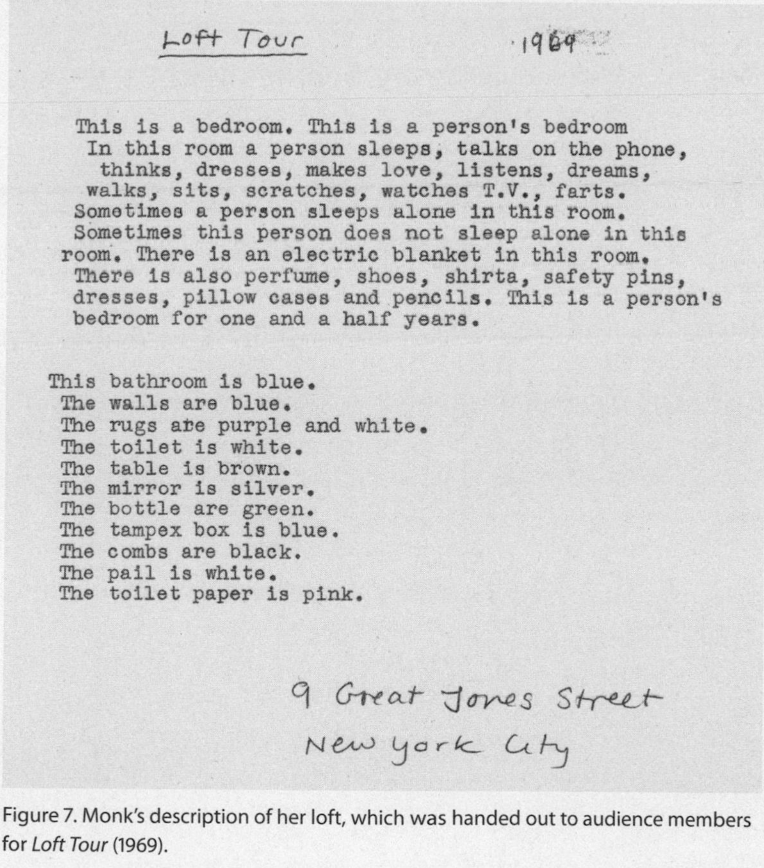

Loft Tour 1969

This is a bedroom. This is a person's bedroom
In this room a person sleeps, talks on the phone,
thinks, dresses, makes love, listens, dreams,
walks, sits, scratches, watches T.V., farts.
Sometimes a person sleeps alone in this room.
Sometimes this person does not sleep alone in this
room. There is an electric blanket in this room.
There is also perfume, shoes, shirta, safety pins,
dresses, pillow cases and pencils. This is a person's
bedroom for one and a half years.

This bathroom is blue.
The walls are blue.
The rugs are purple and white.
The toilet is white.
The table is brown.
The mirror is silver.
The bottle are green.
The tampex box is blue.
The combs are black.
The pail is white.
The toilet paper is pink.

9 Great Jones Street
New York City

Figure 7. Monk's description of her loft, which was handed out to audience members for *Loft Tour* (1969).

Multiplicity

I was interested in the idea of multiplicity as a means of affirming the richness of perception for both the audience and the performers. I wanted to create mosaic forms that included music, movement, images, objects, and light. I sought structures that implied simultaneous worlds. In a sense, these huge forms were musical in that I could play with the counterpoint between the different elements, and by juxtaposing them, I could expand and enrich experience.

When I made Juice: A Theater Cantata *(1969), I decided to use multiple sites over a long period. I worked with three sites—the Guggenheim Museum, the Minor Latham Playhouse, and the House Loft—and the performance of the three parts took place over a month's time. Through all of* Juice, *I experimented with the idea of multiplicity. For each of the three installments, audiences would see objects, movements, and musical motifs appear again and again in a new form. For example, in the first installment, there was a horse and rider in front of the Guggenheim. For the second installment, there was a child on a hobbyhorse in front of the Minor Latham. A week later in my loft, there was a tiny replica of the horse from the second installment sitting on a table in the living room. The change of scale for these repeated images was a way of working with objects, movement, music, etc., to incorporate memory into the present moment.*

Figure 8. Audiences exploring the various scenes as they climbed the spiral for *Juice*. Photo by Peter Moore.

Figure 9. Dancers on multiple levels in the Guggenheim Museum during *Juice* (1969). Photo by Peter Moore.

Figure 10. Audiences witnessed again the costumes and props in the third installment of *Juice* at The House Loft. Photo by V. Sladon.

The Materiality of Time

Right from the beginning, I was interested in time as a sculptural element—how it could be molded, compressed, stretched out, made dense or airy. In my site works, I explored different time structures such as simultaneity, fragmented continuity, cyclical or diurnal time. Overall, time turned into a spatial element; time and space became relative and interdependent.

In Needlebrain Lloyd and the Systems Kid: A Live Movie *(1970), I wanted to play with the filmic notion of time and space in a live performance. I thought that using the techniques of film—close-ups/long-shots, wipes, dissolves, cuts, simultaneity, and framing—would be an intriguing way to explore the time and space of outdoor environments.*

To play with the concept of time, we performed the piece over an extended period—six hours including the dinner break. It began at 4 p.m. in the Arboretum of Connecticut College. Then, after an hourlong sequence, the audience and performers moved up to the large rectangular college green. After another hourlong sequence, the audience had a dinner break. At 8 p.m.,

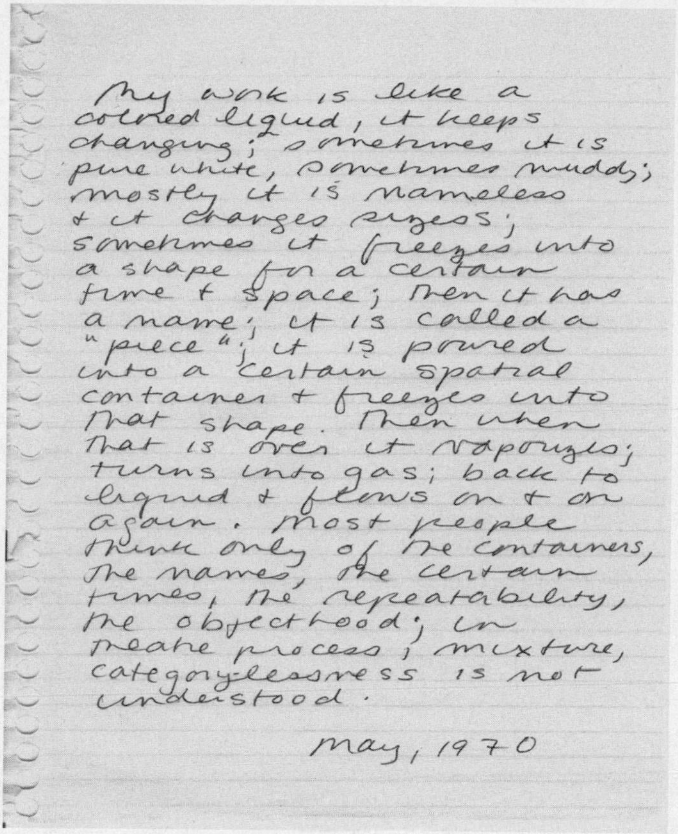
My work is like a
colored liquid, it keeps
changing; sometimes it is
pure white, sometimes muddy;
mostly it is nameless
+ it changes sizes;
sometimes it freezes into
a shape for a certain
time + space; then it has
a name; it is called a
"piece"; it is poured
into a certain spatial
container + freezes into
that shape. Then when
that is over it vaporizes;
turns into gas; back to
liquid + flows on + on
again. Most people
think only of the containers,
the names, the certain
times, the repeatability,
the objecthood; in
theatre process; mixture,
categorylessness is not
understood.

May, 1970

Figure 11. A handwritten manifesto Monk wrote In 1970 about her creative process.

they reassembled in front of one of the buildings that had been in the distance in the afternoon segment. At the end of this segment, 24 motorcycles roared up the hill in formation, surrounded the audience, and led them back to the Arboretum for the last segment. Both evening segments were performed with portable lights piercing the darkness.

Spatial Dialogue

What satisfied me most about working in a nontheatrical space was that the process became a dialogue between an environment that already existed and me. My task was to listen to what a particular space was saying to me. I liked that I was not constructing a reality that would be the same no matter where I went.

Vessel: An Opera Epic *(1971) was an exploration of Joan of Arc as an embodiment of a female visionary who listens to inner voices and acts on them* even in a dangerous world. It took place over a week's time; each weekday evening an audience of 100 would go to my loft on Great Jones Street for part 1 of the performance and then be immediately transported by bus to a garage-style theater, the Performance Garage, for part 2. Then on Saturday, those 500 people would experience part 3 in a parking lot in lower SoHo.

Each of the spaces had a particular visual orientation. For part 1, *Open House*, the space was a long narrow loft with a low ceiling; the audience was seated at one end. The loft was pitch black with images coming out of the darkness and silence. Images began far away as if you were looking down the wrong end of a telescope. Then, little by little, the piece worked its way closer to the audience. All the costumes were black, white, and gray except for the "coming attractions" section, which included short solos in color referring to what would occur in part 2. When audiences traveled to the Garage for part 2, *Handmade Mountain*, they confronted a vertical space or "mountain." For this section, I was particularly inspired by medieval tapestry and painting. As the audience looked up, they saw a very brightly lit and colorful two-dimensional field, sometimes densely packed with events. Part 3, *Existent Lot*, combined elements of the first two parts: it was outdoors in the dark with horizontality being the visual principle, but it was also very colorful and pageant-like.

Figure 12. A "madwoman" comes out of the dark in the first installment of *Vessel* (1971). Photo by Peter Moore.

Figure 13. The verticality of the Handmade Mountain in the second installment of *Vessel*. Photo by Peter Moore.

Figure 14. The pageant of the parking lot in the third installment of *Vessel*. Photo by Peter Moore.

Framing

Most spaces have natural boundaries or frames that contain the images in one way or another. Indoor spaces have walls and ceilings; outdoor spaces may have trees, mountains, or other contours that enclose an area. Inspired by the film medium, I chose to play with both natural and created frames on site; framing became an essential element of my site work. I especially played with distance and scale within a given frame.

> *In one segment of* Needlebrain Lloyd, *a Land Rover filled with performers from The House, moved slowly around the perimeter of the green. At times it would appear miniscule in the viewer's frame, and then it would drive around the green toward the audience, stopping in front of them and obstructing their view of the rest of the piece. Meanwhile a group of people would have entered from very far away, looking like they were only an inch tall.*
>
> *In* Vessel, *the walls of the parking lot were the seeming boundaries, but the frame grew wider and wider, incorporating more and more space within it. Suddenly, beyond the walls, the church across the street lit up to reveal three gray-haired performers, expanding the frame beyond expectations. I originally wanted a helicopter to hover over the parking lot, making use of the sky as part of the piece.*

Figure 15. Exploring the frame with a Land Rover in *Needlebrain Lloyd and the Systems Kid* (1970). Photo by Peter Moore.

Music

I had begun my exploration of the human voice as an instrument in the mid-1960s. As I was working on *Juice*, *Needlebrain Lloyd*, and *Vessel*, music became more and more of a driving force. While I had always balanced each of the perceptual layers and thought of their relationship as nonhierarchical, I became increasingly aware of the overall musicality of my forms. Techniques and forms from music composition began seeping into the structure of the whole.

In Juice, *I used the half-second delay (echo) of the Guggenheim as an inspiration to write music that resounded in that space. One way I worked with that phenomenon was to have the 85 choral voices sound before you saw the performers come up to the railings; it was as if the aural delay became visual. I worked to make the building ring. In contrast to that, the music I wrote for the second installment was more percussive, raw, and primal. I used our large combat boots or work boots as percussion instruments, and I wrote vocal solos, duets, and quartets that had the plaintive quality of folk music. By the third installment, the musical pieces were presented in recorded form.*

In Needlebrain Lloyd, *the music was heard in different relationships to the images. Sometimes the music was heard from far away as one element of a larger image; other times it was the focus of a scene. In the afternoon section on the College Green, I played a piece on my electric organ through the window of a building far away. Later at night, in front of that building with the audience seated fairly close, that same piece was sung by small groups of people sitting around campfires.*

In Vessel, *singing became a metaphor for Joan's voices and the visionary experience. In part 1, music was used to cut through the silent images; then, as the piece progressed, the music acted as a river, linking sections of activity.*

Continuing

Site work continues to inspire me as a way of creating art that lies between the cracks of perception, allowing new hybrid forms to emerge. The titles of my early site-specific pieces reflected that notion: "theater cantata," "live movie," "opera epic." The names became, on the one hand, a map of my exploration and, on the other, a guide for the audience. The seeming contradictions within the titles helped me to gain insight about what I was working on, challenging any preconceived ideas I might have had.

What still excites me about site-specific work is its sense of adventure. Through site work, a collection of performers and audience members can share a space animated by the unique energy of live performance. Once a space is energized, it is never the same again. Site work offers a fresh look at what we take for granted; it reopens the curiosity that is an inherent, fundamental quality of our humanity. Honoring place is a way of grounding us, a way to remain alert to and appreciate the magic of what is.

Figure 16. The main musical theme written by Meredith Monk for the first installment of *Juice*.

2

Joanna Haigood

Joanna Haigood is the artistic director of Zaccho Dance Theatre in San Francisco. From a San Francisco clock tower to airport terminals to the bucolic fields of Massachusetts, Haigood excavates the historical, architectural, and natural features of her chosen sites to reinvigorate our understanding of place. Using diverse movement genres including aerial work and postmodern dance vocabulary, Haigood demonstrates how sites can be saturated with past memories and previous manifestations. Her work has been commissioned by the National Black Arts Festival, Festival d'Avignon, Dancing in the Streets, the Walker Art Center, and Jacob's Pillow, among others, and she has earned such awards as a 1997 Guggenheim Fellowship and a 1999 Alpert Award in the Arts as well as fellowships from the National Endowment for the Arts and the Irvine Foundation. Kloetzel interviewed Haigood on November 22, 2004, in Haigood's spacious dance studio located in an aging warehouse in the Bayview/Hunter's Point area of San Francisco.

An Interview with Joanna Haigood

MK: Do you remember your first steps into the site-specific genre?

JH: There are some vague beginnings. I went to Bard College in upstate New York. The campus was situated in a rather beautiful and serene landscape. The winters there were often very cold and snowy, and by the time spring arrived, the only thing anyone wanted was to be outside. From time to time our classes—composition in particular—were held outside. I always found that interesting. I think that was the beginning of a more focused look at making dances outside of the theater.

In the late 1970s I was a student at The Place (the London School of Contemporary Dance). A couple of my classmates and I created our own choreography lab outside of the studio. We made dances in the streets, on the stairs and escalators at Euston Station, in the subway. We even made a dance for the vegetable section of a supermarket—a short one before security ejected us. This was before getting permits became an established part of the process. It was more of an "anything goes" situation. We never really set a structure for these dances, and they were always improvisational, although the sites and time of day were never random. In all, I wouldn't say these were great intellectual exercises. We were more interested in having fun. Anyway, a few things stuck with me out of that experience. The physical constraints or the body's relationships to specific situations, like stairs, doors, or moving objects—the inherent movement vocabularies in a particular situation or place—became a foundation in my work.

Also, while I was in England, I lived next door to a woman named Judith Holmes. She had been an aerialist for Barnum and Bailey and enjoyed going to see the circus when it came to town. Sometimes she would take me along. I started looking at space differently as a result of my circus adventures with her. The process of exploring these two ideas—movement as it relates to objects or environment and choreography using three dimensions—catapulted me from the theater permanently. Well, let's say, for the most part anyway. Site work became the most engaging work for me.

MK: Do you feel there is something in particular that lures you to the site-specific process?

JH: My mother always wanted me to be an architect. In her attempts to point me in that direction, I became aware and interested in buildings. And although I didn't become an architect, I feel that some of the principles of architecture apply or inform my artistic process.

One thing that continues to attract me to site work is the challenge of working in such diverse environments. Negotiating new materials and situations keeps the creative process fresh for me.

I presume I also like the mountains of administrative work involved as well because that is a big part of making site work. But I am not sure I'm ready to accept that!

MK: How do you choose a site initially?

JH: It varies. Sometimes I'll feel deeply inspired by a place and want to make something there. Sometimes I am moved by an event or by a period in history, and then I try to find a place or a site where that history is relevant. Sometimes I am invited to make a piece by a festival, presenter, or producer. They might be specific as to where the piece takes place.

MK: Could you elaborate on your process? Do you find yourself delving into the sensation of the space or the history or—?

Figure 17. Working in diverse environments. *Departure and Arrival* (2007) at the San Francisco Airport International Terminal. © Stephen Phillips Photography, www.joyoflight.com.

JH: I think I'm interested in all of those things. Usually I try to spend as much time as I can at the site and speak to as many people there as I can.

MK: So you interview people?

JH: Yes, although sometimes more extensively than others depending on the direction or focus of the piece. I also spend a lot of time reading, watching films, and looking at photographs, drawings, and other reference materials. But once I begin the research phase and as other people get involved, information seems to come from all directions.

        I also conduct field measurements. I watch for light and color, and I catalog the types of objects used or that are normally present at the site. I try to map out a series of sections on paper based on parts of the research that most interest me. Rehearsals begin about then, and I start to shape the images and the experience of time.

MK: When you are in the research phase, do you also read historical texts about the place?

JH: I read whatever available history I can, true and false; both are interesting and informative to me. But I do not tend to make literal pieces. My pieces are more impressionistic. They stem from my personal observations and reflections of a place or of certain historical events.

MK: How do you involve your dancers in the research process?

JH: I have many discussions with the dancers, and I share my research with them as much as I can. Sometimes I create a research library for the studio. I think it is important for the performer to have a clear understanding of the context of the work.

MK: Do you find yourself drawing on the narratives of a site?

JH: Yes, I use narratives as a point of reference, but I rarely create work with a linear narrative. It is much more abstract. Sometimes I create visual textures with multiple simultaneous events. Sometimes the performances are self-guided, meaning the audience chooses how, when, and from what point of view to see the performance. Looking at the performances from different perspectives and rearranging the sequences sometimes produces vastly different meanings.

MK: As you work on site, do you feel like you have a certain kind of responsibility to the site in terms of how it is represented or to the community that exists there?

JH: You know, it's a huge responsibility to interpret the minds and hearts of people you don't know very well. You're never going to see the full picture. I feel I have a responsibility to do the best work that I can, to stay inspired, to be as thorough in my research as possible, and to provide the best tools to my collaborators in order to realize the vision.

        In many ways, a place is a poetic expression of a site and the accumulation of the experiences it contains. If you're quiet enough, if you're still enough, you can perceive the resonance of its experience. I guess I would say that that is the responsibility I am concerned with: that place itself becomes the main speaker. That's the condition I try to create for myself and for the audience, a heightened awareness of the place around them.

MK: You mentioned your aerial work earlier. Do you use aerial work in every piece or only if the site calls for it?

JH: First, I decide whether or not it's appropriate or even possible. In general, I am drawn to aerial work because I'm very interested in working the space more sculpturally, using lateral, diagonal, vertical, and horizontal lines as well as perspective and scale as primary choreographic tools.

MK: Do these tools help you alter people's perception of space?

JH: Yes. The aerial work definitely reveals new perspectives! But most

Figure 18. Aerial action by dancers Christopher Love and Sonya Smith in *Inverted States* (2005) on San Francisco's Senator Hotel. Photo by Stacey Prickett.

importantly it redirects an audience's focus to areas that are often over-looked.

MK: Do you feel that your site work also alters people's perception of time?

JH: I like to think of time not only as a system of measurement but also as having varying and distinct qualities. Understanding time is a huge undertaking, but everyone can relate to moments or events when time seemed to be suspended or when everything moved in slow motion or when time "flew by." I am fascinated by this, particularly within the context of a site performance. The site itself can evoke memories of other events; other things like weather, ambient sounds, scent, perspective, and scale also have transporting effects on an audience.

In more traditional forms of dance, music plays an important part in shaping the time experience. The music is often metered and the dance falls into its rhythm and plays upon its nuance. "Real life" also has rhythms, but it can feel more amorphous like a big wave, a whirlwind, or powder. Certain environments bring out different qualities of time. Some are attached to deep emotional triggers; a concentration camp would be a good example here. Some have a strong physical dynamic, like the rushing energy of a large waterfall or a train yard.

MK: Have you run into any kind of dangerous moments in your work, either in how you portray a site or in your interactions with a community?

JH: Danger, no. But I think there may have been expectations of a more literal interpretation. I have also had some problems with people not understanding the nature of the work in the negotiation process or during the time I am working out permits. But luckily, for the most part anyway, projects' objectives and designs have been accepted.

I'll give you a funny example of this. You know, people don't only own their actual buildings and lots, they own a certain amount of air space above the property. Once we were working at the site of a grain terminal. The land-owner of the grain terminal had approved our plans and was familiar with the areas we would be using. One cable or fly line was to extend from one side of his property to the top of the grain terminal, about 400 feet away. For about 25 feet, this cable ran 40 feet above the NYPD's vehicle evidence lot where they stored cars involved in criminal cases. They leased this land from the owner of the grain terminal. This 25 feet suddenly became a big problem because the police department was worried about what we would see when we flew over it. Who actually had jurisdiction over that air space? Was it the lessee, or was it the landowner? It turned out the lessee did. We had just one week to install the show, and suddenly these 25 feet had turned into a giant quagmire for me and the producer. There was quite a bit of scrambling to find the right councilman, police chief, etc., to get a permit in less than the six weeks it normally took. Fortunately, we did. I had a couple of sleepless nights! But, as I learned very early, you just keep changing hats and eventually you'll figure it out.

MK: Such a story really points to site work's ability to make us reconsider our assumptions about space.

JH: Well, it was interesting, because no one had thought of air space as being privately owned; it just didn't click. We were flying over the lot, not using it. But it was a very big deal. There are a lot of things like that—last-minute things that are absolutely critical in site work.

MK: Have you gotten any feedback from your audiences about their postperformance impressions of a site?

JH: Yes, people often say that they will never look at the place in the same way again, or they say things like, "I never noticed this about this place. As a matter of fact I never even knew this place existed, and I've lived in this community for a long time." Sometimes it will inspire them to tell their own story. I think this is the response many site artists receive.

You know, many of us stop fully experiencing our environment after a certain point. We have such tremendous pressure to achieve, to get things done, to move on, that our focus gets very narrow. It's really unfortunate because we lose a lot of the living of life, because we're so busy doing, chasing money, etc. Somehow we're taught to cut off our senses in order to get things done, so we're not distracted by the task at hand. I'm not sure why it happens like that. When you watch children playing or engaging with the world around them, they are open to and interested in everything. But why does that go away?

MK: Getting people to engage with place, time, etc., sounds like a form of activism. Is that a label you would adopt?

JH: I make work that interests me: sometimes it is political work, sometimes it is community work, and sometimes it is personal work. I am not sure I would label it with the term *activism*.

But, with regard to the political, I have a friend who says, "If you're not making political art right now, you shouldn't be making art at all." And a certain part of me agrees. This is a very disturbing time in our country. Every American, not just artists, should be speaking out against the social and political injustices that are rampant in our country today.

But I also think that there are times where it's appropriate to make work

Figure 19. Evoking a new experience of the environment. Joanna Haigood, Jo Kreiter, and Sheila Lopez flying off the San Francisco clock tower in *Noon* (1995). Photo by Theodora Litsios.

that remembers the trees or nature in general. We have become so discon-
nected from the natural world around us. We keep forgetting that we too are
animals, that we are part of a larger natural world or system of life.

MK: And right now, that is political art, in other words, "Remember the tree,
before it's cut down." I think in that context it's amazing what can become
radical. Almost anything.

JH: Exactly.

Looking for the Invisible

By Joanna Haigood

So what is a ghost anyway?

I have spent the best of 25 years examining places for details that would lead to some sort of story or memory of past lives, a clear picture of the distinct forces that I feel still resonate in the present state of things. I am attracted to and truly enjoy the investigation, reading all the physical evidence and traces left behind by people and events. Although seemingly abstract, those curious marks and the relentless wear found in the landscape or in architecture are in fact a tangible and beautifully poetic map of time. Sometimes, when I am lucky, I can sit before the evidence, and I can imagine time unrestrained by order or limits, and all the events begin to exist simultaneously. I can move fluidly, in my mind, in this open-ended dimension, passing from one era to the next without hindrance. But it only lasts for a moment, and then I am back in the here and now.

In our early conversations about the potential direction for the project *Ghost Architecture*, which took place in the Yerba Buena Center for the Arts Forum in San Francisco in 2003, Wayne Campbell and I spoke frequently about our mutual intrigue with time. What if we really had the capacity of transtemporal perception? What would it be like to view the intersection of different events separated in time but not in space? We spoke about how to express this with architecture, using the coordinate system to establish the exact positions of vanished buildings. Maybe by identifying the spot in empty space that was once occupied by a building from the past, we could generate the conditions needed to perceive that open dimension.

With the help of Ann Berman, we began our investigation. We soon discovered that four buildings converged in the location of the Forum just before its construction: the Peerless Movie Theater, the West Hotel, and two apartment buildings. They were built soon after the 1906 earthquake and directly on top of the earthquake debris.

Located at 148 Third Street, the Peerless was built circa 1912 as a nickelodeon, and it continued operating as a movie theater until it closed in 1970. In 1929, it was one of the 4 movie theaters in San Francisco and the estimated 461 theaters throughout the United States that catered exclusively to "colored" audiences. From 1958 until 1970, it was known as the Peerless Girlesque, the Nudeorama, and Ding Dong Dollies, and it screened only X-rated adult films.

The West Hotel was located at 156 Third Street, next to the Peerless, and was

Figure 20. José Navarrete and Suzanne Gallo seen in the multiple reconstructed hotel rooms in Joanna Haigood's *Ghost Architecture* (2003). Photo by Ira Nowinski.

built circa 1908. The 122-room hotel was intended to provide lodging to transient male laborers. Known as one of the finer resident hotels in the area, the West Hotel was sought after by single men working locally and at sea. By 1970, most of the residents in the hotel were over 50 and living on modest pensions. In 1974, all the residents were evicted, and the building was demolished to make way for the Yerba Buena Center complex.

I have always felt that people provide the soul to architecture. They give the architecture a sort of consciousness that imbues it with meaning far beyond its essential functions. When I thought about the West Hotel, it struck me that it was filled with 122 8' × 10' private rooms invested with private activities. In a way they were sacred places, even in their most chaotic condition—private surveys of emotions and their various manifestations.

For most of us, our rooms are places where we feel the safest. They are places where we gather the courage to confront the outside world and where we recover and recharge for the next round. Perhaps most importantly, they are the places we store our memories. We put our memories in our collection of objects, in little pieces of paper that we hang on the walls. We catalog our memories in our habits, in our posture, in our conversations with ourselves. In our rooms, we share our private thoughts, our hopes, and our fears. And we use our rooms to relax and to escape our "real lives" by any means we have available.

I wondered what kind of people lived in the West Hotel.

Anyone who knows anything about the redevelopment of the South of Market area knows something about the battle between the hotel tenants, along with local business owners, and the San Francisco Redevelopment Agency during the late 1960s and early 1970s. It was such a bitter fight that, 30 years later, the mere mention of it can still conjure such high-pitched emotions that it is clear the necessary healing has yet to be completed. It's a sad and unfortunate story, one that reflects our ongoing lack of humane and socially just methods of urban renewal.

When we first met Ira Nowinski in January 2003, he showed us his extraordinary photo book, *No Vacancy: Urban Renewal and the Elderly* (1979). His photographs offered a view of the intimate lives of the hotel residents, their rooms, their clothes, their possessions, their lifestyles, and ultimately their demise.

One photograph stood out during that visit: it was the "Last Resident of the West Hotel." Ira explained that this man had come to the building a few days before the demolition in order to pay his last respects to a place that held profound meaning to him. He was wandering in the halls looking into rooms, perhaps even his own room, and remembering a past that was quickly slipping away. I imagined that from time to time he would pick up a piece of clothing or a picture or maybe just a matchbook that, to an outsider, would appear as a worthless object. But in the instant of his contact, these objects would fill, like the rooms around them, with thousands of moments, creating a resounding chorus of the lives that once passed through them. An Interview/Still Learning, Doing, and Relearning

For months after that initial visit, I spent many hours speaking to Ira about his *No Vacancy* project. And when he spoke about the subjects of his book— Pete Mendelsohn or George Woolf or Eddie Heider or George Hasselbeck or the cat lady, Hope Woodward, or Mr. Bream or any of his acquaintances in the TOOR group (Tenants and Owners in Opposition to Redevelopment)—it was as if they were still alive. I watched him closely as he was transported back in time. I could almost hear their voices. I could almost see them in some common dimension; and always, as he spoke the last words of the story, his love for these old friends would rise, and we would be suspended all together in a timeless moment. Eventually I realized that these people were still alive in their legacy.

So what is a ghost, anyway? Maybe it has something to do with the reconsti-

Figure 21. In one of the rooms, Robert Henry Johnson plays a character/resident of the hotel who takes his own photo in *Ghost Architecture* (2003). Photo by Ira Nowinski.

tution of light from the past, as my friend Pete Richards suggested one day. Or maybe it has something to do with our memory, that invisible vessel that carries us back in time while we're still surely planted in the present. Maybe it is simply the potential of our own curiosity and our willingness to follow it. I can't really say that I know for sure, at least not yet.

3

Stephan Koplowitz

Stephan Koplowitz is a director/choreographer who has developed a reputation for creating site-specific multimedia works in architecturally significant urban sites. Since receiving one of the first commissions by Dancing in the Streets in 1987 for *Fenestrations* in Grand Central Terminal in New York, Koplowitz has gone on to make over 28 site works in such varied venues as Manhattan's Bryant Park (as part of webbedfeats.org), the State of Illinois Building, the Natural History Museum in London, and the British Library. He was awarded a 2004 Alpert Award in the Arts, a 2003 Guggenheim Fellowship, and a 2000 Bessie (New York Dance and Performance Award) for Sustained Achievement in Choreography along with six NEA choreography fellowships. He is the producer/director of TaskForce, an international site-specific touring company, and as dean, teaches for and directs the Sharon Disney Lund School of Dance at CalArts. The following is a dialogue that took place between Kloetzel and Koplowitz in a series of phone conversations between 2005 and 2007.

An Interview with Stephan Koplowitz

MK: Could you talk about your first forays into site work?

SK: My first inkling that the proscenium stage would not accommodate all my goals came early. At Wesleyan University, as part of my 1979 honors thesis in music, I created an interactive dance, light, video, and sound work called *Click Tracks*. It was installed and performed in an old gymnasium. I chose that unconventional space for its size and its ability to allow the audience to experience a multisensory work in a new way.

The audience for *Click Tracks* was divided into two groups. The first group saw the live performance inside the gymnasium, sitting on bleachers. The second group viewed the work in a large hallway adjacent to the performance space through the "eyes" of four video cameras. The cameras were transmitting live images of the performances to four video monitors. There was interdependence among the elements in this work. The sound influenced the lights through sensors; the video could only be seen if a light was on. The dancers reacted to the lights, sound, etc. At intermission, the two groups switched places, thus giving each audience member a different perception of the work. *Click Tracks* was my first attempt at working in an alternative space, and it evoked both opportunities and challenges that would continue to interest and stimulate me as my choreographic career continued.

Then, in 1980, between college and graduate school, I was part of the Jacob's Pillow Dance Ensemble. This group performed in something like 14 different places over the course of six weeks. We performed everywhere from the street to nursing homes to shopping centers to people's lawns to . . . you name it, but we did the same pieces over and over again. It opened my eyes to getting out of the studio and bringing art to the people.

Oddly enough, Elise Bernhardt was having the same experience that I was at the very same time. Elise and I met in 1980 at Jacob's Pillow. Elise, Victoria Marks, and I were all just out of college, and Liz Thompson, the Pillow director, got us involved with the touring ensemble. Elise took on more of a director/managerial role (which makes sense when you look into the future), and I provided some of my choreography to the ensemble and got to perform. Elise was involved in it for the first summer, and I ended up being involved for three summers. Elise claims that was one of her first inspirations to start Dancing in the Streets. Later, our paths crossed again because she commissioned me to do the piece *Fenestrations* in the windows at Grand Central Terminal; that started my career as a professional site artist.

MK: Why does site-specific work interest you?

SK: I love the challenges; I love having to make art completely within the confines of the public sector; I love not being sequestered behind the cloak of the concert hall (although the stage does still hold my interest). Site work also inspires me in that most sites chosen provide a "canvas" never before used as a performance space, a tabula rasa. Going into unexplored territory is always exciting. Transforming a popular public space or a unique private space into a performance space for the first time is a thrill. My goal is to convey that feeling to the audience when they anticipate and then attend a site-specific event.

One reason I have devoted so much time to site work is in response to my experience of how contemporary dance has become somewhat insular in terms of who attends concerts. The habit of making the trip to the proscenium theater is not one shared by all, especially when we compete more and more with home theaters and movies. Also, in our society, certain art forms seem to grow more and more removed from the public eye. Look at how poetry was once a hugely popular art form, with best sellers and newspapers printing poetry and with poets being celebrated in society. That situation has changed, of course, in a way that is similar to the place of contemporary dance; neither is seen as part of the public discourse. So the excitement of doing site work for me is to interject my art into daily life, into the public square, to become part of the public discourse.

MK: Does this ability to be part of the public discourse foster your continued interest in making site-specific work?

SK: Yes, but these days I'm more interested in making site-adaptive as opposed to one-of-a-kind site-specific work. The reason is that site-specific works generally have three or four performances if I'm lucky. Often, they are never to be seen again. Sometimes, I feel as if I've made a career of making the most ephemeral art in the performing arts *ever*. I mean [laughs], I'm not just writing poetry; I'm writing poetry that disappears after you read it. So at this point in my life I'm interested in site-adaptive works because I'm hopeful that they will be able to travel, they will have more of an artistic life, and they can continue to have an impact. Currently, I'm "touring" two site-adaptive projects, *Revealed*, which involves a room-sized camera obscura, and my *Grand Step Project*. I've also created a site-specific touring company called TaskForce, made up of only eight performers, which will tour in the United States, the UK, and Germany. The thrust of the TaskForce is that it acts as a site-adaptive touring group, capable of making site-based work for a series of spaces and sites found within a geographical area and that it is done on a small, more economical scale.

MK: Have you given up on site-specific work entirely?

SK: No, not at all, I'm still very interested. In fact, I got a commission in 2005 from the city of Chattanooga to create a work (*Light Lines* with over 50 performers) for a new pier designed by James Carpenter and built on the Chattanooga River. I'm also making a small work for the Institute for Contemporary Art (ICA) in Boston, and I'm in discussion with the British Museum and the Dance Umbrella Festival for a huge work with video and dancers for the Great Court for 2010. Working in those spaces has been a dream for many, many years.

MK: After you decide upon a site, what is your course of action?

SK: Well, it depends on the project. For both site-adaptive and site-specific projects, I visit the site and think about how the work will be seen by the audience. It's a very simple idea, but in a way it has huge ramifications. If you make your decisions about how to use the site based on how the work is seen, in essence, it dictates almost everything else.

Figure 22. Using large numbers of performers. Dancers in *Grand Step Project: Flight* (2004) at the New York Public Library. Photo by Julie Lemberger.

So once I've made those decisions, the site tells me the scale I'm going to work with. I want to match the scale of the site with the scale of the performers; I think that's very important. Too often I've seen site-specific works where people have chosen sites and created works where the space overwhelms the number of performers they've chosen. It doesn't mean that they haven't made interesting material for those performers, but in the chosen context, their work is not seen in the best light.

MK: Which is why you use so many dancers?

SK: I use many dancers if that is what is *called* for, yes. I don't work with large casts for the sake of working with large numbers. I try to approach each site as though I were an architect, as though I were designing a structure for that site. So the measurements of the site dictate the number of people I feel I will need. I do think of architecture in terms of harmony, that there is a rhythm created by certain design features in a building.

Then I go through this process called "reading the site." I look at the site, and I determine how I want a viewer to see the site. For example, in the Natural History Museum in London (*Genesis Canyon*), I was dealing with the entire entryway or the Grand Entrance Hall as it is called. There was a staircase at one end, there was a stone bridge on the other end, and there were balconies on either side. So I staged that work in four sections: the first section on the steps, the second section on the bridge, the third on the balconies, and the fourth section back on the steps. I had to find a way to direct the audience's focus to each of these areas. Once I decided how to direct the audience's focus, I could start thinking about the theme of the work. So I haven't even come to a literal theme, if there is one, until after I've done all those sorts of structural decisions. And those structural decisions end up influencing how I interpret my theme. The dimensions of the site influence the number of performers I feel are needed. For *Genesis Canyon* I wanted to cover the grand staircase with dancers, create a human "screen." Thus, because of the dimensions of those steps, I needed 38 dancers.

I tell people I work from the outside in, or you can say from the inside out, depending on what you feel is the inside or the outside. I look first at the surface or physicality of a site. I go from that to investigating the history and the context of the site. How is the site currently being used? What do people think of the site today?

MK: So you do some historical research as well?

SK: Oh, absolutely, if the site warrants it. The Natural History Museum in London was built in 1881. It was inspired by Darwin's work in England and was built as a "cathedral to knowledge." So I spent time reading Darwin, looking at the exhibitions in the museum, and studying the history of the architect and the architecture of the time. The work was called *Genesis Canyon* and was about the history of life.

For a work I did in Germany called *Kohle Körper* or *Coal Bodies*, the producers took me on several field trips. I ended up spending three full days just driving around Germany visiting mining museums and coal factories and learning all I could about the history of coal mining. Now, I never would have done that if I weren't involved in that project. That's a good reason why I like doing site-specific work, because it's like making a movie. It forces you into another world, to learn about new subjects often outside of your immediate life experience.

MK: Do you feel that your work stimulates community building?

SK: Ultimately, yes. Almost all of my work has links to the community it is based in. However, my first priority in making a new work is to be true to

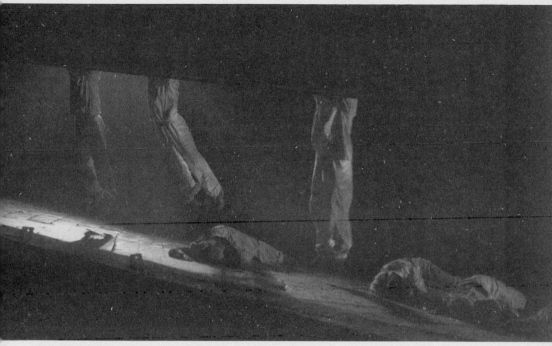

Figure 23. Tumbling down a coal shaft in *Kokerei Projekt: Kohle Körper* (1999). Photo used by permission of Peter and Hildegard Brill.

a central concept. I don't make work about building community or works that reference communities, although I have done that kind of work with my concert dance pieces.

However, that being said, with my site work, I am usually the only person not from the chosen site or community making this work. I don't take 10, 20, or 30 dancers on tour with me, for obvious reasons. I end up making the work with performers from that community. In England, I worked with London-based dance artists. In Germany, I worked with artists from seven or eight countries because of the new laws with the European Union. In Chattanooga, I made a site film that brought together almost every professional dancer in the city. These activities can help foster community. In fact, in auditions, I use this idea of community as a way of attracting dancers to the project. Dance companies have been formed as a result of so many dancers meeting during the process. It's an inspiring part of the work, but not always something that's appreciated or noticed. It's easy to get caught up in the logistics of getting the work produced or the struggle to raise the budget, both of which make us forget at times the lasting value of the collective effort.

MK: Do you feel that your site work ends up changing how people see the environment?

SK: I hope it does, and that's a big reason for me to do site work. I aim to change people's memories and perceptions of a site. My aim is for the audience to never see the site again without having an image of the work in their minds. I know that this is why many producers like to get involved in this art form. They know they are making an impact beyond the theater, sometimes with iconic spaces from their communities.

MK: Have you ever run onto risky ground in terms of how you represent a site?

SK: Yes, but not often. My work tends to be very accessible, and in many ways I am proud of that fact. There are many other artists who do site work that is much more politically oriented or is made to actively express a social agenda.

That said, I did a piece in Chicago in 1991 called *The Governed Body*. It was for the State of Illinois building. It's a huge building; it looks like a UFO landed in the middle of the town. It has one of the biggest internal atrium spaces—20 stories high. The design of the atrium reminded me of a Panopticon, or of how certain prisons are designed. The building houses just about every government agency in Illinois. The work dealt with issues of how governments control our bodies or our minds. It was very abstract, but in essence I was making a living political cartoon using spoken text. I had the dancers chant things like "I want to see the governor" and "He owes me money." People who worked in the building were listening to this, and word got to the governor's office. The day before we were set to perform, I had to take a conference call and explain to members of the governor's office what I was doing. Basically, I had to get clearance of some kind. I don't think they were going to close us down. However, they were concerned that I would insult the government employees who worked in the building, which was not my intention. I was surprised by the reaction. Frankly, I shouldn't have been, given what happened ultimately with relations between artists and government institutions such as the NEA (this was right before all the controversy with regard to the NEA Four). My experience was so benign comparatively.

But I do like to make work that brings out something unique about the site. It's not reverential. I mean, I don't treat the site with kid gloves. It also doesn't mean that the work isn't challenging or doesn't challenge the site in some way. But I'm not purposely bringing a sociopolitical agenda unless the site itself cries out for that. Grand Central is a good example. Grand Central in 1987 was a place that people travel through to reach home, but it was also a place that many people *made* their home. The homeless population in Grand Central was staggering. For some reason, as I initially explored the station, the song "Home on the Range" kept coming to mind. Perhaps this is because Grand Central is one of the few places in New York City where you're tricked into thinking you're looking at a horizon because the space is so large. So the piece was really about that tension between people traveling a distance to get home and people making it a *home*. Home and homelessness I felt could not be ignored. There's some text in the score that references this idea. At one point you hear a knock on the door, and you hear my voice say, "Is anybody home?" This social, public idea inspired the work as much as the visual representation of the three levels.

MK: Does creating site work make you an activist?

SK: Well, am I an activist because I'm an artist and an educator and much of my art is done in public places? In larger terms, I'm going against the grain just by doing those things, no matter what art I create. To be a dance artist, you end up engaging in activist-type behavior. Your art depends on organizing people, their behavior, their bodies. But I'm not an overt political activist or a community organizer. I mean, I tend to shy away from those labels. I am a politically aware person; my father worked for the CIA, and as a result I lived abroad for most of my childhood, during which time I engaged my dad in many conversations and debates. So while I'm not into making polemical or political work, I can't deny that I am politically aware on both a conscious and subconscious level when I make a work. In the end, I'm not going to edit material if it does reference social or political issues.

For example, for the work I made in Germany, *Kohle Körper*, I was not immune to the fact that I was making an artwork in this factory in Germany as a Jewish man. After watching the piece, a German dance producer from East Germany said to my producer, in essence, "If this work had been seen a few years back, there would have been serious trouble." This is because the work ended up actually visually referencing forced labor. I didn't go to Germany to make a work about forced labor, death, and the destruction of lives as a result of forced labor. But I ended up making that work; it came out of me. Sometimes the site just brings up polemical themes, regardless of my initial intentions. For example, the *Grand Step Project* is called *Flight*. It was the first piece I did in New York after 9/11, and I realized that all my experiences since then were informing the work. I made most of that piece on the steps at the

Figure 24. Daring polemical themes in site work. Dancers climb the walls in *Kohle Körper* (1999). Photo used by permission of Peter and Hildegard Brill.

Winter Garden about 200 yards from Ground Zero. You could see Ground Zero from the window behind the steps. The piece starts with someone falling down the stairs. As soon as I saw that image, I knew that there was a connection to falling out of buildings. That's not the main theme of the piece, but it's there, and as soon as I recognized it, I didn't shy away from the image.

So I don't know. Activist? Is Christo an activist? I would say yes, but I don't know if it's the context in which he sees himself. When I was doing *Coal Bodies*, one German critic called me the Christo of dance, which to me is a great compliment. At times, when people ask me what I do as an artist, I will say that my work is a bit like Christo except I wrap my buildings with bodies instead of fabric.

o

Still Learning, Doing, and Relearning: Thoughts on Making and Defining Site-Specific Performance

By Stephan Koplowitz

I'm often asked if it is possible to teach someone how to be a choreographer. My answer is that one cannot become a choreographer, or any kind of artist, merely by taking a class or going to school. While those activities can inform one's practice, experiential learning is what really counts. Art is all in the doing.

When I started making site-specific work, there were very few people I could look to as models, nor were there artists in the field who even specialized in such a practice. However, it was my exposure through films, photographs, and books of the work of Meredith Monk, Trisha Brown, and Twyla Tharp, not to mention the "Happenings" and the Fluxus Movement of the 1960s, that gave me inspiration to even contemplate working outside the proscenium. When I started my professional dance career in the early 1980s, site-specific art was a field without clear boundaries or definitions. After 20-plus years of involvement on my part, I find that I am still contemplating what those boundaries and definitions might be.

Starting a conversation about a definition of site-specific work seems all the more apt given how much more ubiquitous this form of art making has become. I find people designating things as "site-specific" with a loose regard for accuracy and, at times, to the detriment of the work itself in terms of what kind of expectations an audience or critic might have when seeing such a work. *Site art* is a term that takes on different meanings depending on the context, the community of artists making it, or the art form being expressed. In this essay, I explore what I see as the four categories of site art, only one of which I feel is truly "site-specific."

Category Four: Reframing the Known

As a starting point, one may look at all site work as an act of reframing, recontextualizing, and at times reimagining. Placing art outside the conventional platforms (galleries, concert halls, theaters, opera houses) forces the viewer to think of the art differently, even if the art form itself is already familiar. I will never forget watching and listening to the New York Philharmonic's concert performed next to the Berlin Wall in 1989 (on television), or going to a Joni

Mitchell concert (in person) at the Red Rocks Amphitheater, an outdoor concert venue near Denver, Colorado.

Most people do not actively think of these events as being part of the site art canon, but they are related to a form of work that is often seen as site-specific art or at least should be. In this case, the audience is experiencing the "known"—a musical work, performer, etc.—in a different/altered/new context. Works in this category are typically placed in permanent concert venues (Tanglewood, Red Rocks, Jacob's Pillow), and the art itself is usually familiar to the audience. Yet, while work in this category was never conceived to be seen in a specific site (except a concert hall)—in fact, it was not even placed in a site in order to create a new context for the work—such events forever change a person's experience of the work and perhaps of the site as well.

Category Three: Reframing from Studio to Site (Intention Is Everything)

Similar to category four, category three work also involves bringing a created work to a site. However, in this category, the artist's intention differs. While the artist does not create the work with a particular site in mind, the artist (or perhaps producer) does later select a site that will match his/her intention. Elise Bernhardt's desire to have Merce Cunningham bring one of his Events (which has its own predetermined structure and meaning) to a stage placed in the middle of Grand Central Terminal is an example of such work. Elise was not interested in creating a yearly dance festival at Grand Central. She wanted a one-of-a-kind event that would bring particular artworks to the site that she felt were especially appropriate. She believed that Cunningham's Event "fit" Grand Central in a way that would benefit both the site and the work.

Placing an already created work in a new space is, at its core, a legitimate form of reframing. The site gives the work new meaning. The success of such reframing comes down to choosing the right site or finding the right work to match an interesting site. In the visual art world, one gets to experience a version of this by seeing the same art works curated into different contexts (exhibitions) with new intentions. In this case, the "theme" of the exhibition becomes the "site" in which an artwork will be seen.

The strength of category three work is that there is a stronger "bridge" between a performance work and a site; someone made a conscious connection between them, and both work and site were enriched by the connection. Again, work in category three can transform a person's experience of a site, even if the work was not made with the site as its inspiration.

Category Two: Site-Adaptive

In the next category, which I call site-adaptive, a particular site inspires the content and execution of a piece, but it can be performed in similar sites anywhere. Here, the type of site is the constant, no matter where it is located, and the work easily adapts to the particular aspects of the site. I conceived of my work, *Grand Step Project: Flight* (2004), in such a fashion. I made the dance for grand staircases, no matter where they were located. In its first incarnation, we performed the work at six sites around New York City, from the dramatic indoor stairs at the Winter Garden of the World Financial Center, to the sunlit entrance steps of the Cathedral St. John the Divine, to the New York Public Library steps at 42nd Street and 5th Avenue. Steps inspired all content in this major project, with minor variations to reflect the differing sites. There are thousands of grand staircases all over the world, and this work could be performed on any of them.

There are also possible subcategories of site-adaptive work. For example, a site-adaptive work may be one where the structure is the same but the content varies depending on the site. I have created a version of a site-specific event called *Off the Walls* for both the Portland Museum of Art (Maine) and the Hudson River Museum (New York). These two versions were absolutely identical in terms of structure and how the works were made. But, for each version, *Off the Walls* included several discrete performance works (of four to five minutes in length) inspired by particular locations and artworks in each museum. "Guides" (actors) introduced these discrete units and performed soliloquies based on the individual location and performance.

Long term, site-adaptive work has the potential to be the most economical or attractive to make because of the repeatability factor. While such work can have large labor and budget challenges, the bulk of the creative work is completed on one site, and there is room for subsequent incarnations. However, for the last category, we look at a process that challenges all aspects of the process and is, by its very nature, labor-intensive.

Category One: Site-Specific

The final category includes work that is wholly inspired by a specific site and cannot be replicated anywhere else without losing its essence and core meaning. I've created several works that are in this last category. The ones that stand out for me are my three large-scale pieces, all made in Europe: *Genesis Canyon* for London's Natural History Museum, *Babel Index* for the British Library, and *Kohle*

Körper for the Kokerei factory in Essen, Germany. For these works, I developed no creative material until I saw the sites and did site research. Every decision responded to the site itself. The design and functional history of each of these sites is so individual that the works in their entirety could not be done anywhere else. Certain segments could be lifted out, but the work would then become something else (and would fall into another category).

Art made within the third and fourth categories always has the chance to be placed in a new site because the artistic material was made independently; works in the second category are specifically conceived to be performed in multiple sites. But works in the site-specific category are immensely ephemeral; they yield the least "return" in terms of longevity, and they are very labor-intensive. Yet, in my opinion, these works have the potential to be the most exciting to watch. The audience knows that they are participating in an artistic event that has never been done before and may never be repeated. Such works can also galvanize the community around the site to support and take part in the performance because of its historic and unique nature.

Figure 25. Dancers performing on the steps of London's Natural History Museum in the site-specific work *Genesis Canyon* (1996). Photo by Tricia de Courcy Ling.

While I attempt here to give an idea of the various types of site art, the four categories are fluid. A work can start in one and end up in another, and site works at one place may stimulate the formation of works at another. For example, *Genesis Canyon* took place, in part, on a grand staircase in the museum. My experience working on this commission inspired the later *Grand Step Project*. The two works are completely different, but they share some of the same movement techniques involving impressive staircases and choral accompaniment. A similar situation occurred with *Fenestrations*, which, although originally a category one work for Grand Central Terminal in New York, ended up inspiring variations in the windows of Philadelphia's 30th Street Station and the Wexner Center in Minneapolis. So the fluidity of the categories is something one cannot always predict, a volatility that echoes the creative process itself.

Fenestrations: A Practicum in Making Site-Specific Work

Aside from looking at how site work can be categorized, there's the reality of what it takes to make the work. Here again, my own experience has taught me that there are some principles that guide my own working process. The work may change, as may the scale and the location. But over the years there are some principles that I return to each time.

When I was beginning my career as a concert dance artist (my first of eight full seasons at Dance Theater Workshop was in 1987), I was given an unusual opportunity. Thanks to Elise Bernhardt and Dancing in the Streets, I was commissioned in 1987 to create a work specifically for the four levels of catwalks situated inside the huge Romanesque vaulted windows of Grand Central Terminal. It was an assignment that would propel me on my journey of working in sites of all shapes, locations, sizes, and functions.

The process of making *Fenestrations*, a complex and large-scale site-specific work, taught me key lessons; the learning by doing maxim was in full force. In retrospect, it was this project that made the largest imprint on my way of looking at sites.

During my preparation to make *Fenestrations,* I planned to schedule *all* rehearsals in the windows of the Terminal. I thought that was how one made such a work on site. I was undaunted by the scale, the distance between floors, the incessant noise, the crowds, and all of the aspects that comprise working outside of the proscenium. On the first rehearsal day, I had wired all four levels of the windows with a crude system of cheap audio speakers for music playback (bought on Canal Street) and massive amounts of speaker wire. With the help of two assistants, I started working at 6:00 A.M. on a Saturday morning, hoping to get the site ready for a 9:00 A.M. rehearsal. I had purchased five Radio Shack walkie-talkies so I could speak to each "floor" during rehearsals.

I only had a general idea about how to begin my rehearsal, and I assumed the rest would just come to me once we were all together in the real space. I did not think I could actually design the choreography unless I was in the actual space. That was the plan.

As a critical mass of dancers congregated near the information booth in the terminal, a large gentleman dressed in a dark blue station uniform approached. He introduced himself as the station master of Grand Central Terminal.

"Excuse me, what are you doing here today?" he asked with all of his authority.

"I'm rehearsing to make a dance for the windows," I replied.

"I just need to know if you have your certificate of insurance."

"My what?"

"Insurance, liability!"

This being in pre–cell phone days, a dash to a pay phone revealed no existing certificate of insurance. My first rehearsal was shut down before it started. Forty dancers were standing around the busy terminal having their first impression of working with me. With 12 rehearsals to make this entire work, the loss of one day was worrisome. I quickly announced that we would relocate our rehearsal to Brooklyn (then perceived as a seemingly distant and somewhat dangerous borough). I knew a gymnasium we could use as a large rehearsal space. The 40 dancers dwindled to about 32 (8 made their own decision about the quality of this project). The still-interested company followed me across the river via subway. In fact, we were not able to rehearse at Grand Central for another four weeks (eight rehearsals), only two weeks before we were to "open." Forced to conceive and create most of *Fenestrations* in a gymnasium away from the site, I learned a big lesson: *be realistic about both the practicality of creating and rehearsing on site and your ability to conceive and rehearse off site.*

Rehearsing On and Off Site

When dealing with a very large site where performers are separated and essentially cut off from each other in a huge expanse, the choreographic task is complex. The process of teaching steps, staging them, and imparting movement quality becomes almost impossible on site. The process requires at least an hour of time for what might otherwise be accomplished in 10 minutes in a studio.

In the gym in Brooklyn, I marked off the length of each catwalk and created four "lanes" on the floor. Standing on the bleachers in the gym, I could look down on the lanes of dancers and instantaneously give instructions to everyone. Gone was the distraction of the public coming and going in the Terminal, as well as the clumsiness of having to communicate every instruction through crude walkie-talkies. In short, I visualized the site inside my head while working in the gym in a controlled, quiet environment. Rehearsals were extremely productive. By the time we were allowed back into Grand Central, I had mapped out the work's first draft.

Ultimately, being on site was essential. The truth is that we were kept away from the windows one week too long. Once we started working in the windows, I was making changes to the choreography up to the last minute. On some level, we always want more time to complete a work. In this case, we had, in fact, come up quite a bit short. However, I realized that working on site is not always necessary or even beneficial in the early stages of conception and instruction. As I

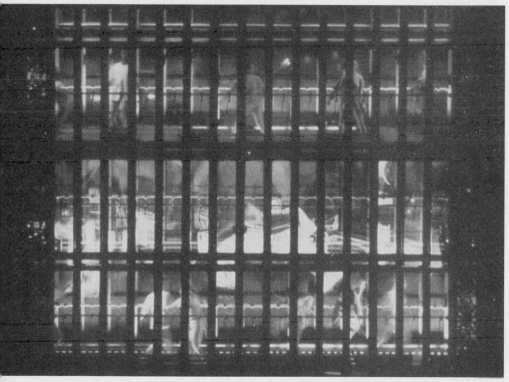

Figure 26. Performing in the windows at Grand Central Terminal for *Fenestrations* (1987). Photo by Tony Giovannetti.

encountered future sites, based on that first experience, I could assess what the proper mix of rehearsals should be, much to the relief of producers or the host sites who often fear that I will demand full access to otherwise busy, hard-to-access sites during the creation process.

The other imprint from this 1987 adventure was also a simple lesson. As they say about real estate: location, location, location. Dancing in the Streets was producing this huge event in Grand Central Terminal with such luminaries as Merce Cunningham, Lucinda Childs, and Michael Moschen. They were all to perform on a prefabricated stage at one end of the Terminal floor (except Philippe Petite, who was to walk a tightrope across the ceiling of the Terminal as a grand finale). Prior to the event, I thought that this platform would be the primary focus, attracting the most attention. My piece, *Fenestrations,* would be a footnote to the evening's program.

When 8,000 people jammed into the Terminal for our first night, only 3,000 people could actually see Merce's company perform. The stage was not high enough to afford sight lines to the other 5,000 people; they were not a happy bunch. It was as though 5,000 people were all given partial view "seats" to a show, but had not been forewarned. When *Fenestrations* appeared in the empty windows, as if by magic, all anyone had to do to see the work was simply look up. There was not one "bad seat" in the house. Thousands cheered, and I had learned another important lesson: *how the audience sees a work is an integral part of a site-specific piece.*

The Audience Factor at the Site: The Key Questions

Since an audience is part of the equation in a site-specific creation, important questions arise: How many people can view the work at one time without obstruction (due to the size and design of the site)? How exactly do they see the work? Must they look up, or down, or at an angle beyond the norm?

Will the audience be standing or sitting or moving after brief stops at subsites? If the audience is standing but not moving, how long can people be expected to stand at one time? Does it make sense to provide seats for your audience? What aesthetic statement are you making by introducing chairs to the site? Does the audience need to travel from site to site? If so, what is an acceptable amount of time and distance?

It is my experience that most site-specific audience members, often without realizing it, bring to site-specific events their built-in concert hall/proscenium expectations and desires. No one wants a partial view "seat," and no one wants to be in an environment that will somehow impede him or her from communing directly with the work. Thus another lesson: *sight lines need to be clearly thought out, as well the clarity and levels of the supporting sound score, so that audience members can enjoy equal access to the work.*

Technical Requirements: Light and Sound

Discussion of sight lines and sound design in relation to overall site performance may sound mundane, technical, or even "academic" in an art-making context. These features may not have the same intellectual, aesthetic heft in the grand scheme of making great works of art, but if they are not attended to early on, it won't matter how intricate, cutting edge, or revelatory the art itself might be. The communication with the audience will be full of unwanted static and the message damaged in the telling. If one fully investigates how an audience will experience both sight and sound of a work in a given space, the art will be more sensitively specific to the site and ultimately seen and heard with more appreciative eyes and ears.

A case could be made that there isn't a difference between what sound/music can work on site or in a proscenium. My own personal bias is that site-specific works need sound accompaniment that is also inspired by the site itself. For example, my work for the Library for the Performing Arts at Lincoln Center (*Informations*, 2001) contained a score by Quentin Chiappetta. This score involved recordings from interviews of the Library's staff that we conducted even before one note of the score or choreography was created. The interviews spoke directly to the legacy of the library, and they were woven into a larger score that included over 80 tracks all culled from the archives of the Library's music/spoken word collection.

Writing scores under such conditions can be a harrowing experience. Often the creation schedule for such a work is four to five weeks. The composer therefore must be able to produce music on an almost daily basis, always staying neck and neck with the pace of choreography.

The importance of lighting in a site work cannot be overemphasized. Lighting is as important a factor to a work as the choreography and music. It is a chance to completely redefine the space in ways that are both transparent and unique. Lighting at minimum helps to reinforce what the choreographer wants the audience to focus on. It carves out the space, creates spaces within the spaces. Frankly, I view it as a secret weapon when making a work; it is the element that fully brings theatricality and pure "magic" to a performance.

The advantages of working with lights are many; the disadvantages are fewer but significant. Lighting is the most costly line item in any site-specific production budget. It is often the case that a given site will have either no electrical power nearby or not enough power. Therefore, power will need to be brought in. In addition, there might be too few natural areas to hang lights, making the expensive proposition of renting and installing lights even more costly. Finding qualified lighting designers is also a challenge, given that the rules of lighting a site are quite different from working in a proscenium or black box environment. I have been lucky to work with two of the best in this field: Tony Giovannetti in New York City, who has lit almost every one of my NYC-based site works since *Fenestrations* in 1987, and Simon Corder, who lit my works in London (*Genesis Canyon* and *Babel Index*) and in Essen, Germany (*Kohle Körper*).

The importance of lighting was most evident in *Fenestrations,* where Tony Giovannetti lit each floor and each of the three windows independently. When the work begins, one dancer appears in the far left fourth-floor window and walks across the catwalk. Suddenly this dancer "disappears," as a dancer magically appears in the middle window of the third floor. This illusion of the same dancer weaving through space from floor to floor was only possible due to the independent lighting on each floor. For *Babel Index*, Simon Corder created a light pattern for the first big section seen from above. The section was inspired by the evolution of writing and the alphabet. Simon's lights gave the floor a texture that mirrored my concept of using the floor as a piece of parchment or stone. The conceptual beauty of working with lights in a space is that, unlike with paint or set constructions, it is invisible and ecologically free of residue. Thus the site is technically not altered.

Conclusion

Ultimately, definitions and categories aside, it all comes down to one thing: Is making site art worth the effort? Are we making art worth looking at? The rise of activity in site forms in contemporary dance during the last 20 years attests to that worth. This increase in work has done much to keep the art form a part of a public discourse; it has helped bridge dance to other institutions and broadened the definition of how art works in our society. Dancers who work on site have discovered that anything that blurs boundaries between art and daily life, that brings people closer together, and that potentially helps connect people to their environment is worthy of the investment of time.

The net result of the site work described here is this: It should make people think differently about the site they are experiencing as well as about the art itself. It should affect people's feelings about themselves in that site and should inform their future interactions with that site. I am drawn to both the obvious and latent subversive nature of this relationship. Art's role in our society is at times taken for granted, but its power to disturb normalcy in all its forms makes it a force to be reckoned with. Site art, and perhaps most effectively site-specific art, is art that seeks in the end to create and cement a bond between the creative act and our world in ways that shift, shake, and disturb our reality.

Making site art demands that one be a lifelong learner, a student in the best sense of the word. My involvement with it helps me remain such an open-minded student, taking in the world with my eyes wide open. Making site art is a process that continues to inspire.

4

Heidi Duckler

Heidi Duckler is the artistic director of Collage Dance Theatre, a site-specific dance company based in Los Angeles. A choreographer who delves deeply into historical and community elements for her work, Duckler adopts overlooked sites for large-scale performances. From Laundromats to historic hotels to an abandoned jail, she unearths the past and, with her sister, Merridawn Duckler, crafts scripts and choreography that resonate in her chosen sites. Heidi Duckler's work has been commissioned by Miami Light, Grand Performances, Roy and Edna Disney Hall (REDCAT), the Hong Kong Youth Arts Foundation, the American Institute of Architects, and Dancing in the Streets, among others. She has been awarded a California Arts Council Choreography Fellowship, a City of Los Angeles Artist Fellowship, four Lester Horton Awards, and three Irvine/Dance USA Dance grants. Merridawn Duckler has published in *Carolina Quarterly*, *Isotope*, and *Green Mountains Review,* among others, and is an associate editor at *Narrative Magazine*. She has been nominated for a Pushcart and for fellowships at Writers@Work, Squaw Valley, Summer Literacy Seminars in Russia, and Yaddo. Her reviews have appeared in the *Los Angeles Times* and the *New York Times* and on NPR's *All Things Considered*. Pavlik interviewed Heidi Duckler on September 16, 2005.

An Interview with Heidi Duckler

CP: What is your definition of site-specific performance?

HD: Well, it's hard to define, of course, but basically site-specific work implies that the content of the work is connected to a particular place. To me, that also means a work in a theater could be site-specific if the content of the piece is related to that specific place. Alternatively, I think that a piece that is created somewhere else and then plopped down in a field is not necessarily a site-specific work.

Sometimes I make work that is re-sited or site-adapted. But I've discovered that a site-adapted work can become site-specific again if the content of the new site is mined. Right now, we are doing a site-specific piece related to the community of Boyle Heights in East Los Angeles. The Autry Museum wants us to bring this same piece to them next year. The content as it relates to the Hispanic and Jewish communities is the source of the work and probably won't change, but because the place is different, the work will be reconfigured. My guess is that it will ultimately relate to the museum where it will be mounted.

CP: You have created works for conventional theaters and for specific sites. How is that process different for you?

HD: When you work in the streets, anything can happen. A car drives by and a hubcap rolls off into the site and there it is. What are you going to do about it? Incorporate it? Ignore it? All these things have an effect. So you make choices as you go.

CP: What kinds of choices characterize your choreographic approach?

HD: Well, there are many ways that I go about creating site work, and, of course, it depends on the nature of the project. I may begin with an emotional connection to the site. Sometimes this is a response to architectural detail or history, or something from my personal past may fuel my curiosity. Sometimes the site finds me, and other times I find it. When a site with a particular history or function becomes available, such as the Subway Terminal or the Ambassador Hotel, then that's a goldmine of inspiration. Other times I have an idea, and I'll look for a vehicle for that idea. For instance, my sister and I were working on a piece based on Kafka's *A Hunger Artist*. We did not know where we would site the piece, but we kept working on it. Finally we discovered that a famous restaurant in Los Angeles, Perino's, was going to be demolished. We said, "Ah! This is the perfect container for that idea."

CP: Do you investigate your sites by reading texts or by conducting interviews with people from the surrounding community?

HD: Yes! Human experience, activity, and cultural memory all contribute to the foundation of a project, although not always in literal ways. For *The Entire World*, I had local mariachis play a postmodern score, linking past and present to provide context for the work. With *A Hunger Artist*, and now *Beowulf*, the text functions as a site. In *Beowulf*, the physical structure of the language has become the architecture of the work to which the dancers respond.

CP: What was your first site-specific project?

HD: My first piece was *Laundromatinee*. It was in a Laundromat built in the 1960s, and the owner agreed to let us rehearse and perform there. We got

Figure 27. Dancers hanging on laundry racks in *Laundromatinee* (1998). Photo by Jeff Kurt Petersen.

inside the washers and climbed the walls. We never prevented the community from getting their wash done, though. And since many did their wash there on a regular basis, they could see the piece evolve and come together. It was fascinating. The audience became really connected to the piece way before we performed it.

CP: Did they give you feedback?

HD: Oh, constantly! There was a little old lady who said, "You girls are getting so good!" I'm sure at first they thought we were odd, but after a while
some of them came to look forward to seeing how the work had developed
and got to know us personally. Our presence eventually became part of their
process of doing laundry. They even took a certain pride in the work when it
was completed. When the performance day came, the Laundromat was filled.
There were at least 100 people there, and some guy decided he had to do his
laundry. We said, "We have this piece, and it is only 20 minutes long. Would
you care to wait?" He said no and did his laundry in the middle of the show.
Everyone loved it. It was terrific!

CP: Was this piece a turning point for you?

HD: Yes, definitely. It was when I realized, "This is what I want to do." Another turning point for me was *Most Wanted*, which was performed in an
abandoned jail in downtown Los Angeles. The audience became characters
in the work. They were fingerprinted, and we took their mug shots. It was
multi-sited and complicated because the audience was divided into groups
and traveled to different scenes at different times. That was a breakthrough
piece for me because, more than any other piece before it, the audience was
integral to the experience. The audience moved through the space with the
performers. That connection between audience and performer is something
I want to continue to explore.

CP: Is it important for you to document your works or leave something
behind in the sites in which you work?

HD: That is a really big question. We do document, but that becomes its own
work in a way. Site work is difficult to document because it is not just what
you see but also what you smell, the temperature, the response of the audience, and the accidental occurrences that happen. It is hard to document with
traditional audiovisual equipment; a webcam and podcast might be a better
answer.

As far as leaving something behind, well, there's memory, and for those
that return to a space we have animated, perhaps they will see or think about
it in a different way. What we do on site is usually outside of the norm for that
site. We may work with metaphor and abstraction. So, because of that, there
is a shift in perspective, and a person's feelings about a place may change. Site
work is about being fresh and alert and seeing the familiar in a new way.

CP: Do you feel that site work, as opposed to work in a theater, allows for
more interaction between audience and performer?

Figure 28. Dancers cling to the bars of a Los Angeles jail cell in *Most Wanted* (1997). Photo by Jeff Kurt Petersen.

HD: It is hard not to have interactions develop on site because the audience isn't passive. We performed in the Los Angeles River in 1995 before there was much talk about river revival here. The show, called *Mother Ditch*, attracted much attention; it was on the 5 o'clock news in Los Angeles. Those on the west side, however, were afraid to cross over to the east side, so we brought them over on a bus. It was such a cultural divide. Some people who had lived in Los Angeles all of their lives said, "Wow, I have never been to this place." Public interest in the river continued from there. It wasn't really the reason I created the piece, but the piece started a conversation about our river and our city in a way I never would have imagined.

CP: What *is* the reason you do site work?

HD: I am a site artist because I am inspired by ordinary life. I love the challenge of walking into a space and engaging what is available to me—a pillar in the middle of the dance floor, or a gravel yard—and integrating it into the performance. When presented with something as familiar as an all-you-can-

Figure 29. Eli Nelson and Elizabeth Nairn performing in the Los Angeles River in *Mother Ditch* (1995). Photo by Jeff Kurt Petersen.

eat buffet, I will find a poetic way to incorporate it into my work. Certain places speak to me, and when I speak back, it is a fascinating conversation.

Site work is alive to me because it is in the present tense, in the moment. It is interesting to me to take that moment and develop it and see if I can make it last. I enjoy the limitations, too. I also love responding to complicated environments that change and evolve and contain a world that is beyond my control. I enjoy working in the midst of life happening, not isolated in a studio. It is very different than working in a proscenium theater, which is more about control.

CP: Do you find that your audiences react to the absence of theatrical conventions?

HD: Yes, absolutely. Site work plays with boundaries. We have had audiences travel down hallways, and suddenly some started opening doors. They couldn't control themselves; they were giddy. They felt free to express themselves, to make choices. And they had to rethink, "What exactly are the boundaries here?"

CP: What is most advantageous about doing site work? What is most challenging?

HD: Well, the most advantageous *and* the most challenging is that I work and relate to people that are not in the art world: business owners, public officials, people from all walks of life. That is frustrating, but also rewarding, because we must find a common ground, a language we can share in order to understand one another. On the other hand, it can make you crazy when someone doesn't understand the value of your work.

CP: How do you decide how to represent a site? Do your decisions about representation ever cause problems with the owners of a site?

HD: We have many conversations with site owners before we start our work. One time we did a piece, *Cover Story,* at the Herald Examiner Building, which is owned by the Hearst family. Their contract included language that set limits on our mentioning the Hearst family in the work itself. So an important part of our process is trying to be clear about expectations up front. For example, at the Ambassador Hotel, where we did *Sleeping with the Ambassador*, they wanted no direct reference to Robert Kennedy's assassination there. In other words, yes, we do encounter controversial subjects, and when I am on someone else's turf, I like to listen to their point of view.

CP: What if the site is considered a public site?

HD: That can be complicated because there isn't just one owner; the "public" is technically the owner. We are doing a piece at the California Science Center, which is a state-owned building, and we have a mandate that states that the work has to be appropriate for kids. Well, what does that mean exactly? Another stipulation is that the public cannot be in any of the documentation. I'm not sure who comes up with all that stuff, but these are examples of limitations when you deal with real-life politics.

CP: Speaking of politics, does activism figure into your work as a site artist?

HD: Well, it's not what motivates me initially. Yet it goes with the territory, because when you bring art to people where they live and work and you connect directly to their own experience, you are an activist. Politics is inherent in my work though it may not be the source of my inspiration. I try to look at a site as a world full of feelings and ideas without a prescribed political agenda.

CP: Do your site works ever converge with redevelopment plans in Los Angeles?

HD: Typically, our work has been in places that are about to be demolished! We were recently contacted about creating a site work at the Dunbar Hotel. The hotel is in the outskirts of downtown Los Angeles in an African American neighborhood. This hotel is where African Americans—often entertainers—stayed because they were not allowed to stay in the white hotels. It was a classy place in its day, and the Community Redevelopment Agency is hoping to refurbish the hotel and bring back its grandeur. Unlike in the Ambassador, they really want us to look squarely into the history of this hotel.

CP: What do you think would happen if you decided to represent this hotel in a way that conflicts with what the owners or city council had in mind?

HD: My take on a place is usually outside the realm of what an owner expects. I research, and I listen. And this material is filtered into the work. But what form will it take? Many sites are filled with controversy. At the time we performed at the Ambassador Hotel, the Los Angeles Conservancy was fighting to save the place; others, including Los Angeles Unified School District, wanted to tear it down. We didn't take sides one way or the other. Most of it has been torn down now. But even prior to our show the public was not allowed inside. Now it's strange to think that our show was the last opportunity the public had to see the place.

Figure 30. Hassan Christopher, Ragen Carlyle, and Marissa LaBog explore the hotel lobby in *Sleeping with the Ambassador* (2003). Photo by Rose Eichenbaum.

CP: How does creating site work affect your relationships with funding agencies?

HD: On one hand, it is good for funding because funding agencies are often interested in creating connections with neighborhoods. So in that regard, Collage Dance Theatre is a good fit for funders—our rehearsals are often open to the public, and our content is related to the neighborhood. On the other hand, dance funding can be difficult to obtain because we are hard to categorize. Funders may ask, "Well, what is this? Dance? Performance art? Theater?" There is really no single category for site work.

CP: Have you ever been challenged by the physical environment—weather, bugs, etc.?

HD: Rats! When we were working on a multi-sited work, *subVersions*, in the subway terminals in Los Angeles, someone on the walkie-talkie said, "Oh my god, 20 rats just ran by my feet!" And, with *Liquid Assets* performed in California Plaza, we were in 10,000 tons of water, which can be dangerous. But all of that is just part of doing site work. It's beautiful, difficult, and unpredictable. When we were rehearsing in the water fountain in the summer, it was great. But then the weather shifted, and it was freezing by the time we performed in September. What do you do?

CP: What *did* you do?

HD: You just go. Or adapt. One critic who wrote about it said, "All I could see were these dancers that were freezing." I wrote back to her and said, "When you look at Balanchine, do you only see how skinny the dancers are? How are you looking at this?"

Oh, and there was another incident when we did a piece, *AfterEden,* at the Marriott Hotel. We took the audience in the freight elevator. One night the freight elevator became stuck in between two floors, so we had to find someone in engineering at the hotel to fix the elevator. This was a month after 9/11, and the audience was freaking out. There was a woman in there who was crying; she had claustrophobia. There was a little open space that I could talk into, so I put my lips up there and said, "Everyone please stay calm. It is OK. We are getting someone to fix the elevator. It is just stuck between the floors." I can't remember how it started exactly, but by the time help arrived, the entire group was singing "We Shall Overcome" inside the elevator. They had gotten inside and become part of the show. I think those people will be affected by that incident forever. I wish the performers could have seen it.

CP: That would have been a great moment to have captured on video.

HD: That is the kind of thing that sometimes happens with site work. It

Figure 31. Sufi Ertur dares hazardous performing conditions in *Liquid Assets* (1998). Photo by Jeff Kurt Petersen.

makes me think about how site work can never be re-created. How do you capture something that is so in the moment?

○

Rabbi Pinchas as a Mexican Wrestler: Adventures in Dance

By Merridawn Duckler

I write scripts for a dance company. Sometimes people look askance at this, as if I've said I write scripts for mimes. They think of dance, even at its most narrative, as the wordless art of the body. But I don't write just any kind of script or for just any kind of company. I write for Collage Dance Theatre, a site-specific dance company based in Los Angeles. Heidi Duckler is the founder. We're collaborators, co-conspirators, and also sisters.

Heidi founded CDT in 1985, after moving to California from Oregon, where we both grew up. As her Web site states: "The company's early works, designed for the stage, dealt with contemporary culture and its artifacts: hairdryers, fast food, used cars." Heidi has loved pop culture objects and environments ever since she was a child, and she has another quality very necessary for a choreographer of site-specific dance—she is very determined. When we were kids she once wore earmuffs for an entire year. People stared huffily at my mother. Allowing her child to suffer like that in the dead of summer! But they didn't know Heidi. That earmuffed babe grew into a choreographer who lacks any compunction about making a dance on top of a Cadillac with an amplified hood or deep underground in a subway terminal.

Me, I'm a high culture junkie. I treat respectable arts, painting, opera, poetry, classical theater like pop culture; they are my everyday, ordinary pals. I think Herodotus is a riot and that everyone should read Genet. I believe vanishing point perspective ought to be part of the standard school curriculum. What makes me an ideal scriptwriter for dancers is that I think the hands and the feet are just as relevant organs as the brain and the heart.

From Breed Street to Casa Mexicana

In 2004 Heidi and I found ourselves sitting on a sunny sidewalk on Breed Street, in the Boyle Heights neighborhood of Los Angeles, waiting for someone to let us into a locked synagogue. In the 1940s and 1950s, some 75,000 Eastern European émigrés lived in Boyle Heights. By 1960 the largely Jewish population had left, and by 1987 this last of the local synagogues, already damaged by an earthquake, had closed. The Los Angeles Jewish Historical Society had decided to restore it for use as a community center for the Mexican community, which is now the dominant demographic of Boyle Heights. CDT had been invited to produce a performance piece to celebrate the building's return.

On the surface this seemed like a natural fit. The company has often involved itself in projects celebrating vanished urban settings, dancing at places as diverse as coin-op Laundromats, the famous Ambassador Hotel, or the Los Angeles River.

But a locked synagogue is symbolic of something else, at least for me, because Heidi and I are Jewish. Heidi is strictly Reform, and I have no history of Jewish observance. But four years ago I decided to attempt to keep kosher, observe fasts and holidays, and quit writing fiction from Friday night until Saturday sundown. I began a graduate program in religious studies, all of which horrifies my secular family and all of which I am hoping to use as foment for the Breed Street project.

The Script

When the audience enters, the ushers hand them either a green or red program. They sit on two sets of risers that face each other with the proscenium between. After the audience is seated, mariachis play traditional music in the atrium with the doors open. HEIDI enters and walks over to a table with two candles and tries unsuccessfully to light them. RICHARD comes walking through dressed as an auto mechanic.

> *HEIDI*: Listen, can you help out here?
> *RICHARD (lowers his facemask and lights the candles with his blowtorch)*:
>   Do you know what these are for?
> *HEIDI*: No.

The day had started with Heidi picking me up at the Burbank airport. As we drove along, the English language seemed to have gotten off at an earlier exit. Every billboard, every sign, every rap song blasting from a passing car was in Spanish. We parked on the street in front of the synagogue and wondered if it was safe.

Danger is always an important topic for us when we are making a performance piece. Here there are real gangs, but maybe Jewish and Latino culture will also be like rivals who fight for ascendancy—maybe the past is going to battle the present and win. In Los Angeles, people spend thousands of dollars to relieve their stress, but we seek tension; it's what feeds and informs both our arts.

Just when my fragile Oregon skin is starting to prickle, a young woman from the Jewish Historical Society comes out to unlock the fence. She takes us around back, chattering all the way into the courtyard. But when she opens the door and lets us into the building, all three of us stand speechless in the dark.

The synagogue is like some old cinema queen, heartbroken, gorgeous, and derelict.

There's a big, intricately carved ark with a blue glass star in the center, flanked by wooden candelabra. On the opposite side of the room, a balcony sits, half-hidden in gloomy shadows. There's a ton of graffiti and gang tags. The pews, speckled with white ash, are strewn willy-nilly like pickup sticks tossed by a giant, petulant child. The *bima* stands in the center, as did most in the early days of American synagogues. Pigeon feathers are everywhere, and the slightest breeze sends them skittering across the floorboards. I usually take pictures to help me understand the spaces, and I take one of a sweet little pile of feathers. Only upon developing it do I see the skeleton of a disintegrating bird underneath.

The source of the cold and the pigeon feathers is a giant open hole in the roof. Smashed boards like ladders from heaven dangle against the robin's egg sky. Despite the traffic that makes up the continual chatter of Los Angeles, the silence inside is profound. The young woman from the historical society shifts her weight from foot to foot as we start to move around, equal parts awe and hand-rubbing glee.

M: Where would the audience sit?

H: We'll put them in the pews.

M: What are you going to do about this? *(points to* bima*)*

H: Dance on it.

M: Let's make it like a Friday service.

H: What, religious?

M: The last service before it becomes secular. We'll follow the order of prayers.

H: Listen, it's not our only community.

M: But we can use the idea of order and disarray because that's an issue for everyone. Look at all the graffiti. It's such a desecration but expressive.

H: I'm hearing mariachi in here.

M: These feathers have to stay.

H&M: Let's have a bar mitzvah!

The space is amazing, ruins and all. This has been a congregation of pigeons and hoodlums. It makes me wonder if anything Jewish really survives without any actual Jews. Outside, the place felt dead. Inside, it's as if the inhabitants just got up in the middle of the service and walked away.

I take a deep breath to remember the smell of old plaster and pockets of cold that never dry from sunlight and pigeon shit and dust, while Heidi stands on the bima and turns 360 degrees, marking her steps.

Later, we return with two other collaborators, the composer Robert Een and the visual artist Habib Kheradyar. Habib is going to use fabric to make the set. He climbs up into the sagging balcony: can they hang sheets from there? Looking up, I think of the women who sat in the balcony, divided from the men. Nothing could be less Reform, nothing further from Los Angeles contemporary culture. Look at Heidi and me, making a piece, with two men deferring, in a sense, to us. But when I see the balcony, I know something still lives up there that wants to express itself.

M: It's where the women sat.

H: That sucks.

M: In the piece, let's divide the men from the women.

We sit on a pew while Bob plays and sings. Beautiful sobs echo from his cello, underscoring his wordless chant. I make some worried marks in my notebook. Will the past let us in, or will we end up like the bougainvillea, clinging to the outside of a fence? This time the woman from the historical society is no longer so friendly. The committee spearheading the renovation of the synagogue is grumbling about a preview of the dance we're supposed to give this spring. In their view it's all too soon. Of course, Heidi can do nothing about that. It's a requirement of the grant.

Site work is often difficult for the choreographer because sites, even in places such as abandoned synagogues, are rarely empty. Heidi ends up with all kinds of unintended collaborators—city permit officials, janitors, nonprofit boards, ordinary busybodies. It's hard for people to think beyond a proscenium with performers onstage and the audience safely in their seats. They have no idea what we're about to embark on.

But, hey, it's not my problem. I'm just the writer! I'm going to take my notes back to Portland and read up on the order of the service in a synagogue. I'll hang up my photos, line up my hopes and fears like so many sharpened pencils, and write.

Continuation of *The Script*

As soon as HEIDI exits, RICHARD walks onto the stage and addresses the audience.

R: I was walking through the old neighborhood when I saw it. I could tell by the dome and the fact that it's on a hill. Also, ask anyone who grew up here, and they'll tell you the same thing. This used to be a . . . (snaps his fingers because he can't remember the word) . . . you know, a . . . you know, where those ones with the (*indicates peyes*) get together. I'm not naming names, but if memory serves, half sat over here (*points to audience*) and the other sat over there (*points to audience*), and you know how it goes. The people over here always want to be the people over there. Except the ones who used to be here? They didn't want to be anyone but themselves.

A few weeks later, I get a call from Los Angeles. Heidi has a certain kind of sparkle in her voice when she is about to tell me something I don't want to hear. Like when she told me it would be fun to black out one of my teeth with our mother's mascara and sell me to the neighbors, saying I was a gypsy child. She has the same tone now. "It's going to be fun to make some changes to the piece!" What changes? Like, for example, the synagogue itself.

It turns out that every time CDT faxes a contract, the Jewish Historical Society balks at signing it. They don't want to support the preview, that is, the showing only a month away.

"Remember how you told me synagogues were usually situated on a hill?" Heidi says, brightly. She describes how she was driving around in tears over the hostile board. Then she suddenly got out of her car and started to walk around. She looked up, and there it was, floating over the horizon, a dome high on a hill.

She started to follow it, almost like a mystical experience. She knocked on the door and a kindly old man answered. It was a community center called Casa de Mexicana. It used to be a church. The officials in charge couldn't have been nicer, kinder, or more accommodating. They'd love to have a performance.

> M: What the hell!
> H: I'm sorry, sis, but we're stuck. The showing is like tomorrow. I can't work with those Breed Street people. They're impossible!
> M: How are we going to do a service in a Mexican church?
> H: It has a balcony. Hey, maybe it used to be a synagogue.
> M: I hate you.
> H: Script in two weeks, sissy o' mine.

I want to tear my hair out. My beautiful ruined synagogue, my ghosts! I can't believe I'm stuck with some ordinary building. All my cherished beliefs of what constitutes Jewish experience are in disarray. I could ask Heidi to find another writer, but Heidi's ears are closed as if she's still wearing those earmuffs.

I call Heidi back and tell her that we aren't doing a religious service. Since I can't use a rabbi, she's going to have to get me someone to narrate the piece. Furthermore, we have to rename the project; we can't call it Breed Street anymore. But that name was perfect! I sulk. Call it Casa Latka. Shul de Whatever. Later, digging in the scraps of paper on my desk, I find one I always call my Jewish koan.

> M: We could call it "The Narrow Bridge."
> H: What does that mean?
> M: It's from a quote.
> H: Well, we are bridging two communities.
> M: Too warm, fuzzy, sickening?
> H: Possibly. What's the quote?
> M: "The entire world is a narrow bridge, but the important thing is not to be afraid."

H: I am afraid. The showing is in three weeks. Let's use it. I'll call Habib and tell him we need a bridge.

I fly back to Los Angeles for the community preview. Habib's bridge is beautiful and strong enough for the dancers to climb on. He wants the bridge to unfurl, aggressively dividing the space. This is the first time it's actually been set up. I'm seeing it for the first time—and so are the dancers. Heidi has been telling people this is a "work-in-progress"; it's more of a work-in-chaos. Dancers hop across the set in long, black Hasidic coats that open to reveal brilliant Mexican serapes. Male and female dancers alike wear black hats with *peyes*. Will it offend anyone? Maybe, if they can see it. The lighting designer is still frantically doing light cues. The mariachi won't play Bob's music, and the folkloric dancers are late. Richard has never spoken the words I wrote in front of anyone until tonight.

The showing is packed. People have come from all over the community, along with curiosity seekers and students from a nearby school. Heidi has had great instincts about the space. Because community is the subject as well as the object, she has put the audience on the stage instead of the dancers. This has the effect of transforming the shopworn, institutional aura of the actual building into something magical, where the active life of the street is also a backdrop that can be glimpsed through the doors.

But despite all our fine talk about two communities, the folk dancers stay in their world, and the modern dancers remain aloof. Lillian and Richard have all the sexual chemistry of two bricks. Why are the dancers falling off the stage? Who are those figures in the fabric? What is that reference to monks?

Continuation of *The Script*

BOB begins to play modern music. LILLIAN is on a ladder on the stage with her back to the audience. She climbs down slowly, and then the other Hasid enter. At first they are tentative and hesitant and isolated, but after a while the movement becomes faster and wilder. They tangle with one another on the floor and take over the stage, separately and in unison. The movement becomes more and more ecstatic, and then CHRIS begins to climb the rope. HEIDI bursts in with the mariachi band. Then the folkloric dancers reenter and do the Machete Dance. Everyone exits except LILLIAN; she is the only one of the Hasidim to interact with the folk dancers. The male member of the folkloric dancers is on the balcony at the top of the bridge and offers the dancers tequila. The dancers cross the bridge each time drinking tequila when they make it across. The music stops.

After the preview, we take our notes away to prepare for the actual opening. It is at this point in our process that I go to Newton, Massachusetts, home of the Hebrew College where I am an online graduate student in Jewish studies. While there, I take seminars every day with two professors. I write in my notebook about one of them: "He's like some angel that fell to earth and immediately started teaching people." He sings, chants, and tosses down Talmudic puzzles at which we immediately start pecking like pigeons. He is a scarecrow of a fellow, with a sweet giggle and a black scowl. In the notebook we're required to keep for the course, I draw his face and underline his aphorisms. *To understand something is itself a religious experience.* From a reading in Maimonides, I quote in big block letters: "For all forces are angels."

Continuation of *The Script*

LILLIAN hangs upside down and takes off her black coat. RICHARD hands her a pair of wings.

R: Then I saw her. I mean the angel. She kept trying to pick a fight. She roughed up a couple in love, got between a group of friends, even shook up some guys just sitting in chairs—you know, just the way you're sitting in chairs. And then—wouldn't you know it—her eyes found me. I'm a lover, not a fighter. I'm a mover, not a shaker. But when the beautiful unknown has you by the nuts, you go. She grabbed me, and I grabbed her back. We fought for hours, and when we got tired, the monks brought us water and wiped our brows. But I pinned her. "I'm not letting you go," I said, "until you answer me." She had no choice. Only we humans get a choice. "What do you want to know?" she said. "What are these for?" I said, pointing to my thighs. And she said, "Pathway to the heart." (*Repeat in Spanish*) *RICHARD and LILLIAN roll in erotic play, and LILLIAN solos while RICHARD watches, but when he moves toward her, CHRIS picks her up and carries her out. RICHARD follows them offstage.*

While I am in Newton, Heidi is busy revising the Bridge show for its actual performance in October.

H: I choreographed the Mexican wrestlers. They're amazingly funny, but how do they fit? No one knows who they are. Lillian says she won't dance until she knows why she should.

M: She's an angel!

H: Who is Richard?

M: He's in love with her!

H: Who is Chris? They're going to wear wrestling robes that have names on them. What names?

M: How come I have to keep naming things?

H: 'Cause you're the writer!

M: Say this to Lillian—she's a Jewish angel. She's no wimp. She's going to mix it up with men and intervene. Let her grab Richard; seize him as he's seized by her. When they wrestle? It's as good as sex.

At the last class, our professor gives us a famous story attributed to Rabbi Pinchas of Koretz, the great follower of the Bal Shem Tov.

M (*by phone at the airport*): OK, I'm faxing you a story, and we're going to use it for the wrestling scene. Richard can say it.

H (*by phone at the next airport*): OK, it came. But if Chris's robe says Rabbi Pinchas, who is Louis?

M: I can't hold my coffee, this luggage, and my phone. Let Louis be the overzealous student.

H: How does that name fit on a bathrobe???

M: That's the only other character.

H: Wait, I got it!

Continuation of *The Script*

Mariachis move around the space playing traditional music to half of the audience with one song and then to the other half with another song. BOB and the other musicians try to follow them, but by the time they set up, the mariachis have moved while the dancers reverse their coats. The audience is also asked to move. HEIDI tempts them with Mexican pastries and dances among them wearing a Day of the Dead mask. When the audience is reseated, they see that the ropes of the bridge have been moved to make a boxing ring.

R: Rabbi Pinchas of Koretz, hell of a guy. But one night there was this fellow—he falls, he rises, he's having a conniption, man. Everyone is very impressed. I mean, you think you read responsively? Well, this one, he and God were like that *(crosses fingers)*. So some of the guys said to Pinchas, "You have to admit this one is really, really seized by the spirit." And Rabbi said: "Yes, the spirit—ha-ruach—has certainly caught hold of him. The only question is just what spirit that is!" *Then RICHARD turns to the audience and calls into the mic like a wrestling color commentator:* And in this corner, Rabbi Pinchas of Koretz! *Dancers act like crazed groupies, cheer and scream.* And in this corner, the Proud, the Indomitable, the Aaaamazing, the Spirit! *Dancers have the same reaction to LOUIS. RICHARD continues in this vein, egging on CHRIS and LOUIS, who proceed to have the silliest possible fight.*

In October I fly to Los Angeles. Heidi has decided that because the mariachi move from place to place in the traditional plying of their craft, the modern musicians should do the same. The mariachis stroll with ease, but Bob and his players have to pick up their chairs and heavy instruments and drag them to the next spot.

The audience members will be given a program so they can participate in the responsive reading. The ushers will give red programs to the men and green ones to the women, although this choice will look random. When the dancers clear the space for the wrestling scene, they'll ask everyone with a green program to go to one side and everyone with a red program to the other. Only upon looking at each other will they see what we have arranged.

Continuation of *The Script*

LOUIS and CHRIS fight more and more wildly, and the other dancers, dressed as Mexican beauty pageant queens, jump into the conflict. Pretty soon chaos reigns. At first RICHARD ignores it, but when all the boundaries break down, he ends up sobbing in the corner because no one is paying attention to the rules. Everyone runs offstage and the fabric of the bridge falls down, right across the table where the folkloric couple is seated, dividing them from each other's sight. On the other side of the bridge RICHARD sees his angel. Soon it becomes clear that some of the dancers are inside the fabric and some out. The ones who are inside reach out with hands and lips to touch those who are outside. They roll them in their arms so they appear to be floating in a sea of fabric. Faces appear outlined and then disappear back into the folds.

Heidi and I want to end with the candles used in the beginning. We like the circularity but fear the hokey. The dancers, now shorn of their coats and clothed only in sexy white tank tops, mount the stage where the candles sit on a table. Their faces are hot and shiny from the kisses and the touching through the semi-porous fabric of the bridge.

Richard stands in front of the candles. I've given him a speech, but it isn't what we want to end on. Dances should end in image. We talk about having the dancers each hold and light candles, but this isn't a dead community with a *yartzeit.* It's a living one with an eternal flame.

H: Should we kill the lights and leave the candle?

M: No, have the dancers blow it out and point to the balcony.

H: What's up there?

End of *The Script*

R (from the stage, surrounded by dancers): Me and the angel, we got a nice place now, pool, couple of kids. They're real angels until about 12, 13. Then they're mine. It's not perfect, far from it, but sometimes we just lie there, in each other's wings. Maybe I tease her a little about the old days: hey, remember what these are for? The sun comes down over the freeway. The beautiful sunset runs to dark. In the old neighborhoods, the ghosts are rising. When I see them walking, I always stop and give them a lift. Hey, how far you going? They say as far as the dome at the top of the hill. They'll already have the candles out, and then they invite me to help, but I don't know if I'm lighting them or they're lighting me.

The night of the opening of *The Entire World Is a Narrow Bridge (The Important Thing Is Not to Be Afraid)* at the Casa de Mexicana is sold out. Everyone laughs when Richard lights the Shabbat candles with his blowtorch. The folkloric couple dances like fire, wrapping up in each other's arms and unfurling away. When Lillian comes down the ladder, we're shocked to see her. Who would expect someone such as she in this place?

The Hasidim dance like perfect, wild ghosts who don't want to be civilized but can no more leave the earth than one can leave a lover. Lillian and Richard roll in each other's arms, as if this were a new way to travel. Her wings lie crushed in a pile like the skeleton of a pigeon. Everyone roars with laughter at the wrestlers. When the audience moves, a woman murmurs behind me, "Hey, look, they've separated the women from the men." Richard speaks his final words. The lights go out, and we sit for a moment in darkness. Then everyone looks at the young, glamorous folk dancers in the balcony with candles; their handsome, sober faces are beautiful in the glow of the candlelight.

5

Ann Carlson

Ann Carlson has been attracted to unusual sites from her earliest efforts in the performance world. After her university experiences in the West and then performing with Meredith Monk in New York in the 1980s, Carlson went on to create site-specific performances from the most intimate to the grandest of scales. Borrowing from the disciplines of choreography, performance, theater, and public and conceptual art, Carlson's work is project-based and often organized within a series format. Carlson has received more than 30 commissions and numerous awards for her artistic work, including a 2009 USA Artists Fellowship, a 2008 American Masterpiece award, a 2003 Guggenheim Fellowship, a 2003 New York Foundation for the Arts Fellowship, a 1995 Alpert Award in the Arts, and a three-year choreographic fellowship from the National Endowment for the Arts. Kloetzel interviewed Carlson on July 1, 2005, at a coffeehouse in New York City.

An Interview with Ann Carlson

MK: What do you think of the term *site-specific*?

AC: People laugh at me, but I used to say that everything is site work. You know, from a young age, I started feeling like whether I was working in a theater or whether I was working outside a theater, they're both really the same. But I also used to be a little annoyed by the term *site work* because it seemed to privilege concert stage–based work. Actually, I think the issue is really that the term is a bit watered down at this point—domesticated, easily dismissed. So I just like to call it all work.

MK: Categorization can be problematic on so many levels.

AC: Yes, but I do love the possibility in site-specific work, or site-sensitive work, or site-responsive—however it's named—that people will happen upon an event or a public performance work. I love the opportunity for passersby to "stumble" upon something they didn't expect. In work inside a theater, people are deliberate about attending and they are familiar with their role as spectators. I enjoy the potential to upend all of that. In the last four years or so, or at least since *Geyser Land*, I've only made one piece in the theater; everything else has been sited in one way or another. I guess I've become almost pathological about being in a theater. I feel held hostage most of the time. So, more and more, site work has become my practice. I'd like to just say that's where my work is now; it's no longer "sited" in the theatre. For most of my work life, and I know a lot of artists feel this way, it's the job of others to categorize the work you do. So I just try and let it go.

MK: It's intriguing to watch the waxing and waning of site work since the 1960s and 1970s. Coming back to New York these days, I'm always amazed at how many artists who were dedicated to the theater space are branching into site work.

AC: Well, I think that could be due to issues of economics and access. You mentioned the 1960s and 1970s; I'd say initially there were economic issues, a refusal of the marketplace. But it was also the issue of access for the spectator. There's the potential for a sort of anarchy in site work that was attractive to people then (and now), as well as the benefit of working outside the usual presenter context.

MK: What would you consider your first site work?

AC: Hmmm. I guess I would say one of my first site works would be the *Real People* series, the series of performance works made with and for people gathered together by profession—lawyers, security officers, the *Geyser Land* poker players, etc. These works are based around people's passions, why they do what they do, and what gestures and movements define and express those passions and activities. The series examines stereotypes and looks for the vulnerability and the humanity embedded in people's work and identity. I did a piece with lawyers and fly fishermen, and then went on to work with so many different kinds of people—nuns, teachers, physicians, etc.

MK: Was the *Real People* series also performed in the performers' actual workplaces?

AC: Yes, the fly fishermen performed on the lake, the corporate executives in the office, etc. You see, we would rehearse in their workplaces, and whatever was generated would emerge out of wherever they were. So there was a very common kind of "sitedness" in those pieces.

Strangely enough, the first piece in that series, "Sloss, Kerr, Rosenberg & Moore," happened in the theater and included four attorneys with their shoes glued to the floor. But they ended up performing the piece in a lot of different places. In other words, it could be re-sited in a theater or a gallery;

it could be outside; it could be anywhere. I didn't make the work thinking that, but that certainly interested me—to make something that could exist anywhere, so that it could have an incredibly fluid, dynamic life.

But the interesting layer about the *Real People* pieces was that they almost forced themselves into various sites. For example, one of the lawyers decided that he wanted to perform the piece at his wedding reception, just completely out of the blue. So they got up and did it where the musicians were performing at their reception. Suddenly that work was not just site work. It was being sited in their lives in a certain way. It functioned almost as a contemporary folk dance; in other words, "Let's mark time. Let's mark these important events by doing these movements." And because it was so tied up with their identity as attorneys, there was a kind of delight and an ability to be bigger than that identity, but also sort of reduced to it.

MK: How did you begin to notice the "sitedness" of this work, especially since this piece was done in a theater?

AC: Actually, thinking back on it, another piece from the *Real People* series,

Figure 32. Lawyers John Sloss, Charles Kerr, Scott Rosenberg, and Thomas Moore perform in a *Real People* piece, "Sloss, Kerr, Rosenberg & Moore" (2007). Photo excerpted from video/performance work by Ann Carlson and Mary Ellen Strom.

"Catch and Release," the piece with the fly fishermen, was my first official site work—in the more traditional use of the term. The lawyer piece was first performed in 1986, and a year later the fly fisherman piece was mounted. I thought of "Catch and Release" as multiply sited, in a way—it happened on a pond in Maine, but also (I like to think) in the body of the performers themselves. As choreographers, perhaps the first "site" is the body and all the visual, cultural, and behavioral signs ingrained in the body that impact the work. It circles out, I guess, from the site of the body to the context of where the body stands.

MK: Was there something in your background that inspired you to explore this expanding context?

AC: I started this process in undergraduate school. I made a piece with runners and then with football players on the practice fields. I enjoyed working outside even then, but also it was a way to invite people (in this case football players and runners) to participate in these performances by siting the work where they were comfortable. As I think about my work over the years, there's a blurring of site and people and content. . . . I'm reminded of when I made a kind of protest piece on a huge American flag during the first Gulf war. It could be done anywhere as long as I could lay a flag down.

MK: In other words, you were taking your site with you?

AC: Yes, and that's a theatrical convention, really, to take the floor wherever you go. In this instance it was a huge 40' × 30' flag that could house the performance.

MK: Do you also create works that you feel can't move between sites or that can only exist in one site?

AC: Yes, for example, *Geyser Land* could only exist in Montana. And that's where I think that "sited work" and "site-specific work" part ways. *Geyser Land* was very site-specific. Actually, we were invited to do the piece in Japan. But while we could set up the strategy, it would be a really different work because in *Geyser Land* we were investigating that particular strip of land between Livingston and Bozeman, Montana.

        Strangely enough, when I was making a piece on horseback, I felt like *that* was a very site-specific piece. The back of the horse was the site. I would think of myself on that horse working with the landscape and the surface of the horse and also the history of the horse and how this horse got here and what he stood for and what I stood for . . . all those layers that we pick apart when we make a site-specific work. We understand what the site is emblematic of and all of that. You know, sometimes I feel like wherever I find myself there's a site there.

MK: Is that why you find yourself drawn to the "series" approach to creation?

I know that you have made a number of pieces under a series title, such as *Real People*, *Animal*, or *Night Light*. These series seem to draw on a similar strategy for multiple sites.

AC: Yes, I love that, thinking up a strategy that has sort of a multi-life, not unlike the fluidity of the lawyers performing at Lincoln Center and then at one lawyer's wedding. For example, reenacting historical photographs was a strategy that I used in the *Night Light* series, but then it became embedded in *Geyser Land* as well.

MK: With respect to the *Night Light* series, why was it important for the re-created photographs to happen on the sites where the photographs were first taken?

AC: Because it created a space-time collision. What's there now, what was there—that kind of history/present juxtaposition. You know, it's like an out-of-the-ground type of memory or out-of-sync diorama, particularly as chain stores take up so much architecture. The *Night Light* strategy asks, what was here before it was a Starbucks? The photo being staged on and as close as possible to the site where it was originally taken is vital. It's that collision between a historical moment and what's there in contemporary life, and it points to the fact that we're making history right now. The *Night Light* strategy emphasizes the circular continuum of historical events.

MK: You seem consistently inspired by the history of spaces.

AC: Sure, and I'm interested in whose history is being told for each patch of ground we explore. I mean, even the earth as its own organism responds to a cacophony of influences and events. The *Night Light* project points to this ground as having some active role in the formation of memory and history. In working on *Geyser Land*, one of the profound things was to see that—to my eye—the landscape or the patches of ground we were exploring had changed very little from the time period of most of the photographs to the present. Or the changes were so miniscule that as urban folks we couldn't see them.

MK: So do sites choose you, or do you search for them?

AC: It's a combination usually. Most of the time, I get caught up in my own ideas, and I try to follow them as far as I can. Usually I come up against roadblocks, and then I veer into another idea.

MK: Would you say that this was the case for *Geyser Land*, that the train and the landscape in Montana helped you realize an idea you were already exploring?

AC: Well, that was really Mary Ellen Strom's, idea, and I jumped on board. Mary Ellen, my partner, is from Butte, Montana, and her dad worked for the

Figure 33. Archival photo (c. 1926) of a man with a luggage cart at the train depot in Livingston, Montana. Reprinted courtesy Gallatin Pioneer Museum, Bozeman.

Figure 34. Reenacting the historical photo of the man with a luggage cart at the Livingston Depot in *Geyser Land* (2003). Photo by Mary Ellen Strom.

railroad. She had this great idea to explore the moment in history when the beginning of film and the railroad "collided" and to investigate this specific swath of contested landscape, the Crow Indians' last holdout before the railroad broke through. She was also driven by her personal history, a love of that landscape, which I also share. All these interests intersected with that land and that past, and it all started to crystallize. There were just so many layers of entry there.

MK: Does the notion of responsibility, especially toward a site you're attached to, enter into your creation process?

AC: I would hope so. I mean, I feel like I have the responsibility to have everything line up, in a way that feels resonant to me and to the other people collaborating. "Line up" is maybe too linear. [laughs] But to have everything layer together in a way that makes sense. I guess ultimately what we're projecting needs to make sense to the participants and to the viewers. I look back on the piece you and I did together (*Geyser Land*), and I realize that most of the audience who participated in that piece couldn't think clearly about the solo that you were doing along the train aisle. I remember being excited when you appeared because I thought, "Oh, good, someone who is movement and dance-trained and has an experienced aesthetic." I could just give you the structure of a woman being overwhelmed by her first experience with train travel, and we could make it right there. But most people thought you were nuts or were irritated or something along those lines. I think back on that, and I realize that I didn't really take responsibility for the audience. Well, you can't ever know exactly what an audience's reaction will be. But I didn't take full responsibility in terms of crafting the improvisation in the form that matched the rest of the work.

MK: Yes, it seemed to stand out as the only dance that was happening either on or off the train.

AC: Well, I think dance is any conscious movement, so there was other "dance" in *Geyser Land*, but not of the modern dance, abstracted aesthetic. I think it would have helped to have an intermediary activity that would have broken down and/or explained a little bit of what you were doing. You know that space between pedestrian behavior and abstracted movement. This becomes even more of an issue in site work when the majority of theatrical conventions might be absent. For example, by putting the poker players in the corner of a train car with the light on them, it helped theatricalize what they did in their everyday lives. But going from that to your highly aestheticized movement material was too big a jump.

But getting back to that question of responsibility. You know all of those things that we weigh as makers, all of the things that go into being a responsible citizen, go into being a responsible maker. Sure, we may push the audience a bit, but we need to consider that pushing. I mean, I'm interested in people not shutting down toward the work because it's so outside their experience that all they can do is say it's crazy. For example, for your solo in *Geyser Land*, I think that people couldn't really handle it in the way that we could as dancers who are trained in that concert dance model. I mean, we already disassociate from our bodies in a certain way; we see the body as a theatrical vessel symbolic of more than individual selves. But most people don't experience that. So, to me, having you lying there in the train aisle had all of these filmic references. But a real woman lying scantily dressed in a real train in a real aisle that someone couldn't step over had very different references for them. They didn't see you as just a body. They saw you as a real woman in trouble or crazy. So, in a way, maybe we're getting back to those privileges of the concert stage.

MK: Do you ever feel that frustrations like that might draw you back to the concert stage?

AC: I don't think so. You know, since 9/11, I've had a harder time making sense of art making; it's more complicated to understand the meaning of art in this post-9/11 context. A lot of people got fired up, saying that making art is all we need to do, that it's the only thing that makes sense. But at the time I felt exactly the opposite. My first response was that there's nothing to make now, that there's been a kind of denigration of the soul. And so just now, four years later, I'm finally coming to a point of realizing that since that time, I've only made site work. I've stayed outside, where you would think it would be less safe. But it seemed more solid somehow. I've had a hard time being indoors. My "animal" self is more on the surface.

MK: That's intriguing. Is this a recent discovery?

AC: Well, I don't know if I would call it a discovery. I just noticed it when someone asked me for a videotape of my recent theater work and I discovered that, since 2001, I had mostly been making work outside. And then I met a few people who were here in New York who had similar responses to 9/11. It seems like there's been a sort of backtracking for a lot of people, trying to understand how that event focused or impacted their lives and work. So I think site work—you were saying maybe there's an uphill growth of it again now—I think there must be a relationship to 9/11 in the city here.

You know, I didn't think about this before, but the truth is, if you're not in a building, you're not vulnerable to the building, whether it's a theater or anything else. Now when I consider it, of course I stayed outside; we're not safe inside a building.

MK: Actually, you weren't just outside of buildings after 9/11, but outside of New York altogether, right?

AC: That's right. I didn't realize that until now. It makes sense. Perhaps for me, that's what site work has become—a post-urban running to the safety of the outdoors.

o

Thumbprint

By Ann Carlson

> What if you found a portal to a parallel universe? What if you could slide into 1,000 different worlds? Where it's the same year, and you're the same person, but everything else is different. And what if you can't find your way home?
>
> Quinn Michael Mallory (season five opening monologue from *Sliders*)

There's rarely time or reason to trace back through the process of making a work. Once in a while someone will say, "Where did you get that idea?" I'll pause and try to come up with an answer. But when one project is done, I'm usually well on my way to the next, and like birth or amnesia, it's almost impossible to remember how an early work got started.

I do remember *Night Light*, however. It began with a thumbprint. I spent weeks photocopying my thumb and enlarging it. I poured over the uneven radius of lines, which led me to think about the individual body and its imprint, the remnants of a physical impression, the record of our body's time here on earth and its lasting impression on history. A thumbprint is a site specific to that individual; it has a connection to a particular gene pool, and through those identifiable swirls and circles, the thumbprint has been used to single out people with uncanny accuracy. I began to reflect on the thumbprint as a tiny topo map, a little maze, a fossil, and a miniature pathway toward the center of something. At some point, still thinking about the print as topo map, I tried overlaying my enlarged thumbprint on a map of Manhattan. The topo map juxtaposed with this geographic map held some resonance.

As I walked the New York City streets to and from the photocopy machine, I remembered seeing footage of a public lecture given by Albert Einstein. He was explaining his theory of relativity in lay terms. "All of time exists in the present." Those words kept echoing in my mind, as I imagined a potential collision of time and space that might occur in a dream, in a book, or even on a street corner. What if this collision was visible? What if people who walked here 75 years ago emerged from the sidewalk like in a pop-up book?

This Page

Lucretia Wilkerson was furious. Her sister had the 40 acres that they owned in common logged without telling Lucretia. They made $40,000 from taking the trees off the property; half would go to Lucretia, but she'd never wanted it logged. Her plan was to build a little cabin and retire up there in 25 years or so, as soon as she got her son out of the house and found somebody to marry her again. Flouting her long-term plans, Lucretia moved with her 10-year-old son, Justin, back from Missouri, both to get her money and to express her outrage to her sister.

I started taking walking tours. The guided tours of historical crime scenes were good; the walking tours of radical political history were better. It was thrilling to stand and stare at a building that was the site of a rally or protest that changed policy. How benign the building looked in the midst of all that history. On another tour, the guide kept telling stories about buildings and what went on inside them in years past. It felt as if he could make everything up and we would all just nod and wait for the next building and the next story. The slippage of "truth" in the historical record was a source of entertainment in these walking tours. These tours held the thrill of a theatrical drama mixed with the allure of a bedtime story. They were like seeing through a window into some parallel universe, where the events were still going on.

Another type of window into history is the diorama. I love dioramas, particularly the dusty, predictable ones at the Museum of Natural History. These big windows into another place or time—all that dusty fur and fake flesh. How alive I feel when I look into them. How much they stand as mementos of a time that has passed or of a wilderness that stands waiting and alive while I stand and look through this window. Those dioramas hold an uneasy invitation into that taxidermied moment, stuffed with a sense of victory and progress as well as death and decay. It's a strange mixture of colonized curiosity, dramatic entropy, replicated stage design, and papery wilderness.

Once Ben was contracted to remove the trees, it took about four days. Most of the trees were blue spruce pine. The machinery that Ben used to fell each tree was a D420 Logger Pro, a massive piece of machinery that was part tank and part crane. Ben sat in the cab and manipulated the eight-foot jaws that grabbed around the lower trunk of the tree; the blade, almost invisible, emerged from underneath the engine and sliced through the tree's trunk—75 years of growth cut in seconds. Ben powered the machinery forward, carrying the felled tree a few feet to the horizontal pile of trees he'd already cut. He dropped tree after tree onto the pile. This went on until most of the trees were gone; he left some lodge pole pines that now stood like light grey toothpicks—skinny, sickly remnants of what was, just moments ago, an abundant mountain forest. After a modest and controlled burn of the area, all that remained were messy blackened slash piles and plastic Gatorade bottles. Ben drank four Gatorades a day and chewed Rolaids, a trick he learned from his cowboy brother. The combination repelled heat exhaustion in high altitudes, and he could work faster and longer. He made up the cost of gas for his Logger Pro in the first three hours of the job, and the rest he pocketed as income.

I began to consider archival photography as a resource for a modern-day diorama. I imagined New Yorkers on their way for a coffee or a meeting running into a woman selling newspapers as if it were 1895. I combed photos at the New York Historical Society, the Public Library, and the Municipal Archives. I looked for clear evidence of where the photos were taken, thinking to restage them on the exact same spot. Some photos were easy to place but boring to look at. Most highlighted the obvious racism and classism of archival documentation. Would this project be reconfirming who was/is omitted from the public archives? I was naively shocked at who wasn't in most historical societies' photo archives. Women were in short supply, and people of color were hardly present. I decided to fall forward into the idea anyway, to display the omissions—perhaps as an act of reconciliation or a reminder of some kind.

Eventually, three events pushed this project I call *Night Light* into a workable idea: a demonstration of the theory of relativity, a love of dioramas, and a desire to reveal the time/space collision in a performance-based event emerging from the streets of Manhattan. The central strategy of *Night Light* (at some point it seemed clear that the project needed to occur after the sun had set) developed into the restaging of archival photos in the tradition of tableau vivant. Performers cast in likeness to the original photo and costumed in exact replica to the original photo stood in stillness on the spot where the photo was actually taken. *Night Light* staged this collision between the historical moment that the photo represented and the present. Seen in the context of a walking tour, this project became a template for a four-year journey through four U.S. cities, the woods of the Berkshires, and the mountains of Montana. At the root of the project was a three-dimensional occurrence transposed into two dimensions and then turned back into three dimensions. As the project evolved, *Night Light* also became a postmortem comment on photography itself. What *Night Light* pointed to—more than history, really, or how history is told, or by whom—was the apparatus of early photography itself. As we were staging one photo on the corner of 6th Avenue and 23rd Street, a young man walked by and stopped. I overheard his cell phone call: "Hey, you gotta see this. They're restaging an Alice Austen photo right here. Come down quick. Corner of 6th and 23rd. Yeah, the young woman selling newspapers." The literacy of the passerby amazed me.

This project had the unexpected benefit of giving employment to numerous dancers in various cities. I realized early on that the rigorous training of contemporary modern dance technique provided the groundwork for an ability to "pitch stillness" and to perform stillness in a deep and focused way. Thinking of motion on a continuum that begins with energized stillness, dancers in this project had a particular resource to call upon. Not that all the performers had dance training, but time and again my experience was that this project was particularly poignant when dancers performed the roles in the restaged photos. In the context of a "dance," *Night Light* shifted the locomotor movement to the spectator, heightening the sense of the present moment, of being a performer in the dance of the everyday.

These Words

It hadn't exactly been her idea, but she knew she had to publish if she was to have any credibility. Even though she worked in a field that in its practice was mostly nonverbal, the only way to gain a foothold in the context of the academy was to trade in the currency of written word, with theory, explanations, findings, descriptions, and ideas, written in ink, bound with glue, lasting forever. The moving body was her passion. She loved to dance, and she considered herself lucky to have a job in a university. The meetings were tedious, but she could dance, choreograph, and teach others about dance, day in and day out. So when her friend and colleague asked her to collaborate on a publication about site-specific work, she jumped at the chance. Site-specific projects had always been a particular interest of hers. So they invited choreographers to write essays and edit their words and photographs into a volume that might enlighten future artists and thinkers in this way of making work. It would be a good contribution to the field, and she could list this publication in her impending tenure review.

The scale of the New York City version of *Night Light* was enormous. Horses and people and awnings and barrels and black/white and gray scale. There were so many people to costume and to cue to be still. Then there was the rain, the wind, and the theatrical lights to set up and take down multiple times in one evening. The producers of the event, Dancing in the Streets and The Kitchen, were incredible supports, securing permits to be on public sidewalks and streets, gathering countless volunteers, arranging for people to buy tickets and to know where to go. They took care of all of those logistics, details, and unpredictable occurrences that can enliven, deepen, and expand the potential of an outdoor temporal performance event, but can also ruin, deplete, soak, and shut down months of work and planning in one windstorm.

Ben sold the logs to a mill and lumber operation just 26 miles down the interstate. These particular logs were then hauled to a mill outside Tacoma. Four small publishing houses contracted with this mill to buy paper for their publications. The mill had a reputation of "green" milling, meaning they didn't process their logs with arsenic or dump the runoff water from the operation into any river or stream. They piped their runoff down to a local landfill, where the dirty water was eventually strained by mud and rock, worms and rainwater. It fed the grove of blue spruce that lined the edge of the forest around the mill.

We staged eight photos in the Chelsea section of Manhattan. These ranged in time from 1895 to 1972. Tour guides along the way told their own stories of shopping and partying and falling in love on those streets. Looking back, the tour was too long, plus it rained, and half of the performances were canceled. The tour guides needed more direction, but the costumes were brilliant and the performers were astounding, holding their positions for 45 minutes to an hour without moving. Most spectators were excited and enthusiastic, happy to relax after the two-and-a-half-mile walk left them at The Kitchen, now turned into a café/bar.

They finally got an OK from the publisher. She'd had dinner with her ex-boyfriend, a radical environmentalist. They broke up because he was opposed to expanding his carbon footprint by having children. She told him about the book project, and he had suggested a "green" publisher, a company that contracted with environmentally conscious paper mills. She felt happy to have the publication become part of a sustainably conscious practice. It made sense. It took almost four years to gather the interviews and essays— some 100,000 words written by 16 artists working mostly in the United States.

Figure 35. Archival photo of immigrant railroad workers, the so-called Gandy dancers, laying railroad ties in Montana in 1946. Reprinted courtesy Gallatin Pioneer Museum, Bozemen.

Figure 36. Using the *Night Light* strategy in multiple sites. The "Gandy dancers" in *Geyser Land* (2003). Photo by Rachel Kulick.

After New York City, versions of *Night Light* were presented in Chicago, San Francisco, Boston, and Beckett, Massachusetts, as well as along the train tracks between Livingston and Bozeman, Montana, and most recently in Middletown, Connecticut, at Wesleyan University. The project had a conceptual framework that was realized anew in each location. I learned more with each event and cleaned up mistakes made in previous versions. We uncovered similar "holes" in the history of each historical archive and discovered incredible talent, interest, and enthusiasm for the project everywhere we went.

This Book

I finally held it. The book jacket and binding were beautiful. I leafed through it and skimmed words written by friends and colleagues. I smiled because I remembered how much I had worried and labored over the essay, how hard it was to work on. How intimidating it felt to write and simultaneously how soothing it was to type. I'd so enjoyed Cambodia: A Book for People That Find Television Too Slow *by Brian Fawcett; it tempted me to try the structure of a multiple narrative on a page, fiction against nonfiction, keeping at least two stories in front of the readers' eyes at once. How exhilarating to see the two voices appear in my own words in this book. The photos had printed up well; the book felt heavy in my hands. I put it on top of the pile of things on my desk and went outside.*

Each project holds in its layers some kind of beckoning, for the makers, the critics, the curators, the producers, performers, technicians, designers, and for the spectators—deliberate or passing by. In my experience, this beckoning continues even after the event has finished. Perhaps the success of an event is measured in the lasting strength of this beckoning. It's a call to remember, renew, and rethink how we see, perceive, and imagine this time and space we occupy. A reminder to reconsider the environments we live in and share with one another and to listen to this land we stand on together.

2

Environmental Dialogues
Sensing Site

Figure 37. Communing with site. Olive Bieringa in the Paris version of *GO* (2007). Photo by Thomas Greil.

What is it about the public sphere that intrigues the site artist? Site choreographers often assert that art in public spaces can impact the largest number of people and can help shape social and cultural dialogues. Olive Bieringa, Otto Ramstad, Leah Stein, and Marylee Hardenbergh would all concur that public spaces offer a jumping-off point for such dialogues. Yet, before vaulting into a verbal exchange, these site choreographers believe we need to be physically receptive and responsive to place. They want us to see, hear, smell, and touch—in other words, tune into the site on a sensual level. When making site work, Bieringa, Ramstad, Stein, and Hardenbergh find ways to interact with public places that activate all their senses. Then they model this approach for audiences and passersby. These choreographers do not always select public spaces that are at the forefront of a community. In fact, much of their work exists in places at the edge, overlooked places that would seem unappealing or perhaps even embarrassing for a community. Weed-filled parking lots or undeveloped plots between buildings, sewage plants or gritty city streets, these choreographers want us to notice spaces from the revered to the disregarded, connect to them sensually, and then explore our current treatment of such places.

Olive Bieringa and Otto Ramstad began the BodyCartography Project in 1997. In their earliest works, they enjoyed inserting themselves into heavily trafficked spaces—malls, outdoor eating areas, and storefronts—altering audience perception of place by walking very slowly or incorporating blindfolds and out-of-place objects to travel through the space. More recent projects have focused on city sidewalks and the people and objects that exist along these sidewalks. Unlike many other site choreographers, Bieringa and Ramstad are not always concerned with obtaining permits to perform in public spaces. They often gather with performers in public areas, forcing city officials to ponder what is and what is not "appropriate" behavior in these places. As such, their work provokes people to consider other possibilities for interacting with and perhaps legislating public spaces. At times, their work takes on large environmental issues such as global climate change; at other times it may dive into a particular person's understanding of a section of pavement. Yet, from their most intimate to their most expansive work, they want people to experience place in unusual ways and to consider the benefits of sensual and kinesthetic interactions with place.

In chapter 6, Bieringa and Ramstad examine their interest in testing boundaries, particularly that between public and private space. They contemplate how and why our movements are controlled in various places, and they question the institutions behind such control. They also reveal their interest in liminal spaces, where nature is reclaiming the built environment. By describing their work in such spaces, Bieringa and Ramstad draw attention to the concept of the in-between in many of their endeavors. In Bieringa's essay, "Between Landscape, Self, and Other," she exhibits the fallout of testing boundaries as she delves into her solo *GO* (2005), performed on an urban sidewalk. As she interacts with shopkeepers, barbers, and homeless people, among others, she perceives her privilege of whiteness and considers the intersection of visibility and race. Her article accentuates the difficult questions that site choreographers ask of themselves and the places they inhabit.

Leah Stein also probes our relationship with public spaces. Her love for the environment, both urban and wild, began at a young age, and dancing on site was a logical extension of this love. Stein began creating site work in the early 1990s, and although she has made work for rose gardens and revered parks, she finds herself returning again and again to the disregarded spaces in urban areas. She feels a certain sympathy for the overgrown parking lots or crumbling buildings of the past. Often beginning with movement improvisations on site, she encourages her dancers to explore the site and find physical and sensual ways of relating to it. As they come across odds and ends, she directs dancers and musicians to experiment with them to bring the voice of the overlooked place to the fore. In her opinion, such an approach fosters a connection and sensitivity between dancers and place that is communicated to the audience. As she explains, her hope is to offer "a different way of being on the planet and of being sensitive to environmental and human issues." In her site works, which at times take on a meditative quality, people and place seem to come to a quiet accord, one that speaks of a hopeful future for humans and the environment.

In her interview, Stein talks about her delight in facilitating people's "heightened sensitivity" to sites of all kinds. As she ponders her numerous performance projects, her attraction to unremarkable sites shines through, and she celebrates the yearning of the natural environment to reclaim such places. While Stein makes work for a variety of sites, she notes her discomfort in interacting with "over-designed" spaces. In her article, "Of Grass and Gravel," Stein explores her fascination with the merging of architectural structures and the natural world. Reflecting back on her childhood impressions, Stein uses the concept of interfacing with nature, sound, and urban spaces to highlight humanity's inherent curiosity in the mysteries of our environs. Her site-specific efforts to renew that curiosity point to the site choreographer's desire to connect to place in fresh and innovative ways.

For Marylee Hardenbergh, celebration and concern for the environment activate the majority of her work. Well-known for her 2006 piece, *One River Mississippi*, Hardenbergh has made over 25 pieces in which water plays a significant role. Yet, while she is consistently lured to water, it is not always in the form of iconic rivers. From barges on the Mississippi River, to wastewater treatment plants, to lakes, to water towers, Hardenbergh makes us question our use, and potential abuse, of water. Hardenbergh feels that one of the most effective ways to cultivate concern for the environment involves bringing the audience into the work itself. Influenced by the Movement Choirs of Rudolf Laban, Hardenbergh directs her dancers to include audiences in the work through activities such as manipulating fabric or simple movement patterns. Hardenbergh fundamentally believes that audience participation changes people's investment in and sensual understanding of place. Recently, Hardenbergh has received support for such a claim; in a survey conducted six months after one of her river works, 60 percent of audience members believed that "they were better stewards of the river."

In her interview, Hardenbergh delves into her efforts to foster public appreciation of place. She details the benefits of ritualistic activities that allow audience members to discover the attraction of varied sites, and she describes her unusual tactic of using large machinery as "performers" in her work. In her article, "*One River Mississippi*," Hardenbergh discusses her monumental site work along the Mississippi River. Hardenbergh chronicles the frustrations and satisfactions in coordinating the 550 performers to perform at seven sites simultaneously. As she contemplates how to cultivate a community's awareness of place, she observes that the most dramatic changes in terms of environmental or cultural issues often spring from the sense of community and of joy that site work generates. Her journey down the Mississippi emphasizes the ability of site choreographers to join people and place in satisfying and celebratory ways.

As Bieringa, Ramstad, Stein, and Hardenbergh create work on site, they exhibit a high level of hope for the human-environment relationship. For them, the site-specific process effectively opens their own and their audiences' visual, aural, tactile, and kinesthetic senses to the world around them. By employing tactics of site improvisation and audience participation, these choreographers believe that they can promote sensorial receptiveness to the environment, and they see such receptiveness as a crucial step for creating respectful and responsive behaviors. Then they rely on human instincts to complete the process. In short, Bieringa, Ramstad, Stein, and Hardenbergh believe that site work, in unlocking our sensory channels and natural curiosity, will bring people to care for places, both venerated and overlooked. In their work, the site dance genre functions as both a model and a guide for future human-place exchanges.

6

Olive Bieringa and Otto Ramstad

Olive Bieringa and Otto Ramstad are directors of the BodyCartography Project, a site-specific dance and improvisation company based in Minneapolis. Since 1997, the BodyCartography Project has created more than 150 performance events in sites from Russia to Japan to New Zealand. Investigating lagoons, city sidewalks, and mountaintops, Bieringa and Ramstad's ventures tease out the distinctions between private/public and urban/wild through workshops, performances, site films, and installations. Their works have received awards in the United States, New Zealand, and Europe, and they were recently featured on the BBC for their work with Cheshire Dance and Crewe Station. Bieringa and Ramstad were named 2008 Public Art Saint Paul Sustainable Arts Fellows and the Project has enjoyed support from the Archibald Bush Foundation, Multi-Arts Production Fund, Jerome Foundation, Minnesota State Arts Board, Creative New Zealand, and Forecast Public Artworks. Pavlik interviewed Bieringa and Ramstad on September 7, 2005.

An Interview with Olive Bieringa and Otto Ramstad

CP: Is *site-specific* an appropriate term to describe your work?

OB: We have played with the terminology a lot trying to decide whether we want to call our work site-specific or place-based or various other things. It keeps coming back to site-specific because it is a term that is the most accessible or known. When I make something that is site-specific, it is really generated from that site. It is not something I could just do in any outdoor locale. I could make something in a bus stop and perform it in a train station, for example, but that for me is not site-specific. I would call that location-specific. I think the term *site-specific* means different things to different people and that for many people it includes the historical aspect of the site. Our practice has been very physical and very present. Even if we do read about the history of a site, our process is not about reenacting or illustrating that history. Our practice has been about what is here right now in this space and how we respond to it. We generate material from that point, although history does provide us with a wider context for awareness.

OR: I would also say that our site-specific work is about using the space we are in, in that moment. But I don't feel we need to impose a reductionist view on other people's ideas of site work. I was in a festival in Duluth called *Dances on the Lake Walk* that was set in a rose garden. Many of the companies chose to work on the flat lawn so that they could bring pieces they created in the studio. To me, those pieces were not really site-specific. They were just pieces performed on a lawn. I have never thought about this before, but I guess that work could be site-specific in a bourgeois, high art, rose garden way. [Chuckles] In fact, many of the pieces were like the garden itself, cultured and ordered. But we used the actual environment when we did our piece.

CP: What attracts you to making site work?

OB: For me, there are many layers that draw me outside. I think initially there was a desire not to be making art in the commodified context of a theater. There I would have had to spend my time and energy on publicity and trying to get people to come and see the work. But if I perform out in a public place, then I can expose my work to a whole new audience. All my energy can go to the art making rather than the production and publicity aspects. If, early on, I had the ambition to produce a saleable product to be noticed by the media or by the dance hierarchy, then I probably would have made more work in the theater.

But once I started to do site work, I realized that I was so engaged and inspired to work in the public realm. It is still exciting for me to figure out how to generate and frame work out in the world in different kinds of environments. That act of framing and collecting material from the places we work has become the source material for much of our work.

CP: Speaking of framing, I know that the BodyCartography Project has created a number of dance films on site. Can you talk about your first film venture?

OR: The first site project we did on film was *Wharepapa*, which we created in the mountains of New Zealand. We put together a cast of people from the local and surrounding areas; in other words, they were specific to the site. One of the women in the cast was the organizer of the tour, and with her connections we were able to show the film in lots of public places. We showed it outside of museums and inside and outside of cafés. We would show the film, and then we would do a live performance wherever the film was screened. At one town we showed the video on the back wall of a café with a big storefront window. The audience then turned around to look out the window to watch us performing out in the parking lot. It was a very banal space in contrast to the fantastic space of the mountains in the video.

After the show, we would fan out into the audience and talk to people about what they thought about the project. We asked if they had been to the site (Mt. Arthur) where we had made the film and, if so, whether they thought any differently about it now after seeing this video.

CP: What was your most rewarding piece?

OB: Perhaps *Lagoon.* It was a piece we developed in New Zealand in 2003. It took place in an urban park and lagoon in Wellington. It is a large space and

Figure 38. Kilda Northcott performs in *Lagoon* (2003) in New Zealand. Photo by Matt Mueller.

called for a large spectacle. The piece had big group unison choreography on a hillside, people climbing down walls, jumping off bridges, and hanging out of boats. Around 2,500 people came and they said, "Wow, dance can be like this" or "Wow, this space can be used in this way. I never would have imagined it." The piece won the Pelorus Trust Creativity Award at the New Zealand Fringe Festival.

OR: *Lagoon* was also rewarding in terms of integration with the public

OB: Yes, it was. But while making spectacle is great, on an artistic level I think there are other questions to be exposed. Working in more intimate spaces with subtler movement allows for a different range of possible interactions with pedestrians or with a place.

I have been working on an hour-long solo recently where I choose a beginning point and an end point over five or six city blocks. I am inviting as few people as possible, not more than 20, to come and watch me improvise along this route. For me, on an artistic level, that is far more exciting, challenging, and interesting.

CP: Do you feel that there are any people or practices in your backgrounds that have influenced your creative paths?

OB: I was exposed to a lot of conceptual art, land art, performance art, and theater works that really inspired me. Growing up in New Zealand in the 1970s and 1980s, I was involved in a number of large-scale community performance events such as the work of New Zealand theater director Warwick Broadhead. I saw companies like Welfare State, which was an English theater group that was big in the United Kingdom. One of their pieces took place in the sand dunes where they built a whole village. It was an all-day, wild, community, environmental theater experience. I was also exposed to artists like Richard Long, James Turrel, Christo, Laurie Anderson, Bill Viola, Fluxus artists, and Sankai Juku. Later influences include Maya Deren, Kazuo Ohno, Judson Church artists Steve Paxton and Deborah Hay, Meg Stuart, Benoit La Chambre, Forced Entertainment, and numerous filmmakers and musicians. I also saw a piece by Meredith Monk out on Roosevelt Island.

In terms of our practice, the Tuning Score that Lisa Nelson developed with Karen Nelson, KJ Holmes, and Scott Smith, among others, lends itself beautifully to site work. Improvisational practices in general lend themselves to working outdoors due to their sensorial awareness practices. Also, release technique, tai chi, contact improvisation, Body-Mind Centering®, and working with dancers with disabilities are all important components of our practice.

OR: My mom is an artist, and we were always creative at our house. Also, when I was in high school, I was really involved in graffiti and painting illegally. I thought of it more as public art. In Minneapolis, where I grew up, the railroad tracks were set down in a trough through the middle of the city. We used to paint down there, so it kind of seemed like cave art.

      Skateboarding also encouraged me to engage with the city in a creative way. I still see potential space because of skateboarding; I look for places to slide and jump on or off of.

      But I think it is hard for me to name my influences. When I work, I like to assume an almost isolationist perspective. I try to clear my head of influences and allow myself to be instinctive in the process. After this initial step, I then consciously seek out other information.

CP: Is that what you do with sites as well?

OR: Yes, in our site work, I am also resistant to adding in material or ideas immediately because I want to see something pure. Maybe this is part of my perfectionist tendency. I want to address the primacy of the material. Often, you only get one chance to do this without adding in your other perceptions. Of course, your perceptions from other contexts can't be completely filtered out, but you have this chance in the beginning to address the space without excess baggage or concepts. I like to take advantage of that moment because it is a fantastic process of discovery.

CP: When you are looking for sites, what catches your attention?

OB: It's a very intuitive process. Otto and I have driven and walked around many areas, looking for something that feels engaging visually and physically. Often these places have multiple levels, textures, curious soundscapes or socialscapes, and are visually arresting. We also look for places on a usage or context level that have something interesting happening in them. Sometimes liminal spaces that have no social function have been really interesting to us, a floating concrete breakwater, for example. We have made a lot of work on the edge of the water so we can be in or out of the water or in boats. So a site may present itself over time, someone might suggest one to us, or it might come with a commission.

CP: I noticed you have been working on site at military bases. What is your attraction to them?

OR: Military spaces seem really decontextualized to me. I have never been in the military, and I have never seen what happens there. In fact, I have never been to any active military bases, only ones that have been closed down. They are empty and weird spaces. After a while, you can identify certain militaristic

Figure 39. Wilhemeena Gordon et al. performing at the water's edge in *Lagoon* (2003). Photo courtesy of the *Dominion Post*.

objects at the site, but there are still some things that I never identify, and so it allows me to be creative and make up my own ideas of what they would be used for.

I also like military spaces because most often they are falling apart. I like the energy of places where the human-made structures are coming apart and the natural plants and animals are coming back. Of course, we can see in New Orleans that nature does not need that much time to take things apart.

OB: We have been dancing in military spaces since the BodyCartography Project began because they offer a lot of room for the imagination. They are places that nature is reclaiming; they were built for war, but nature is burying their history. In New Zealand, Australia, and all up and down the West Coast, there are forts that were built to protect the West from the Japanese, but a gun was barely fired in any of them. So they are these horrible, resonant, and beautiful spaces that are accessible.

When we started working in military spaces in New Zealand, California, and Washington, I said, "Whoa! I feel like we now need to go to Japan to gain more of an understanding from the other side of the war." I wanted to contextualize the spaces, not just take them at physical face value. On our first journey to Japan, what we discovered after some research, travel, and translation was that very few military structures existed and what was there was not very accessible to foreigners, much of it still being occupied controversially by the United States military. What was not occupied or destroyed by the U.S. military with carpet and nuclear bombing was far out on small islands or in the countryside.

OR: One of the spaces we went to was a military poisonous gas factory on Naoshima Island in Japan. That was a really intense space. During the war, everybody on the island was excited that the factory was being built because it was going to provide jobs. But they had not been told what the factory was going to produce. Many of them signed up for jobs and started working there, and they still did not know what the factory was producing. The safety equipment was not good, but the workers did not worry because they didn't know about the gas. Many of them came down with terrible diseases and died. When the war ended, some people committed suicide because they thought the Americans were going to come and kill them for making poisonous gas. It was just horrible, and I had no idea how I could work in that space because of those feelings. I felt shut down. It is interesting because it was so visually beautiful, but my feelings based on the knowledge of what happened there were so terrible.

CP: Is this history affecting your creative process?

OR: So far we have mostly worked with the physicality of the sites without the cultural context. That was our main focus and still is to a degree. I am not into emotive work and am somewhat resistant to the modern dance idea of making works about something. I am a very kinesthetic person, and I create a lot of material based on that. We look for what we can perceive here and now through our physical or kinesthetic senses. But now we wonder: have we picked up some of the historical or cultural information about various sites without knowing it?

OB: Yes, I think so. It is really rich material, and our first research trip to Japan just brought up more questions in terms of the direction of the project. It is a cultural and historical education for us. Right now it feels like a 10-year project. We are developing a collaborative team of Japanese, New Zealand, and American artists to generate personal, historical, and improvisational material for live performances and film.

CP: It sounds like you have gained new insights from working with people from various cultures. Is there anything that particularly strikes you about working in different countries or with different cultures?

OB: I love working in different countries because I get to see how different social rules, legal laws, and ideas about space manifest within a culture. In the United States, for example, there is so much paranoia about what people do in public space. I think this fear has been initiated, in part, by insurance companies as a way to build revenue; they try to build fear that somebody—the government, the city, a corporation, or an individual—could get sued if someone gets injured. In New Zealand and Brazil, for example, there is far more responsibility placed on the individual for their own safety. This makes the working process easier, since individuals have more freedom, but it is also less charged politically. This is changing as multinational insurance companies extend their reach around the world.

    In the United States, it is a big deal if you want to do something without asking permission. You learn about all sorts of things when you try. You learn that half the pavement in downtown San Francisco is owned by the bank and that the other half of the pavement belongs to the city. On the half that belongs to the bank, I can't lie down; I can't fall; I can't sit. I can't do anything that would look like vagrancy or like I am a crazed person. I have to walk. I have to keep moving. So for me that brings up a lot of questions and a lot of issues around personal freedom, the freedom of expression, and what is acceptable behavior in a public place.

OR: Yes, on some level, all of our work is an expression of freedom. It is about physically being able to do what you want, when you want. It is about going underneath unconscious social agreement; this is a political act. I do this not only when making a project but also in my normal life. I try to be open to doing what I feel like doing wherever I am. I do not mean this in terms of doing things to or at other people. But if I feel like lying down, then I will try to do it, especially in places that I'm not supposed to do it.

CP: Have you ever run into any conflicts with authorities?

OB: Once in San Francisco, we were fined while working at the Sutro Baths. We were there documenting a performance with a camcorder amid hundreds of tourists with camcorders. But we were the ones who were ticketed for having an organized dance event on federal property without a permit. They also told us that we needed $5 million worth of insurance coverage. The following year we got the insurance and the permit, and the show went on.

CP: Have you ever found yourselves or put others in a compromising situation?

OB: I can think of one example when we were doing this weekly lab in San Francisco in 1999. As a group exercise, we decided to investigate the differences between performance, ritual, and research. So we separated into three

Figure 40. Olive Bieringa exploring boundaries on site. The BodyCartography Project, San Francisco (2000). Photo by Patricia Zura.

groups and worked in different places. One of the groups chose to work on a street corner with these guys who were selling books. It was the booksellers' regular spot. They were really excited about what the group was doing, and people began gathering on the street corner to watch. All of a sudden, the booksellers were completely visible, highlighted by this large group of dancers and audience. The cops showed up and ended up taking the booksellers' stuff and closing them down. It was horrible. No one had thought that would be the result, but it was like, "Wow, that was a really stupid thing to do." That is an example of choosing a location without having awareness and sensitivity for the particular situation.

CP: Generally, what is the response to your activities by spectators?

OB: Spectators standing next to you will sometimes talk about you like you are an object. People think when you start running, jumping, and flying around the street that you no longer feel or see or have any awareness. There is a fear that you are going to run into a car, but, of course, when you are in your dancing body, you are far more cognizant of what surrounds you and what you can work with and what you can do with your physicality. There is a disconnect in people's minds as to what happens inside the dancing body.

OR: But, over time, we have developed a process of engaging with the audience. Often, with our unadvertised, spontaneous work, people want to know what it means or what it is. They ask, "What are you doing?" It is interesting to ask them back, "What *are* we doing?" Many times they have a lot of ideas, but they just don't trust that they know what is happening. I think that is a function of Western, expert-based culture. It is a given in postmodern art that the meaning is up for grabs, but this idea has not seeped into general culture.

OB: People generate meaning about performance all the time, but they do not think their interpretation is of value. How can we let the general public know that what they are experiencing is of value? For me, it has really been about how to interface with people and ask them what they are seeing. During one of our slow motion improvisations in Nicollet Mall in Minneapolis, I asked a man, "Well, what do you see?" He said, "Well, I see ancient people and modern people and the ancient people are taking time to . . ." There is a whole story there already.

CP: What a creative response. Have you received additional comments?

OB: Most of the time people get really jazzed up about what they experienced. Some say, "Yeah! Wow! I want to play like that." Either they want to get involved, or they want to start dancing, or both. They also realize that the space is beautiful or inspiring, and they want to start moving through the world seeing beauty like that every day. There is a level of playfulness and physicality, as well as the revealing of the site, that I think excites people. It is about being in the world in a different way.

OR: One of the things that is nice about public interaction in site work is that it actually *happens*. Sometimes the feedback is integrated right into the middle of the performance. I think it should be like that all the time. People should be able to say, "Hey, where did you get those shoes?" or "Wow, you look really different to me." Taking ourselves out of the established context of the ritualized theater space really helps this interaction.

We noticed in San Francisco that the people that interacted with us were homeless people or often people of minority groups. When you are an economically disenfranchised person or a minority, you stand out and you are "other than," so you are someone to be seen. We found that for these people, it wasn't such a big deal to interact with us and sometimes join us. Of course, this is a generalization, but it was an interesting thing that we found working in public sites.

CP: Do you consider your site work activism or yourselves activists?

OB: Yes, I think so, in an indirect way. I think an activist message is inherent in the process of getting people excited about their bodies. They realize that dancing is not only a physical activity for trained movers. Often, we offer free performances in accessible locations and sometimes community-oriented, inclusive, or audience participatory projects. On a personal level, being in my full embodied self out in the public sphere is definitely a form of activism.

CP: What are some of the advantages of doing site work?

OR: One of the advantages is that there are physical skills that you can develop by dancing on site, more so than in the studio. You can experiment with different surfaces and objects in nature. Once we started dancing outside, I realized that all of dance is a scientific experiment based on this control principle of a flat floor. No one really talks about that. I have heard people say,

Figure 41. Olive Bieringa and Otto Ramstad of the BodyCartography Project improvise on an unusual surface (2003). Photo by Eric Ramstad.

"Let's see what we can do physically with bodies in space." But no one ever says, "And let's do it on a flat surface." I don't think anyone considered that; it was just a given. I have found that when you are not working on a flat surface, you can feel your reflexes improve. This is just one example of how the site-specific process can push you.

Another advantage of doing site work is that we are doing something different and visible. We get to feel integrated with the community. We can go on tour and actually inhabit the places we go. I have friends in large dance companies that tour around the world, and all they see is the neighborhood around the theaters. When we tour and perform site work, we get to meet people from the art community as well as other local people.

CP: Does creating site work affect your chances of obtaining funding for your work?

OB: I think it has not generated much funding for us. Site work is often undervalued within our current cultural models. Some people think that it is something that happened in the 1960s and we don't need to be doing it anymore. In general, funders want you to rent a theater and have great box office sales as a mark of success. Site work is often free and, in their eyes, only costs money to produce. The irony of this is that theater work is expensive to produce, and because our overheads are less and our site work is self-publicizing, we sometimes make more money presenting outdoors through donations than we would in a theater.

But I did not think about funding when I began this work. For me, making art in public places and working site-specifically is about realizing the world is my studio and theater, and that the issues that are important to me in my art-making practice make sense in the context of the street, the parking lot, the harbor, and the military bunker.

○

Between Landscape, Self, and Other

By Olive Bieringa

BodyCartography: The Mission

As the BodyCartography Project we investigate the body's relationship to the physical, architectural, climatic, technological, and social landscapes that we inhabit in urban/wild and private/public contexts. This is the material of our work. We activate space and challenge social and perceptual limitations of physical freedom. We engage and provoke audiences in diverse contexts.

Making Work in the Public Realm

The BodyCartography Project is not creating political theater, but our work is irrefutably political in its act of reclaiming public space, spaces which are often choked with consumerism, fear, or intimidation. We aim to engage people in a kinesthetic sensorial experience where the body has previously been rendered mute to understand the causal effect our actions have on others, whole communities, and the environment.

In 1997–98 while living in both San Francisco and New Zealand, I became interested in how my somatic, perceptual, and improvisational dance practice could interface with an audience beyond the small experimental dance community; I wanted to discover how it could work in direct relationship with a wider social and physical world. When working in urban/wild landscapes, dance makes a new sense. The dance dialogue between self, other, and environment has an inherent logic and implications beyond the metaphorical in terms of how we relate to others and the environments we move through and live in. In 2005, I developed a solo entitled *GO* to intensify this dialogue.

Advertising GO

> *Olive Bieringa is planning to dance her way along Nicollet Avenue from downtown to Franklin Avenue. During this most unusual rush-hour commute she'll kinetically respond to curious pedestrians, busy intersections, and many of the other random events that make up daily life in the concrete jungle. None of Bieringa's steps will be planned: The performer (who is also the co-director of the BodyCartography Project) will be improvising to the rhythms of the city as well as an on-the-spot soundscape created by Bryce Beverlin II, who will "play" the street. Bieringa, who has performed* GO *in Brooklyn and Seattle, often enters shops along the way, interacts with passersby, navigates obstacles, and challenges the idea that the inspiration for dance can be contained within theaters and studios. Free. 5:00 P.M.—Caroline Palmer*

> WED JUN 28—*City Pages*, A-List, Minneapolis, June 2006

Finding Meaning

My current solo practice *GO* is an improvised solo that takes place along a street on a predetermined route for a very small, ideally invisible audience. *GO* is an investigation of the *space in between*. It is an investigation of the ongoing journey between our inner and outer landscapes and the ecological entwinement of self, other, and environment.

GO *Audience Score*

As the performance begins, you are invited to watch from the sidewalk from behind or in front of the performer. Stay together in groups of three or less. Shift your perspective. Follow your curiosity. Give the performer space and watch from a distance. Sometimes come close for a more intimate experience. Track sensation in your body. Allow space for natural sound. The performance will be approximately 60 minutes. Have a great walk.

GO is providing a vehicle for me to spend physical and performative time with all kinds of people in an urban context. As I dance, who do I meet? Who is the most open to interacting with me and interested in what I am doing? The guy who accepts and ravenously eats my partially eaten Wendy's hamburger? The dance insiders who follow me? The man in the matching pale blue suit who stands awkwardly next to me at the traffic lights? The group of East African men who come outside to watch in amusement? Who are the people that don't want to be seen but are highly visible? Questions of class, race, and otherness surface.

I have the privilege of being white and can therefore choose my invisibility and maybe my "craziness." As one African American witness commented at an earlier BodyCartography event: "Man, I just scratch my nuts and they take me to jail. What do you clowns think you're doing?"

GO is a delicate improvisational score. I do not rehearse. Before I perform, I sometimes ask the local business owners whether as part of the performance I can enter their stores. Many are resistant and suspicious. Maybe those with the most at stake? Some embrace the idea fully, like the African American barber who asked me what kind of music I would want him to play. This work is less about my dancing and more about creating containers for people to see the street and reveal the life of what is already there.

The work was first performed on Nicollet Avenue in Minneapolis in 2005. This avenue moves from a clean straight-suited downtown, past banks, fountains, and hotels. Crossing the street we pass a large housing project with rolled out turf, a strip of "ethnic" restaurants including an East African coffee shop, a theater, a barber, a corner store, a white hair salon, an army surplus store with a space helmet in the window, and the transgender youth center. Crossing the freeway we pass empty lots, a hardware store, a 99-cent store, a drug rehabilitation clinic, another barber, a church, and arriving at Franklin Avenue at Arcadia, a hipster café. The work has also been performed in Seattle's University district, downtown Brooklyn, and presented by the Santa Cruz Institute of Contemporary Art on Pacific Avenue in Santa Cruz. One year after the initial performance

Figure 42. Olive Bieringa experimenting with the "givens" in an environment in *GO*. ©Sean Smuda, 2006, www.seansmuda.com.

on Nicollet Avenue, I performed it as a simultaneous solo with multidisciplinary artist Bryce Beverlin II. I danced while Bryce sonically played the street. From this piece we developed the short film *Nicollet Avenue.*

From a physiological perspective *GO* explores the relationship between self and environment, balancing inner and outer sensing through parasympathetic and sympathetic aspects of the nervous system. *GO* is an empathy practice with the public I meet, the pavement I crawl over, and the streets that I cross. In this practice I am working with a kinesthetic response to what is entering my body through my skin, mouth, nose, ears, and eyes. Our sense of movement and touch evolve simultaneously. Our skin and our brain develop from the same embryological tissue. The skin demonstrates this intimate connection through a reflexive expressiveness—blushing, for example. To quote Deane Juhan in *Job's Body*, "The skin acts as an interface, a permeable membrane, between our bodies and the world, our thoughts and our physical existence. By rubbing up against the world, we define ourselves to ourselves." As I move I am literally leaving traces of myself, my own skin, across the tarmac and cement. Smell and taste are present in car fumes, strawberry bubble gum from the corner store, the urine-covered pavement, sparkling Perrier with lemon, freshly laid lawn, hair product chemicals, bleach in the fountain, one mouthful of hamburger, and woodchips. The sound of traffic is endless, disappearing from my focus and returning as I approach the bridge over the freeway. I am not a suicide jumper, no matter how mesmerizing this river of traffic below appears. I hear hip-hop over a car radio. I hear my own breath and heart as I dance inside a cardboard box. I see a wide street filled with people walking in every direction, rubber sealing the cracks in the pavement, the grass stains on my seersucker suit, a lonely shopping cart, people sleeping in a public plaza, an abandoned lot filled with weeds, five cop cars approaching with sirens wailing, a bus full of curious eyes, my jacket hooked on top of a stick flying in the wind.

My street guise is part camouflage and part clown. A light blue seersucker suit that almost blends into the beginning surroundings of the piece, at least in Minneapolis. As I progress further down the street, the costume becomes more and more absurd as it becomes out of context, stained, and animated as a prop or character itself.

Interaction, Interruption, and Exposure

Spending time in the American public landscape can feel naked if one thinks about the thousands of potential eyes and ears from such sources as occupied buildings, surveillance cameras, and mobile pedestrians. Most people, I suspect, do not think about those watchers consciously, but rather hold themselves in a certain way in public subconsciously from years of training and societal pattern learning.

GO performer Bryce Beverlin II

How can two strangers from different cultures/classes share this moment in time and space? How do I engage you in a physical dialogue? Do we have time to find a breath together, a glance, a physical call and response? Can I read the space in between us fast enough to give you more space so I don't frighten you away, or do I need to come closer, offer a physical challenge, ask you the time, invite you to join me for a dance, convince you to take my gift of an empty box or a large block of cement, ask you to play me a tune or together negotiate a dangerous street?

He laughs when I offer him food and takes it with delight, claiming he suspected I was up to something when he first saw me. He sits burning his bills on a bench at a busy intersection and offers up a seat to me, saying we share the planet. On a street corner she joins me in a swaying curvaceous dance for a fat full moon. He marches off in a harassed fury, repeating over and over, "How stupid!" He sat watching for a long time in his taxi, talking to me, moving his taxi gently alongside as we moved down the street. Dancing my way out of the hands of the Brooklyn police officers who left laughing. Together we waited at an intersection for the lights to change. Polished cowboy boots reflecting the light of a street lamp. His Spanish, my English. Breathing. Smiling. She dances with a real estate sign in two hands and music filling her ears. I join her with my suit jacket as my dance partner in my arms. Flipping it every now and then in the air. Grabbed tightly on the wrist by a Santa Cruz police officer. Where is my ID? What do I think I am doing? The practice continues . . .

As the movement conversation continues on the same street over time, how will these relationships evolve and change?

Affecting a Larger Politic

As a social and physical practice, *GO* exposes issues of freedom and engagement. As Bryce Beverlin II, a performer for *GO*, noted, "To move and mold the notion and practice of public behavior while simultaneously understanding and accepting the impetus of that examination to be of well-established societal roles and rules is certainly an undertaking, but can be very rewarding to both the artist and the public persons."

The work provides space for embodiment and relationship to be explored in a cultural context where art, play, and creative process are undervalued. Audiences have the liberty to walk away whenever they want. They are also invited to value the multiple meanings they generate from what they experience, be it absurd, ugly, challenging, or hilarious, constructing their own urban myth. Here we stand on this empty street corner, all kinds of people, together for this moment watching this person dance inside a cardboard box to the rhythm of the passing traffic as the sun drops below the cityscape behind.

7

Leah Stein

Leah Stein, the artistic director of the Leah Stein Dance Company, loves to engage with environments in both wild and urban spaces. For the past 15 years, she has made site works in and around her hometown of Philadelphia, as well as in places as varied as a defunct train yard in Poland or a parking lot in British Columbia. She particularly enjoys collaborating with composers, poets, and sculptors and uses these collaborations to create multiple avenues of access to place. She has been awarded grants from Dance Advance, the Leeway Foundation, and the Pennsylvania Council on the Arts, as well as a Herald Angel Award at the Edinburgh Fringe Festival. She has been in residence at the Yellow Springs Art Institute, the American Dance Festival, and the Winter Pillow. Kloetzel and Stein spoke on July 7, 2005, in a crowded coffee shop in Philadelphia.

An Interview with Leah Stein

MK: I know that you began to do site-specific work in the 1990s. What attracted you to move outside the theater?

LS: A lot of my inspiration for making dances came from the natural environment. The forces of nature and the physics of movement were my impetus at that point—as metaphor, as immediate bodily experience. In the early 1990s, with two good friends, I drove across the country and went to the Southwest for the first time. I was so taken by the landscape that it completely altered my idea of what it meant to be on the earth. It was so wild, so unlike any landscape I had ever imagined, particularly Bryce Canyon and Canyon de Chelley. I know it's so romanticized and sensationalized, but I was young and impressionable. The different landscapes all across the country—the open space, the prairies, the red rock, the strata, the layers of earth—made such a big impression on me.

   For example, at Mono Lake in California, there are salt deposits that form below the surface of the water, and they push up from underneath to

Figure 43. Karen McMahon Hedley and Leah Stein improvising at Bryce Canyon. Photo by Sorrel Alburger.

form these huge salt towers. I was so inspired by these irregularly shaped, figure-like towers that I created a piece called *Strata*. In the piece, we worked literally with weight and pushing from underneath to create height; we explored the idea of gradual change and the image of piled layers using the walls and floor and beams in the space.

MK: Did you perform it on site?

LS: No, we did it in an art gallery. It was a 20-minute piece, and we did it three times in a row. It was a very slow piece, and the audience could come and go as they wanted. I was working with geological time. There was a lot of pushing up of bodies against the walls, and it created a whole different feeling of gravity and movement.

MK: Would you call that site-specific dance?

LS: Partially. It was inspired by a specific landscape, but we made it for a particular room in the art gallery. Later, we did it again in the studio and used the elements that were there—a pole, a wall, etc.

MK: So site-specific work has the potential to move away from the original site?

LS: There's an element that's moveable, and there's an element that's specific. So when you move it, it changes to whatever's specific about the next space. But there are some elements that can be maintained from one place to another. What's odd is that *Strata* was site-specific, but it wasn't inspired by the art gallery in which it was performed. The art gallery was transformed by another site. But eventually I realized that I just needed to do the whole creative process out of the studio.

MK: How do you select sites? For example, what drew you to create the piece by the canal in Manayunk near Philadelphia?

LS: I remember the day I started looking around for the site for the Manayunk piece, *Return*. I knew the kind of juxtapositions I wanted of architecture and nature, or wildness and weeds, or maybe remnants of the past. I entered Manayunk along the water, and I just started wandering around. I'm really interested in unremarkable places, places that might not be the highlight of an area. To me, these less considered sites have a lot of life in them. It was the beginning of my "you-can-find-something-interesting-anywhere" stage. I like places that haven't yet been designed or where the design is disintegrating. They have so many qualities that are interesting for me as an artist. There is a real richness of possibility because there's something going on that people aren't trying to control.

MK: Once you choose a site, what initially guides your process?

LS: I think "resonate" is an important concept for me. I ask myself, how does this place resonate? I pay attention to how the elements of the environment interact—movement, sounds, textures, colors, etc. On what levels do these elements resonate? How can we embody it, play with it, push against it, stretch it out, and show the other side of it?

I did a piece called *Falling from the Sky* at Longwood Gardens, which has a very cultivated beauty. I was nervous in the site because it's overly designed. I was not sure what to do because it's already so manicured. The piece ended up being very expansive; it covered so much ground. We started in a field, and then we went through a series of walkways and hills down to an Italian water garden. The Italian water garden was very formally designed, and it was interesting to pull at this formality. The section ended with all the dancers suddenly dropping to the ground, and at that exact moment the fountains all came on with a big splash. It was quite a humorous moment. Adjacent to the formal water garden was a large pond. A line of performers danced along the

Figure 44. Performing in the cultivated beauty of Longwood Gardens in *Falling from the Sky* (2000). Photo courtesy of Leah Stein Dance Company.

edge of the pond in the distance, and the piece ended with a dancer (Josie Smith) in a canoe accompanied by a trombone player (David Champion).

There are so many different things to focus on in any site, so a choreographer has to decide what is important or what should be highlighted. Is it the historic development or the design of it? Or is it the political and social history that happened there? I had such a strong feeling about Longwood Gardens because it is owned by Dupont, an oil company. Then I found out about the pesticides and herbicides they use there, and I got really upset. I'm not really subversive, and I don't really do that much social/political work outwardly. But I feel like I really want my concerns to be communicated even if they don't have a social label. I have these little ways that I rebel. In the case of *Falling from the Sky*, I tried to push it as far as we could go.

MK: Do you generally do research on your sites?

LS: Yes, this has always been true with my work. I do research, and I learn about the site, and then I let it go. Sometimes this research comes out really clearly in the work. Other times it is more peripheral or woven into the fabric of the piece in an inconspicuous way. It depends on the site.

For example, for *Return*, I did a lot of research on the site because Manayunk has such a long history. The neighborhood is so old, and there is an even longer recognition of the past through the Native American names, like Manayunk. I discovered that there is a strange tension between the people whose families have lived in that community for generations and the new Main Street of Manayunk, which is so upscale. So my research for that ended up being quite extensive, but it didn't actually manifest in a literal way in the performance.

MK: Do you ever include community members in your work?

LS: Yes, in *Falling from the Sky*, we included a local group of children; actually they were the children of the Mexican migrants who worked on local mushroom farms. I really like to have community members involved in site projects. Once I started inviting people who were not necessarily professional dancers to perform in my projects, I began to want more community involvement.

Community involvement infuses the piece with a different tone. I think that the audience becomes more included in the performance. It helps to soften the audience/performer line because the audience sees themselves in the community participants. And then the performers (and audience) become changed by the experience. They have a new and lasting connection to that site.

MK: Didn't you do a number of pieces at Historic Bartram's Gardens in West Philadelphia with people from the community?

LS: Yes, I did a residency at a high school in southwest Philly. When I went into the school, I was really nervous because I was a white modern dance lady going into a multiracial, inner-city school. But I worked on basic movement principles, ideas, improvisation, and some contact improvisation. I was surprised because the kids were very open. We went to Bartram's Gardens and explored the site. I had them go off and choose a place, a sound they heard, and something they saw to bring back and discuss. For them, the site was far from their high school in the inner city, and it was as if some of them had never walked on grass; they were worried about their shoes getting muddy. It was a massive site experience for them, partly because it was collaborative. I let them generate movement, and we worked together to create the piece. It was really rewarding to have their direct input. By the end they had a whole different feeling about the site; it truly became their site.

Actually, the year before the piece with the high school kids, I went and worked with the kids who lived in the projects right next to the site. I integrated them into the piece. The kids' lives were raw; they were wonderful and inspirational to work with. The creative process felt like the most important thing in order to encourage and engage their imaginations.

MK: Did you talk to them about the history of Bartram's Gardens and about the contrast between the wealthy white man's garden and mansion and their housing project across the street?

LS: Actually, the history was not my focus, but it did come out as hard issues came up. For example, we talked about the impulse to fight back because otherwise, if you don't fight, you get beaten up. That was challenging to hold a line about justice in the face of such unjust circumstances. My goal was for them to feel like they were part of something, something that was theirs, too, even for a short time.

MK: What kind of input have you received from your audiences and/or community performers? Do they discuss a newfound connection to the places in which you perform?

LS: Yes. Audiences and performers tell me afterwards that they've known the place so long in a certain way, but to be part of a creative process on site changed their connection to the place. Their connection deepened, and they also discovered new things about the site.

For example, I did a piece called *Corner Lot* in a little parking lot in the Old City part of Philadelphia. I loved the site; it was this little gritty corner. After seeing the piece, people saw and perceived something that they wouldn't have seen in that overlooked lot. People started to see connections to their lives on a personal level; the lot was really transformed for them.

We did another piece in South Carolina called *Watermark* right outside of a university library. There was a reflecting pool in front of the library, and we did a whole section with books. We even had books floating on water. We also performed a section on a staircase, dropping books down it, etc. Afterwards, people said things like, "I've taught here for 20 years, and I have never noticed that staircase, and I will never look at it the same way again." That is not an uncommon response. Many times people revisit sites where a piece was performed and are able to connect with the site again, as though it was still ringing with the performance.

MK: When you work on site, are you concerned about having an approach that is respectful and sensitive to the place, the history of it, and the community that surrounds it?

LS: Well, I like to have as much information as possible going in. For example, for the Bartram's Gardens pieces, I went on a tour and learned about the gardens and how the trees were planted over 200 years ago. Learning about the site helped me develop a relationship to it. I like to create a definite con-

Figure 45. Josie Smith, Leslie Dworkin, Darla Stanley, and Jillian Bird performing in a Philadelphia parking lot in *Corner Lot* (2000). Photo courtesy of Leah Stein Dance Company.

nection to my chosen sites as well as a respect for the history of that site. I think the more sensitive we are in the process, the richer the work is. The way that I work, I don't come in with a preconceived idea; I generate ideas from the site. I believe our sensitivity and connection to the site comes across in the performance and that the audience becomes more respectful and aware of what's around them.

MK: Has the audience ever been annoyed or upset with your presentational choices?

LS: Not typically in urban sites. People are used to all kinds of events in a city, and they're not as precious about where things are performed. But in other sites . . . For example, in the piece in South Carolina, *Watermark*, some people had really strong reactions to us putting books in the water. They thought it was too destructive. We were using these old books that we bought at a thrift store. But people still had a strong response to that.

But I've had really great experiences, too. In our final performance in a festival in Poland, we moved from one site to another and ended up in a parking lot with garages. We had an active, big movement section where everybody finally came together for a simple ending. A man pulled up in a car in the middle of this and wanted to get into his garage. This had *never* happened in the two-week rehearsal process. He put his arm out of his window, and I think a performer whispered some information to him about what was going on. He just sat there, elbow out the window, and watched a large group of 30 dancers and four musicians dancing in his driveway. He appeared captivated and happily patient. From the audience's perspective, it almost seemed planned.

MK: It must be interesting to take site work into cultures that are new and/or unfamiliar.

LS: What I noticed about working in Poland was this incredible group mind. I could give them a task, and about 10 or more people could all work together. During the process, I really wanted someone to work with the space on top of one of these garages. It was possible to get up there, but nobody wanted to do it. There just wasn't a star system in Poland, like in the United States. There weren't people who wanted to stand out and be the one who would jump on top of the garage. And so we didn't, and that was fine. But then a funny thing happened. During the performance, there were these kids who were heckling us before the performance began. Then, during the performance, they ended up sitting right there on top of the garage. It was great. In the beginning, someone was going to ask them to get off, but I said, "Don't. It's OK." When the performance started, they became really engaged in watching, and they moved to watch each section. So I ended up getting that element that I really wanted. I like pushing those boundaries because I like having an element of wildness and unpredictability in my work.

MK: What was the most unusual site you've ever worked in?

LS: Actually, it was also in Poland. At another location, we did a site work called *The Train Project* in an old train garage that was abandoned in 1989. It was amazing because everything was still there, like tickets, oilcans, tools, everything. It was definitely one of the most unusual sites I've ever worked in. There was this young Polish guy, Piotr, who lived nearby and was there every day. He knew everything about the trains; he loved the place. We befriended him and communicated by drawing pictures. We seemed to understand each other in some miraculous way. We eventually invited him to be part of the piece. It was a wonderful experience because our understanding expanded and his experience expanded. This is one of the true rewards of site work.

MK: Do you feel that doing site work has changed you personally?

LS: I think doing site work expands your awareness and attention to all aspects of life. It spurs you to ask, "What is happening? How do these elements interact? How do they relate? What 'story' do they tell?" Somehow that is a big enough dialogue or investigation that it's started to live in my creative process, even in the theater. But I am still drawn to create dances on site. My imagination is continually active and engaged by the challenge.

MK: Does your site work ally you with activist organizations?

LS: I just had a meeting this morning with a graphic designer. She's going to be part of the upcoming Philadelphia Earth Charter Summit. We talked about artists forming alliances with organizations or movements who share similar concerns, be they social, political, or environmental. It's about attempting to integrate or build bridges between the artist's work and political or social movements. I'm really interested in seeing how I can strengthen my work, my active voice in the world through alliances to what I believe in. So, yes, I do think of myself as an activist. I have a lot of concern for life on this planet, the impoverished state of it, and for how we treat the earth and each other. I feel like my work reflects this statement in a quiet way. It might not be in the title, but it does reside in the process and in the realization of the work. It offers a different way of being on the planet and of being sensitive to environmental and human issues.

○

Of Grass and Gravel

By Leah Stein

In the open space between two buildings on a city street, I see a vast world of possibility. Like the start of an engine, the unplanned space triggers my imagination. My body responds immediately. Gestures emerge. I see evidence of the history of what was there coexisting with the new life beginning to emerge. I notice the natural world mingling with architectural remnants of concrete and brick walls. As I ponder the graffiti-covered and crumbling surfaces, I begin to imagine a dance taking place right there in partnership with the wall. I instantly see the shape and contour of the ground, the meeting of metal, cement, fences, dirt, rocks, ragged and open edges with a pile of sticks here and a lost shoe over there. The textured walls collect various colors and patterns that catch my attention like a sudden flash. My body instinctually reacts and tells me that I am more "a part of," rather than "apart from," the landscape. I look for the tiny tendrils, if not an entire field of weeds, pushing through the cement and from between bricks with that eternal effort of green life. This interface of the natural environment, unplanned and unstoppable, cohabitating with urban life, reminds me of the inseparability of people and the environment. That inseparability is at the core of my passion for making dances on site.

Interfacing with the Past

The natural environment has been a close friend of mine since I was very young. Running out the front door and hearing it slam behind me represented a kind of unnamed freedom that still rings vividly in my memory. There is an old family movie, 16mm, showing me happily patting dark rich earth around my foot as if I were planting it in the ground. This was filmed before I had ever had a dance class.

When I was seven, I was lucky enough to be introduced to dance in a big empty airy barn out in a field in the Hudson Valley. Sometimes our teacher, Brenda Buffalino, would take us outside into the tall grasses for part of the class. Dance, I learned, was about moving in a big space with others, where the interior and exterior spaces were equally important.

Both indoors and outdoors, I was drawn to light and shadow. As a child, I particularly remember noticing the patterns of sunlight on the walls in my house changing with the time of day and season. I was so awestruck by this discovery that I took black-and-white photographs of these dancing patterns of shadows on the living room wall. Through these images I found a new world that made that wall seem like a living thing.

I also remember my own personal study of topography from the school bus window. Throughout the changing seasons, I would study the movement, the changes in texture and color, and the land masses on the way to and from school. I am sure that I chatted with friends as well, but there were many times when I was quietly engaged with the passing landscape. One memory, in particular, stands out in my mind. On my first ride on a new bus route, we passed some apple orchards. Between two of these orchards, an open area formed a depression in the land. It was filled with a quiet fog still hanging in the cool of the early morning. The beauty and simplicity of this image has stayed with me all these years, igniting my creative process.

Interface of Architecture and Nature

The first dance I created in a college composition class was outdoors. I chose a location with a concrete wall lining the back of the space and a young tree a good distance in front of the wall. At the time, this combination of geometric and organic elements represented a vital and stirring relationship for me. It reflected my own internal tension between the concrete or planned and the organic or instinctual. This relationship between structure and openness, between clear landmarks, concrete guideposts, and organic unfolding, drives most of my dances.

I find that I continue to be compelled by the interface between architecture and nature, as well as by the connections, contradictions, and infinite possible relationships that emerge from it. For example, in *Return* (1994), I chose an area along the old Manayunk Canal outside of Philadelphia. The site offered an activated balance between the natural world (people came to walk the tow path for this experience of "nature") and the "designed" world (it was the home of the historic Manayunk bridge, a noted icon for its immense size and compelling design). Along the cement-lined canal, where weeds and trees are gradually taking over, there are several bridges, small and large, as well as a 20-foot-tall stone wall, standing alone among the trees and weeds.

I created the structure of the dance to mirror this combination of natural and architectural elements. I juxtaposed choreographed material with improvisational structures, all of which were made in direct response to the environment. Using the stone wall, for example, dancers climbed up, wedged between a tree and the wall. Their backs were pushed against the tree for support as they walked with their feet and hands up the wall where they perched for some time. For my early works, such as *Return*, we developed certain structures, such as "moving/still," "passage," and "tread," that allowed people to travel long distances in a dance, far beyond the standard length of a dance studio or theater stage. These structures, which propelled dancers along the vast stretches of the canal, for instance, helped connect patterns of people with the environment in ways that made the landscape a totally equal player, not simply "background."

Another dance, *Bardo* (2005), was created and performed in a large empty lot on Broad Street in central Philadelphia. The title comes from a Buddhist term that means "in-between space," or suspended time, and often refers to the time between life and death. I chose the empty lot in this work for its embodiment of this concept. This open lot between two buildings was being taken over by "urban nature," a mixture of weeds, gravel, and debris. The mixture of elements was like a dialogue of multiple voices. The everyday, unremarkable collection of things, the unplanned combination of textures and colors, the ambient sounds—all seemed to talk to each other. I saw the potential to create something new based on what was already there.

For the performance of *Bardo*, the audience sat on round stools near one end of the site in a gravel area. They turned on their seats to follow the dance as it moved in a counterclockwise direction. The 18 performers moved through the space, along jagged brick walls, down the distant alleyway that lined the end of the site, up to an exposed support beam, and under long plastic tubes native to the terrain. The performance began in the light and ended after dark, referencing the transitional, in-between concept of *bardo*. Movement ranged from intimate and barely perceptible gestures to the sharp, rugged throwing of dusty rocks against metal.

During the creation of *Bardo*, I began to experiment with site-video. As the dance progressed from dusk to dark, an abstract video image of moving light and shadow (playing continually but imperceptibly at the beginning of the dance) gradually came into view on a rough urban wall. The flickering band of video by Edward Dormer highlighted rhythmical elements in both the choreography and sound score. As night fell, the projected video image became more visible, and it appeared as though the building surface itself were moving in waves. Audience members were impacted by these images and commented that what had been

Figure 46. Experimenting with elements on site. Michele Tantoco, Olase Freeman, Karen Bookbinder, Josie Smith, and Jillian Bird in Leah Stein's *Bardo* (2005). ©Jacques-Jean Tiziou/ www.jjtiziou.net.

invisible to them at the beginning of the dance became a mesmerizing source of calmness in the dark. Throughout the dance, Toshi Makihara quite literally "played" the site, making an original sound score that created a feeling of spaciousness as well as precise specificity.

Interface of Movement and Sound

The sound score in site work is always an equal element for me. Sound can create sudden shifts in attention, open the space, focus a moment, elicit an energy or emotion, and essentially bring the sounds of the site to life. The theater is quiet; all sounds are chosen. But on site, sounds and movements already exist. I am continually interested in the continuum between movement and sound on site, especially the overlap where movement can almost be heard, and sound can almost be seen.

In *Bardo*, Makihara used two 5- or 6-foot-long wooden dowels to play the 30-foot diagonal support beams that attached to an exposed brick wall high above the ground and reached down into the ground. The hollow, metal, ringing sound of Makihara's playing reverberated through the entire site. The physical movement required of him to play or create this sound was often as equally interesting as the sound itself.

In *Return*, there was a section under a low bridge where Makihara and another musician, David Forlano, "played" a wide graffiti-covered wall with different length sticks. The visual energy of the graffiti in combination with the sound of the percussive playing (an elaborate rhythmic improvisation) was even more engaging because of their physicality. They would reach and lunge and bend to play, or strike with their sticks, as much surface area as possible, creating a very dynamic movement section. The "ceiling" of the bridge created a powerful acoustic chamber, so the sound rang with clarity.

In *Junebug*, created in 1998 at Historic Bartram's Gardens, Makihara played a giant gong down by the water's edge where a cider mill had been carved in stone. He stood on an outcropping of rocks and swung the gong in full reaching sweeps with one hand while holding the mallet in the other. He would strike the gong with large expansive gestures, activating an entire scene of movement. The power and force of his own "dancing" was inseparable from the sound he was creating.

In my work, dancers also function as sound makers. While exploring a site, I find movements that create sound and integrate these actions into the work. For example, I may have dancers shuffling their feet in gravel, dropping stones into buckets of water, or performing movement sequences whose rhythmic pat-

Figure 47. Performers and sculptural installations under a bridge in *Return* (1994). Photo courtesy of Leah Stein Dance Company.

terns emerge through impact with a resonant wall or floor. In *Corner Lot*, which was performed in 2000 in a small corner parking lot in Philadelphia flanked by two very tall old brick walls, the dancers had 20-foot-long copper pipes that created beautiful sounds when dragged or rolled along the surfaces of the site. For me, when working on site, sound and movement operate on an undivided continuum; dancers and musicians activate this continuum as they jointly create aural, visual, and kinetic textures.

Interface of the Body and the Land

I recently read Frank Lloyd Wright's 1954 book, *The Natural House*. He talks about creating organic architecture that integrates the landscape into the design and even the function of the house. This is exactly how I feel about making dances. I remember visiting Falling Water, his house in Bear Run, Pennsylvania, which was built over a waterfall. This experience made a huge impression on me. It made me realize that I could look at landscape and people in a collaborative context, rather than as two distinctly separate entities. Wright discusses the power of the horizon line as an important symbol for people; it provides a foundation, but also offers a sense of expansiveness. I often think of the horizon line or feel it kinesthetically when generating movement ideas. It helps clarify relationships between movement and the environment. Sometimes extended arms may define the horizon line, or forearms may rest on this horizontal plane like a leaf on the surface of water.

The interface of the body landscape and physical environment fascinates me. Just as the environment carries a record of its life geologically, architecturally, and culturally, the body does as well. Sometimes they correspond with each other bringing out likenesses, and sometimes they are in sharp contrast. An early work, *Departure* (1993), performed in a large open meadow, explored this synthesis of dancers and the surroundings. Four dancers moved with large, slow steps as though their bodies were full of air. They seemed to mesh with the movement of a strong wind in the surrounding trees and waving grasses. In contrast, the very slow-motion procession at the end of *Bardo* (inspired by one section of Kurosawa's film *Dreams*) moved from the empty lot into the active nightlife. There was a tension, a strangeness, and also a striking sense of the unexpected that made this procession oddly compelling.

In *Junebug*, I enjoyed playing with a direct correspondence between body and landscape. I distinctly remember noticing the gentle slope of the land with all its irregularities and allowing it to give rise to several choreographic ideas. There was one small depression in the ground that appealed to me. It looked as though an animal or object had rested there long enough to make a lasting impression in the earth. The grass had grown evenly over this concave dip, making it barely visible. We found a moment when the children involved in the project could roll a dancer down the hill, right into this gentle dip. She fit perfectly, curled up into the "dip" as though it had been made for her. Many people remembered this moment of the performance. Someone even asked if I had dug out the earth, because the perfect fit seemed too great a coincidence.

Conclusion

The juice of my creative process is found in the mix of unexpected elements with the studied sense of form. I am continually inspired to mix the spontaneous with the well-crafted. On site, this juxtaposition is inherently present at all times—the planned and the unplanned, the known and the unknown. As my relationship with sites deepens, I sense a powerful dialogue between typically contrasted elements (nature, architecture, urban landscape, people, sound, movement) that provides the ground for my dances. I tap into the sense of interconnectedness among these elements. As I dive into this interface, I find meaning, even community, in what can be a fragmented and strangely disjointed modern existence. There is a Japanese Buddhist term, "Esho Funi," which means: oneness of self and environment. This idea is a core principle for me. I continue to make dances on site, integrating the unexpected, the deeply investigated, the seen, and the unseen, to create a shared sense of place and to connect people more deeply to themselves, each other and the environment.

8

Marylee Hardenbergh

Marylee Hardenbergh is the artistic director of Global Site Performance and is an artist-in-residence at the Center for Global Environmental Education at Hamline University in St. Paul, Minnesota. For over twenty years, Hardenbergh has created works for such unusual sites as a sewage treatment plant in Minneapolis, a war-torn Parliament Building in Bosnia, and on mooring cells in the Mississippi River. She often includes such unique performers as cherry picker drivers, Bobcat operators, firefighters, canoeists, rollerbladers, and sewage workers as she attempts to transform the audience's experience of the environment. She has received a Fulbright scholarship, an NEA two-year choreography fellowship, a Soros Foundation grant, and five McKnight fellowships. She also received an Exceptional Service Award from the American Dance Therapy Association in 2006 for her community performances. From her home in Minneapolis, Hardenbergh conversed with Pavlik on October 19, 2005.

An Interview with Marylee Hardenbergh

CP: When is a dance site-specific?

MH: For me, a dance is site-specific when the music, the costumes, and the movement vocabulary are created especially for that site. They emerge from the site itself.

Look at the two words making up the term. *Specific* connotes made-to-order, for that particular thing. *Site* denotes the place of the performance. Therefore, a choreographer cannot create a dance onstage and then take it outside, or do a dance in one place and then move it to another place. Those kinds of migrating dances merit the word *site-adaptive*.

For my site-specific works I use performers from the site. To take a group of Minnesota dancers to California to create a site dance there is not as true to the site as making a site dance with dancers from California. I believe that a site-specific choreographer should find dancers and performers from that site. That might also include people who regularly inhabit the site like cyclists, skateboarders, and rollerbladers.

CP: How do you go about starting a new site work?

MH: When I start a new site-specific piece, I drink in the site, which to me includes all natural and human phenomena interacting with it. I really believe that in each of the sites that I choose, there is a lot of beauty already there. Even though it may be an overlooked, forgotten, or dirty site, there is so much beauty there, and I love to bring out that beauty through the dance.

I go to the site and make a pact with it. I say, "I'll come and visit you each day for 30 days straight, and then I want you to yield up your secrets to me." So I go to the site at different times of the day, in all weathers; I just go and sit and look.

First and foremost, I consider the visual. I work hard to decide the date and the time of day for the performance, so that it becomes site- and time-specific. I focus on the viewing angle for the audience. Is the moon going to rise there? Where is the sun setting? I only use natural light. Thus the lighting design is provided by the sun and the clouds. All that studying pays off when people say, "Man, you are so lucky! That moon coming up behind that fire truck was so great." I once attended someone else's performance, and we all had the sun in our eyes. Of course, I asked myself, "Why would a choreographer do that? It was difficult to see the dance."

CP: What triggered your impulse to move outdoors?

MH: In 1982, I volunteered to create a dance for the faculty performance at the University of Minnesota. I was a member of the faculty teaching Laban Movement Analysis. Two weeks before the show, the head of the dance department came in to watch. She was shocked at how, in her mind, the dance looked messy. Right there she said, "You can't be in the show. We cannot have your piece in the faculty performance."

I was mortified! But one of the other instructors, a visiting artist from New York at the time, said to me, "Marylee, being in the faculty show at the University of Minnesota is not a big deal. Just do the piece when the dancers are ready." One of my dancers, who worked as an architectural historian, said, "Let's do it in the Landmark Center cortile," referring to an interior courtyard of a building in downtown St. Paul. So we did. In fact, we did it twice in front of the same audience because the dance lasted only 11 minutes. I wanted the audience to see the movement from two perspectives, so I said, "Watch it one time from eye level. Then go up to the second or third floor and watch it from the edge looking down." I had not choreographed the dance from the aerial viewpoint, but when I saw the video, the patterns struck me as so beautiful.

This really opened my eyes to alternative sites for dance performances. If I had not been kicked out of the faculty performance, I might never have realized, "Oh! I like these dances out of the proscenium!"

CP: Where was your first site-specific dance?

MH: The first dance that I choreographed for a specific place was *Solstice Falls on Friday* at St. Anthony Falls in Minneapolis in 1985. I had nine dancers performing on nine 20-foot diameter concrete mooring cells that are part of the lock and dam system in Minneapolis. The audience stood on a bridge looking down at the dancers performing on the mooring cells.

Before I created any of the movement for the piece, I made the costumes to match the circular concrete "stages." When the dancers lay down, the costumes formed perfect circles of cloth to match the circular stages. When the dancers stood, they could manipulate the cloth using nylon rods sewn into the perimeter. Half of each costume was red and half purple; I even dyed the

Figure 48. Performers on mooring cells in *Solstice Falls on Friday* (1985). Photograph by James O. Phelps.

two shoes to match. I also commissioned music to be composed for the piece. So all was created for the site: the music, the costumes, and the movement.

CP: Do you ever involve your audiences in your site works?

MH: Yes. most of my performances use a great deal of audience participation. My intention is to create a strong, interactive bond between the site and the hearts of the audience members. If they are participating, they tend to feel more invested. I also want the audience involved after the performance proper. For example, at the end of the *Mother's Day Dance,* a work that I produced for three years, we handed out color-coded streamer wands. The great-grandmothers made an inner circle with silver streamers. The grandmothers made a circle around them with yellow streamer wands. The third circle was made up of mothers with pink streamer wands, and finally the fourth circle was made by anyone who ever had a mother. They held green streamers. One woman told me afterwards that she attended with her mother, and that as a result of having been at the performance, her relationship with her mother was transformed. In the past, her mother had shrugged off the children's attempts to honor and pamper their mother on Mother's Day. However, after the dance publicly valorized a large group of mothers, the mother allowed the children's affection to sink in.

CP: What is it about public spaces that entice you?

MH: While I admire dance theater, I am sold on the idea of choreographing for outdoor (and sometimes indoor) sites. Dancing outside brings dance out to the public, most of whom do not attend dance performances. My pieces have been good ambassadors for dance.

I also like that element of surprise when people just walk by and happen upon a performance. I prize capturing the "accidental audience." That could not happen if I were presenting a dance inside a theater.

CP: I know you also enjoy working with large machinery in your site works. Do you find that this links you to new audiences?

MH: Yes, many of my performances use machines. When I choreograph with machines for the first time, I meet with two or three operators and ask them to show me what their machines can do. What is their movement repertoire? Then I take the moves that I think will work and put them into the choreography. Once I incorporated an operator of a cherry picker for *Urban Sky Harvest* at the farmers market in Minneapolis; he worked trimming trees for a power company and said after the performance, "Being in your performance was exciting because it was really the first time ever that I was able to put my machine through its paces. In the streets, I can never spiral up at 360 degrees like that." After that same performance, a woman came up to me crying and

Figure 49. People stopping to photograph Hardenbergh's *Urban Sky Harvest* (1991). Photo by Gary Phelps.

said, "My husband works at the Park Board, and this is the first time, after 20 years, that I have been able to understand what is so inspiring to him about these machines and why he even likes his job." After another of my shows, one of the operators said, "You know, this art stuff isn't so bad." That's exactly the reaction I am looking for.

CP: Are there any main issues that site work helps you address?

MH: For the most part, my overarching intention is to create beauty, joy, and a sense of community. But because my site work is outdoors, environmental issues have edged their way into my dances. I began to look more seriously at the degradation of our environment.

After the 1994 Duluth performance of *Bridge Dancing,* where there were 4,000 to 5,000 audience members, I began to understand that this art form was indeed a powerful one and that I could use my art to raise awareness of the environment. A few days later, I was looking in the phone book, and it opened to Metro Waste Control. So I called them up. After I was transferred about 10 times, I finally reached a guy who understood that I might have something to offer them. I mounted a dance on a sewage treatment plant the next year, and the video of that dance won a national award for educating the public! So while my first dances did indirectly address ecology issues, my later dances began to embrace them head-on.

Other issues have also crept into my work. In 2005, in my *Solstice River* performance, I explored a treaty signing between two Dakota chiefs and the U.S. Army. This first treaty in 1805 marked the beginning of the end of Native American use of the tribal lands along the Mississippi. For the project, I included some of the Dakota people in the work. On the first night of the performance, a Dakota dancer who was to hold a cloth representing the river and the land that the "white folks" would take forgot to bring the cloth into the performance with him. I spoke with him afterwards, and he assured me that he would remember the cloth the next night, but again it was forgotten. My hunch is that a reenactment of the land being taken from their tribe cut too close to the bone.

That said, some of the audience members came up to me afterwards and said, "Thank you so much for bringing the Dakota back to this land." It had been 200 years since they have been welcomed here.

CP: Are there any significant artists that have helped shape your artistic process?

MH: Without question, Irmgard Bartenieff has had the most influence on my creations. During the 1970s, well before the concept of site-specific dance came into my mind, I studied Rudolf Laban's concept of Space Harmony with her. My knowledge of Space Harmony has deeply informed how I look at spaces and how people can move within those spaces. I also learned about Laban leading movement choirs for thousands of people dancing together. This was a stunning thought to contemplate. I was further inspired by dancing in movement choirs created by Bartenieff. I watched her create them, and her method influenced how I work with people.

After creating site works for a few years, I discovered a photograph in the Walker Art Center in Minneapolis at a Bauhaus exhibit that helped me to see that my work was not outré. I vividly remember standing in front of a 1920s photograph showing Oskar Schlemmer's dancers atop the new Bauhaus building in Dessau, Germany. Oh, I thought, here is someone else who puts dancers up on buildings or architectural spaces. I stood in front of that photo for quite a while as feelings of relief and recognition washed over me and tears came to my eyes.

CP: What logistical issues arise when presenting or creating site work?

MH: The most challenging issue is getting permission to use the site. All sites are owned by someone, so site-specific choreographers have to get permission to use the beach, the building, the bridge. In fact, I needed two whole years to get permission for my first site-specific dance! I always get permission before I plan too much, because I got burned once. A building in Minneapolis caught my eye, so I called the building management office and told them about my work and specifically what I wanted to do. They seemed to accept the idea, and I put in a month creating the dance. Then I called back to discuss the dance date, and they said they needed to check with their legal department, who in turn absolutely refused, saying, "Oh my god, your dancers, what if they fall off the edge?" I pointed out that the dancers would perform on a 30-foot-wide ledge. A dancer would only fall if she took a running leap from the spot I had given her. But the owners still denied me, and I lost a month's work.

CP: Does research factor into your process? Do you interview anyone in the community?

MH: Generally, I do not conduct many interviews as part of my research. I am more interested in the architectural and historical aspects of the site. I learn who built it and what it was used for. For example, I have gone to the architects of buildings to ask, "What rhythms do you see in the façade? This is what I am thinking. What do you see?" Sometimes the architect might say, "Oh, I would connect the twenty-first floor to the twenty-third floor." And I will appreciate those insights. But for the most part, I study the visual aspects of the site.

    In the programs given out at the performance, I also write in a lot of information about the site and its history. Is that history always incorporated into the actual movements? Not always, but sometimes history does find its way into the piece. So, yes, I do research, and the research informs the performance.

CP: Earlier you mentioned some of the responses you get from audiences about your work. Could you expand on that?

MH: People often make a point of discussing their reactions to my work. After my 1985 *Solstice Falls on Friday* performance, for example, a stranger telephoned me right afterward and said, "I am sorry for bothering you at home, but I just wanted to thank you for giving the river back to the people." Of course, I felt flattered, but I did not understand. He explained, "Well, did you feel a sense of community on that bridge? No one wanted to leave. Your dance gave us a community sense that this is our river."

    Audience members typically feel their perception of the site changes. People have approached me 10 years after seeing a dance and said, "You know, whenever I drive over the bridge, I still see the movement and the color, and I'll never forget it."

    In the audience's perception, the site and the performance get very deeply connected. One of my all-time favorite comments comes from a Duluth dad who said, "I just wanted to tell you that I took my daughter to see your performance before she was able to talk. When she started to talk, every once in a while she would pop out with 'Daddy, let's go down to the water and watch the dancers.'"

More broadly, we have done surveys for two years after the *Solstice River* performance. We want to teach people to become better stewards of the river. After six months, 60 percent of the people in a follow-up survey said that they felt that they were better stewards of the river. Respondents noted that their understanding of the bridge's history, the river environment, and the overall site improved by attending.

CP: Those are impressive figures.

MH: Yes, by doing site work I have discovered that dances on site don't just disappear; they leave lasting impressions.

○

One River Mississippi

By Marylee Hardenbergh

On June 24, 2006, seven cities danced together down at the Mississippi River. At precisely the same moment, thousands of miles apart, large communities of dancers performed in a free, public art event, melding the art of dance with ideas of ecology and community. After four years of preparations, local radio simulcasts musically united the dance performances. Employing the tools of beauty, healing, and joy, our seven audiences realized the unity of their local sites with the larger whole of the Mississippi River.

My first image for this piece—of thousands of people moving together along the Mississippi—came in a meditative moment after I had spent two weeks rafting down a stark Alaskan river. In my mind I saw dancers connecting through simultaneous movements and props; I envisioned a huge needle held aloft, perpendicular to the flow of the river, threading the dancers together with a virtual ribbon. I saw 40 bridges, each one filled with large audiences. I began work immediately, holding focus groups of environmentalists, community organizers, and dancers and contacting cities along the Mississippi.

Then I came down to earth. Instead of 40, I finally settled on 7 sites, a mammoth task in itself, but surmountable. For many years I have been creating an annual dance, *Solstice River,* at the Mississippi River in my hometown of Minneapolis. The June 2006 performance of *One River Mississippi* was *Solstice River* on steroids. For *One River*, I not only extended the concept to stretch along the length of the river but also added simultaneity into the bargain.

One River Mississippi encompassed seven simultaneous performances in seven venues along the river beginning with the headwaters in Itasca, winding down to Minneapolis, the Quad Cities, St. Louis, Memphis, New Orleans, and ending at a site near the river's mouth at the Gulf of Mexico. Our original final site was in Venice, Louisiana, but since our site was still underwater due to the effects of Hurricane Katrina, we moved to beautiful Woodland Plantation in Plaquemines Parish, which was the farthest southern site that had electricity and telephone service in 2006.

In *One River Mississippi,* I started with my spark, and then over the many months, the concept continued to metamorphose. I followed a string of contacts, be it dealing with the U.S. Army Corps of Engineers for permissions, environmentalists for consultation on key issues to spotlight, or sound engineers to advise on the technical aspects of the music. I also had to arrange for choreographers, dance therapists, Reiki masters, and the like to create a performance. All of their input flowed through me, got filtered, and became part of the overall flavor of the final performance.

The dance's intention was to create synchronous energy and understanding of the interconnectedness between communities and an ecosystem. It gave the people of this ecosystem the opportunity to work together to honor the "One River" that spans our nation. Due to the communities' witnessing of the devastation inflicted downriver by Hurricane Katrina, our event became quite timely, and it engendered a new sense of commitment to the Mississippi ecosystem as a whole. There were a vast number of participants in this piece. We had 500 performers and 10,000 audience members.

The central theme of *One River Mississippi* was using dance to connect many communities to the sites in which they live, to create a sense of place. The mayor of New Orleans, C. Ray Nagin, put it best in his letter of May 2005 when he wrote to me voicing his support of the project: "This is a chance to strengthen the ties between our cities and awaken our consciousness to the environmental impacts associated with our existence. All too often we forget that our connection to the earth is a connection to each other, and these simultaneous, site-specific performances will create a sense of interconnectedness that transcends our local community relationships, reminding us that we are all one in a great, eternal whole, so we must protect and nurture our bonds."

In engaging community members, dancers, environmentalists, audience members, as well as other choreographers in the project, my hope was that people would learn to love the river and begin to relate to the world around them with renewed eyes and hearts. I hoped to inspire a greater sense of empowerment and responsibility in taking care of the river.

Discovering Site

Studying the visual components of a site is integral to my process, in part because the audience is very important to me. When I examine a site, I consider whether the audience has good viewing—no sun in their eyes, no visual occlusions—before I will choose it as a performance place. Then I map the site, taking a visual and physical inventory. I take photographs and then make copies of the photos so that I can draw on them. I envision where I might put dancers in relation to the vertical or horizontal lines in the space, and I see the direction and flow of the dancers' movement in the space. I interpret the patterns of what already exists in the design and look for articulate spaces for movement. Choreographing not floor patterns but patterns for cityscapes or landscapes, I imagine my placing of dancers as fashioning a "constellation effect."

It was an engaging question for a site-specific choreographer: how could I ensure that each piece was specific to its locale, but also connected to six other sites? In this case, each site was linked by the Mississippi River, yet often they were drastically different. For example, in Itasca we had only a 20-foot-wide stream to work with. But by the Quad Cities we had a long stretch of the now quarter-mile-wide river to manage. In Memphis, we performed on an island with the cityscape in the background. When we first went to the site in New Orleans, there was a wooden wharf where we improvised; later, a huge cruise ship was moored right at the wharf, blocking the view of the river. Was that going to be part of the choreography, or was it going to be removed? The cruise ship was there to house university faculty whose homes had been destroyed. In the end, the cruise ship was gone, but there was a new barrier, so the dancers still could not be on the wharf. Since I regard the site as "the boss," the special elements of that site had to be taken into account for each rehearsal.

I chose the seven sites with the help of a local choreographer from each town. My initial thought was to allow the local choreographers to choose their own locales for the dance. A dance critic told me it was a must for me to go to each of the sites and to choose the sites myself. I smile as I think of this now. At the time I did not have funds to fly to all of the cities a second time. The funding sources for our planning grants rejected our application for further funding. But an angel of a private funder turned the tide. I thank the artist Christo for this because for the first 20 minutes of the meeting in Minneapolis with the donor, we shared our experience of seeing his work, *The Gates*, in Central Park in New

Figure 50. One of the many locales for *One River Mississippi*. Photo by Joe Maciejko, courtesy of Ballet Quad Cities.

York City! The donor spoke of how magical Central Park became and how the community felt united; the board member who had set up the meeting for us told her, "Well, that is just like Marylee's dances! The audience doesn't want to leave, and there is a strong sense of awe in the audience." In fact, years ago, a news article labeled me the "Kinetic Christo."

Heading Up a Team

In the final days, each of the seven sites had quite a team working together: choreographers, project managers, environmental advisors, dance therapists, radio station personnel, Reiki masters, and sound system companies. The environmentalists were the first people I met with in each city, two years ahead of the performance. Then the choreographers came on the team in different ways. Some were recommended by the environmentalists I had met. Some of them were recommended by my Dance Therapy network. One I cold-called after scouring the web. Three headed up dance departments in universities.

We convened once in Memphis and once in St. Louis. We worked long hours during our precious days when we were together physically. My goal for many of the exercises was to create group cohesion among the choreographers and to develop common strategies for creating site work.

I had to figure out how to balance acting as overall artistic director and encouraging participation and a sense of ownership from the choreographers. Dancing together during our meetings, I was able to create a sense of togetherness while maintaining respect for the individual choreographer. My job as one of the co-choreographers was to make an overall structure and to choreograph the final unison sections. The choreographers and I also had conference calls monthly, then every other week, then weekly for the last few weeks. Connecting through voice was essential since we could not be consistently in one another's presence.

Structuring the Work

In the end, my design for the structure was to have each site use its own site-specific music for twenty minutes in section 1 and then switch to unison music in later sections. Choreographers chose such local music as Miles Davis in St. Louis, Johnny Cash in Memphis, and Louis Armstrong in New Orleans. Section 2 was a four-minute collection of musical excerpts from all seven sites, in geographical order. Section 3 was performed to an original score composed by Lee Blaske to celebrate the entire Mississippi River. I worked with him on the structure; it began small, as the river does at its headwaters, then grew in strength, becoming industrial here and meandering and lazy there, until it became grand and majestic and burst out into the Gulf of Mexico for the finale.

After great difficulty, I procured the use of a radio station in each locale and had sound systems at each site tuned into the broadcast. The radio stations did a marvelous job of synchronizing the music. I sent them all instructions to begin section 2, the unison music, at precisely 7:37:00 whether or not their site's section 1 had finished.

Since we had seven sites, each site took a color of the rainbow. The first time I visited St. Louis, one of the local choreographers mentioned that there is a theory that there are seven chakras along the Mississippi River and that St. Louis was the fourth, the heart chakra. Each of the seven chakras also has a color. So it was that Itasca had red, Minneapolis orange, and so on, down to violet at Woodland Plantation. These colors were used in costumes and props at each site.

When my dancers are spaced far apart, I use unison and synchrony to create and highlight the relationship between them. In this piece, there was a sevenfold synchrony that united the river communities. The movements were based on phrase material from each of the seven choreographers.

Figure 51. Using fabric to define vast spaces in *One River Mississippi*. Photo by Bruce Goodman.

My aesthetic also depends on the use of fabric to extend the human form of the dancer, to define vast spaces, and to draw the audience's attention to lines of energy. The presence of the dancers and fabric creates new visual patterns for the audience, calling their attention to connections and places they would not normally notice. In Memphis, large panels of fabric emerged on a parking ramp across the water and brought the audience's attention to the cityscape. In St. Louis, streamers of fabric cascaded down the walls of concrete, connecting the top of the levee to the river's cobblestones. In Minneapolis, the audience on the bridge helped "hold the river" with the "Blue Highway," a piece of blue fabric 1,200 feet long that unfurls along the length of the bridge. The audience, from 80-year-olds down to children, ran to grab hold and connect.

Drawing in the Audience

Following are some quotes from the audience:

> *St. Louis:* "*Everyone was so pleased to be there and be a part of something meaningful and beautiful . . . and thought provoking. We continue to find something new to mention even a week later.*"

New Orleans: "It was a once-in-a-lifetime thing, and it was really great. Congratulations!" "I feel grateful, joyous, and elevated to a special plane of existence."

St. Louis: "What you created and spread in this project has changed the energy of all who experienced the process and the evening's event. People's hearts and awareness of the connection to one another and to the beauty and the spirit of the river are aroused and strengthened."

St. Louis: "Thank you so much for this amazing experience that encompassed mind, body, and spirit and also gave such a connection to nature and mankind up and down the river. I was blown away with the experience and the connections that happened throughout the day, especially knowing it was happening in six other sites!"

Memphis: "This was a great opportunity to feel the connection to our brothers and sisters, north to south, all ages, races, and belief systems."

Plaquemines Parish: "Ya'll really brought us to the river. I really feel closer to the river. Our audience had ownership. They became part of the event." "So I, too, was changed by the river, the people, the beauty of the creativeness of others. It was majestic, awesome, and flowing."

I love to create experiential community events where both the audience and the dancers transform their relationship to the place. As a choreographer, I want to present the audience with gifts: inspiration, beauty, and a sense of belonging. I want to offer them a connection to the earth within the city and the opportunity to appreciate the natural cycles of the moon and sun, which often go unnoticed in the night lights and hectic pace of the city.

Dance is the best medium through which people can feel related to the earth. The art of dance shares the same language of time and motion, as do the earth, the moon, and the sun. The celestial bodies move. The human body moves. The audience is also invited to move, invited to be more than witnesses. For *One River Mississippi*, a dance therapist was present at each site, and they taught the audience a roll-roll-reach movement before the performance started. The audience was invited to join in the dance when they saw the dancers performing that very same movement in the finale. Several audience members commented that they could feel the other audience members up and down the river and that they felt swept away by the power of this. Some of the New Orleans viewers said they

Figure 52. Audiences in Itasca, Minnesota, joining in with gesture in *One River Mississippi*. Photo by Melanie Mertz.

felt the support and love that the communities upriver were sending down to them, and this touched their hearts. When, months later, I saw the video of the seven audiences and dancers performing that last simple repeating phrase, I cried with joy to see in real-life pixels what I had dreamed of all those months ago!

I wish to thank my artistic collaborators, the choreographers of the seven sites: Elaine Hansen in Itasca, Jenny Moore and Bernadette Knaeble in Minneapolis, Johanne Jakhelln in the Quad Cities, Beckah Voigt and Sarah Anne Patz in St. Louis, Kimberly Baker in Memphis, Barbara Hayley and Monique Moss in New Orleans, and Angela Hammerli in Plaquemines Parish.

3

Revering Beauty

The Essence of Place

Figure 53. Eiko & Koma in *Snow* (1999). Photo by Philip Trager.

Every site-specific choreographer expresses a desire for audiences to notice place. Many also want us to contemplate the effect of our behaviors on our surroundings. They may wish audiences to commit to environmental efforts or defend a historical structure that resides at a site. Some want us to consider the role of particular places in historical events or encourage us to see place as a background for human achievements and failings. Yet there are some site choreographers whose most ardent desire is for us to pay homage to the sheer beauty of place. These choreographers want to alert us to the details that characterize a place—the light, the plants, the architecture, even the dirt. For these choreographers, including Eiko Otake, Sally Jacques, Sara Pearson, and Patrik Widrig, each place shines in its own way and, with a little help from the site choreographer, we can learn to appreciate the wonders of the world around us.

Eiko Otake has been making site work with Koma Otake since the 1970s. When they first started, they performed on site mostly due to financial reasons; theaters were too costly to rent and outdoor sites were free for rehearsals and performances. But more recent works have grown from a deeper sympathy with place, as well as a greater interest in the accessibility of such sites. Unlike the majority of site works discussed in this volume, Eiko & Koma's pieces since the mid-1990s have appeared at multiple venues. In other words, when Eiko & Koma create a piece, that same piece may travel and be performed both in a lake in Minnesota and in a river in eastern Pennsylvania. This type of work, which many scholars and site artists would call site-adaptive, relies on the commonalities between sites, in this case, the common occurrence of water. Other pieces by Eiko & Koma draw on shared characteristics such as a dirt pile, a tree, or even a modified trailer. These commonalities, Otake believes, can escort viewers into an appreciation of the "primal elements" of place.

In chapter 9, Otake discusses her interest in site-adaptive work. She sees Eiko & Koma's site-adaptive pieces as bringing a kind of "nakedness" to place; the work points to the beauty of form, rather than to practical function or commercial use. As she states, her desire is for the audience to see a site as "a landscape with its own memories, rather than the usability of the place." Otake also celebrates how site work can communicate with a mixed group of devoted and happenstance audience members, a point fleshed out in her article, "Feeling Wind, Feeling Gaze." As she discusses the ritualistic elements in Eiko & Koma's pieces *Breath* (1998), *Caravan Project* (1999), and *Offering* (2002), she champions site work's ability to upend our culture's link between valuable art and high ticket prices.

Sally Jacques has been making site works for her home city, Austin, Texas, since the mid-1980s. In her earlier works, she often adopted an overt political bent; she made pieces near or on the grounds of the Austin State Capitol to protest issues such as homelessness, the AIDS crisis, and the Gulf War. In particular, she was interested in exposing the unpleasant underbelly of social and political inequities. Yet, even as she actively addressed social and political issues, she found that images of beauty were as resonant in her work as the more explicit messages. For instance, in her piece *Inside the Heart* (1991), which explored the themes of violence and greed in relation to the Gulf War, the final image was of doves flying into the night air. During the performance, instead of flying away, one rested on her finger a moment—a heartwarming image that has remained with her. Jacques has focused on creating such images of beauty by turning more and more to aerial work. In *Requiem* (2006) and *Constellation* (2007), Jacques sent her dancers soaring overhead off of imposing edifices in downtown Austin. For New Year's Eve 2006, Jacques' company, Blue Lapis Light, created *Angels in Our Midst*, a piece that featured aerial dancers swinging back and forth across a huge image of the earth projected onto the side of a downtown hotel. Jacques believes that such enchanting moments stay with people, satisfying a spiritual hunger that lives in all of us.

In Jacques' interview, she revels in the ability of site-specific dance to join mystical beauty and popular acclaim. As she describes the risks and wonders of aerial site work, she opines that such work allows her company to experience a level of collaborative interdependence that mirrors the interdependence of the natural world. In her article, "The Making of *Requiem*: A Site-Specific Dance Opera," Jacques depicts one example of this interdependence. To create her piece *Requiem* at the unfinished Intel Building in Austin, Jacques needed to navigate the vagaries of city institutions and federal offices, as well as collaborate with electricians, designers, and dancers. As she charts her progress through these nuts and bolts toward the realization of her vision, we gain a sense of the enormity of producing site work as well as the engineering ingenuity of her collaborative team.

In 1987, Sara Pearson and Patrik Widrig formed their company, PEARSONWIDRIG DANCETHEATER, in New York. The company performs both theater works and site works, with the majority of their site works traveling from site to site. Similar to Eiko & Koma, Pearson and Widrig feel that adapting a site piece to different venues can be both enlightening and effective. Their site-adaptive pieces often include the same materials from site to site—for example, 300 oranges, two knives, and Italian folk music for the piece *Ordinary Festivals* (1995)—but the movement phrasing and structure of the work change with each new place they encounter. Pearson and Widrig believe that site works help them discover the underlying presence of a place or, as Pearson explains, "the key that the place is singing in." She finds that no matter whether they are working in a Buddhist temple in Japan or on a rowboat in Central Park, place speaks to them and imbues their work with a beauty that resonates in the community.

In chapter 11, Pearson and Widrig share their first steps into the site art field and demonstrate the benefit of persistence for the continued development of the genre. They also analyze the distinction between space and place as one that helps guide their creative process on site. In Pearson's article, "The Honeymoon is Over," she explores a recent site experience at Wave Hill in the Bronx. Detailing PEARSONWIDRIG DANCETHEATER's efforts to create a site work on the vast lawns of the New York garden estate, Pearson reflects on the very different experiences of a single phenomenon—in this case, grass—that can surface in a site art process. While Pearson may lament the romanticized view of site work, her article points to the site choreographer's passion for both the obvious and hidden beauty found in outdoor sites.

The site choreographers included in this section have a tendency to ruminate on the soul of a place or on a site's mystical presence. Whether their interest is in uncovering the essence of place or the spirit of space, they often sound in awe of the sites they choose. Further, although they are interested in the particularities of sites, they have an investment in discovering the "universality" of place. This is an unusual sentiment for artists who pride themselves on understanding the individuality of place. Yet these choreographers do not see this as a problematic division. For them, a specific site—in all its beauty—acts as a microcosm of a larger voice of "place," and it is the job of the site choreographer to help this voice come forth. In other words, these choreographers believe that the site process, both site-adaptive and site-specific, can restore people's communication with place by enhancing their admiration of it. By actively reviving humanity's wonder for the world, these artists attempt to offer a recipe for an emotionally and spiritually satisfying human experience of place.

9

Eiko Otake

Eiko Otake, of the well-known group Eiko & Koma, has been performing site works on and off since the 1970s. Since 1995, Eiko & Koma has actively conceived and performed many site-adaptive pieces that attempt to integrate landscape and body. Their site works grace rivers, cemeteries, and museums around the globe; they inspire audiences of varied nationalities through their dances that verge on ritual. Eiko and Koma Otake were awarded 1996 MacArthur fellowships, the 2004 Samuel H. Scripps American Dance Festival Award, the 2006 Dance Magazine Award, and the first United States Artists Award. Eiko Otake is one of 11 founding artists of the Center for Creative Research (CCR) and a CCR resident artist at Wesleyan University. Otake spoke with Pavlik from her home in New York City on October 6, 2005.

An Interview with Eiko Otake

CP: You and Koma have created a significant amount of work both on site and in theaters. Will you talk a little about what differentiates your work in the theater and on site?

EO: Every work performed in a place, even a theater, calls for some kind of preparation, an awareness of the specifics of the place. So whether indoor or outdoor, I regard our performances as both site-specific and time-specific to a degree.

CP: Could you discuss your choreographic process?

EO: We have a framework for the choreography such that performances with the same title deliver more or less the same content, but our choreography is often not set in detail. We have somewhat of a ground design, which comes along with the concept and subject of the piece. For example, in *River,* we become part of the river. We are born, bloom, and die in a river. This is the concept of the piece. For the design, we come from upstream with driftwood and then float downstream with driftwood, leaving the audience with only the river. But we adapt the piece to the space we are in; sometimes this requires many changes to the basic design. We always try to seek a deepening of the relationship between the site itself, the concept of the work, and our style of moving.

CP: How do you choose sites?

EO: In New York, where we live, we can visit a site many times and take a whole year to imagine ourselves in it and prepare. But when we are on tour, the situation can be quite different. We do not have the same kind of control. But we always participate in choosing the site. We don't just perform where producers dictate. We correspond with the producers about what we want and need, and then they choose several sites for us to consider. When we arrive, we examine these sites and choose the final one. The process is a dialogue with the producers about our conceptual or technical needs and their

Figure 54. Eiko & Koma float downstream at the end of *River* (1995). Photo by Philip Trager.

logistical needs. There have to be common desires and strategies when you are presenting site work. There are also basic considerations: the accessibility of the site, the safety needs of the audience and staff, the availability of electricity, and the legality, whether it is legal to perform there and what is allowed to happen there. We have to research and discuss all of this in advance. We enjoy this kind of collaboration.

CP: Have you ever been in a position where none of the sites that were offered felt right?

EO: Oh, yes, many times.

CP: So what do you do in that situation?

EO: We just do our best, meaning we put forth our best effort within the given time and choices. We are not necessarily looking for a place that is just right. We are looking for a place that is workable. This is another reason we really prefer to have our own structure and concept because we are looking for ways we can bring something to a place rather than just being inspired by the place. Then when we get there, we will de-prepare and re-create. That is a joy of site work.

CP: After you decide upon a site, what draws your focus initially?

EO: Let me give you an example. For our piece *River*, producers have already looked for a site with water that matches our requirements more or less. So, once we get there, the first thing we do is a safety check. How safe is it? Can the audience sit by the riverbank? How safe is it for the audience to leave the performance site after it gets dark? Usually the audience comes to the performance in the light and goes home in the dark, as we prefer to start our dance in twilight. This is because when we perform from dusk to dark we can dance with nature's grand lighting design; as it gets darker outdoors, our lights feel brighter, all without the aid of a lighting cue.

We also investigate the safety of the performance area. It is not only a water quality issue. It is also about how much debris is in the riverbed. There may be broken glass, or there may be sharp objects such as cans. Sometimes we teach a workshop, meet nice people, and ask them to clean the river with us. Or we do this with local crew members. It is nice to work together with local people on the site of a performance and to spend some time together that way. So the safety issue is number one.

CP: What other issues come to mind?

EO: Number two is a visibility issue. How can we be visible from the audience? Are the audience's sight lines adequate? Because Koma and I are in water, it is important that people can really see us. Otherwise, we are only frustrating the audience, something we don't want to do. We also consider:

What time does the sun set? How is the natural light in a site? Is it hard to see us if people are facing toward the setting sun or its afterglow? How can we enhance the performance with our own lighting system and not make it feel like an intrusion? What is the noise level of the site? How do our viewers arrive? What will they see before, during, and after our performance in that site as landscape and environment? We also check how many insects there are and how cold or hot the place might be.

In the case of performing the work *River*, we need to consider which direction the river flows because we like to move from upstream to down during the performance. That direction of the river flow is common knowledge among the local audience members. That direction gives us a subtext that we cannot have in theaters. In theaters, stage right is not that different from stage left from the audience's perspective. But in the case of *River*, the direction of the water's flow creates an unmistakable story and texture.

CP: How does a site's accessibility affect the work?

EO: We structure the piece differently if we know it is in a site where people can just happen upon it. If the site is reasonably accessible and the producer does a fair job publicizing the event, there is a different mix of people; there are always the people who just happen across the performance, and there are those who come intentionally. That brings nice tension and freshness to an event. I love this. The audience members are affected by each other and by both the specificity and some commonalities of a site they are in. If the site is a busy place, some people may just stay for five minutes and leave because they did not necessarily come to see our performance. We should not be discouraged by this, but rather believe that some unexpected five minutes could affect people as profoundly as a whole evening in a theater. Even when they do decide to stay for a while, we do not control their time frame of arrival and departure. Each audience member's beginning, middle, and end is different. On the contrary, if the site has no everyday traffic, then we assume all audience members come purposefully and on time. They expect to see the whole work as we conceive and design it.

CP: How important is the history of a site to your work?

EO: Some site-specific choreographers study and include historical information in their work. But I prefer to hear about a place by chatting with local people, not necessarily interviewing people. When we teach a workshop or when we work with local production crews, we get to hear about a place, a river, etc. We do not always use that information in creating the piece, but it helps us feel a little closer to a place, or imagine what the audience members might feel or remember about the place.

One reason that we do not focus on a site's historical events is because we look for some kind of commonality between the places we perform; we focus on the primal elements. For example, when we perform in a particular part of the Delaware River, we certainly end up knowing about its history. But in the end, what we like to bring to the audience is the very essence of the river; we show what connects one river to another river—water that runs. Visually and soundwise, we do start by addressing the specifics of a place, but the darkness of the night usually brings out the core of the place, so that River X becomes all rivers. As performers, we want to be metaphorically naked, and we want the place, our "stage," to be metaphorically naked as well. We do not want to force-feed, but somehow the audience seems to see and feel that nakedness.

We want to have recognizable references between what we offer, say, in San Francisco and what we offer in Minneapolis. The choreography or what we do in each place may be different because of the specificities of sites to which we adapt the works. Yet there are things or feelings that are common between the sites. In the case of the work *River*, it is the driftwood prop, and in *Offering* it is the dirt as a set that helps bring the recognizable visual similarities and themes. If two people see the same piece in different sites and then they talk over the phone, I want them to find a kind of intentional commonality in the work they have seen. So in that way our work is site-specific in its happening, but not in the concept or the feel. That is the way we have chosen to work.

CP: In some of your writings, you mention how your site works foster an altered relationship between the audience and a site. Can you discuss this further?

EO: I will talk about performing *River* in the Delaware River at Easton, Pennsylvania. We performed in the area of the river roped off for swimming during the summer break. We performed around sunset. People came to the place with a sense of familiarity. However, twilight or night was not the time they usually came to spend time at the river. So when we started the performance, they suddenly realized that they have seldom seen the river without worrying about where their kids were or if they had put on sunscreen. Then the time changed, and we started to lose natural light. By the time the piece was finished, it was totally dark. We floated downstream and that was the end of the piece; we disappeared. We brought in a little bit of electric light just to see the mist rise from the river. It was just so beautiful.

CP: Do you think this impacted the audience?

EO: Beauty brings people wonder, awe, and reflection. Afterwards, one woman said, "All summer, I have been bringing my kids to this place, and I have never seen this river as a 'river.'" She meant that when she comes with the kids she is *using* that place. At the performance, she sat and was given a chance just to look at the river itself and at us as something that lives in the moment in the river. In that function, Koma and I did not show only dance. Dance is only the window to view the river. Not that this is the main thing that we do, but I think it is a good part of our artwork, to give the audience a sense of a place and of a time. The place itself carries beauty of its own; it is not only a place to be used for function or for fun. I don't want people to go home being taught a lesson. But I do want them to experience another way of looking at the place.

In Minneapolis we performed in a lake. They use the lake for water sports like boating and water skiing, so during the summer the lake is very busy and loud. People are running all over the place, and in the background you have jet skis and motorboats, but you can't stop them because it is a public place. So we mobilized a bunch of people to give leaflets to those people who do the water sports in late afternoons and early evenings. The leaflets announced the time of day that we were planning to perform. It said, "We are performing at this time. During that time, would you be willing to come to a performance instead of doing water sports in the background?" People cooperated, and it gave us a way to connect to the local people.

CP: Have you received other feedback that audiences do experience a new way of seeing a place?

EO: Yes. People often tell us how they pass the site and remember us, the rain, or whatever it is that happened in the performance. What we are after is not making a historical event but making a story—not a logical story, maybe something closer to a small myth. Maybe 80 years from now someone will say, "Well, you know, these very strange people came from upstream and then did something and then they floated downstream. I did not see it, but my grandmother saw it." Back in old Japan, people tended to live in a place for a very long time, and they had lots of stories attached to places. That was part of the way human beings inhabited a place. People understood that human lives were affected not only economically and politically but also emotionally and culturally. They knew that a community was not only defined by a horizontal sense of space but also by a vertical sense of time. Time would live and breathe in a place. Generally speaking, in contemporary life in developed countries, there are not as many mythic stories that are passed on through the centuries. But I like to imagine we become one of these strange stories or myths that people continue to talk about.

CP: When did you and Koma create your first site work?

EO: We created our first site work in the late 1970s, shortly after we came to America from Japan. In starting our career in America, we performed not necessarily where we wanted to perform but where we were allowed to perform. We performed outdoors because doing so usually did not cost us anything. Also very early on, Elise Bernhardt, then director of Dancing in the Streets, produced us in a park in Brooklyn. We did it because we were invited and we were young. Why not? We would do anything that seemed exciting at that point. But each time after we performed outdoors, we felt a little frustrated because we did not get the same kind of attention from the audience as we did in the theater.

But that changed in 1980 when we performed in a site by the Hudson River, near the World Trade Center. We performed in an event produced by Creative Time. This was before that part of downtown New York was developed, so instead of seeing all the buildings, we could only see the two towers that were our backdrop. The dunes that were the landfill were our stage. We performed on top of the dunes, and the people were sitting underneath looking up at us. We then tumbled down the hill toward the audience and continued our dance, lit by four fires that got brighter as the night fell. We had maybe a week to prepare in the site, and we did a lot of crazy things like digging a hole, hiding it, disappearing into it with a big sand splash, and experimenting with how to build and sustain fires. In that performance, Koma and I felt for the first time that with enough time to prepare, performing outdoors could be enjoyable.

However it was not until we started working on the piece *River* that we actually started to take site work more seriously. *River* was the first outdoor project that we ourselves produced and toured. Curiously enough, we conceived *River* in the Catskills while working in a barn-theater without air-conditioning. When we got tired of the heat, we noticed there was a beautiful stream by the theater, and we wondered why we were sweating in the theater when we could be in the stream. We realized then how much of our adult years we had spent in theaters! That was 10 years ago. From then on we have always had site work as a very important part of what we do.

CP: Did your decision to create site work affect your ability to raise funds for your work?

EO: Although we have had our share of hard times, Koma and I have been

Figure 55. Eiko & Koma performing near the World Trade Center in *Event Fission* (1980). Photo ©Johan Elbers 2009.

very lucky. In recent decades, every project to which Koma and I put our energy has gotten some type of support and exposure, whether it was an indoor piece or an outdoor piece. Economically, however, the most difficult thing about site work is that usually we like to perform for free. Outdoor performances create more pleasure and surprises when no admission is charged. This means the producers do not have box office income, and they have no money to pay us except through their funding. For producers, to be able to expect box office income is at least a helpful start to create a budget for a presentation. So producing performances outdoors requires extraordinary effort by presenters. As a consequence, outdoor work is harder to get booked and harder to make fiscally rewarding.

CP: Have you ever been asked to do a performance by tourism and/or development agencies?

EO: No, we have not. In fact, we have mostly worked with those interested in preserving a site. In conceiving the tour of *River*, we worked with environmental groups. But that interaction was prompted by us. When we first started to perform *River*, we asked our art producers to bring the leaders of local environmental activist groups on as potential co-producers. We were interested in promoting and provoking a kind of intersection between cultural activists and environmental activists. The environmental activists and our art presenters tend to live as different tribes in the same community, but they are alike; both are pro-active, spirited, and keenly interested in their community. I wanted them to work together. This was also beneficial because local producers and activist groups can usually work out sensitive local political issues while they prepare for our performance. We allow for information sharing or discourse to be scheduled within the same week of our performance. However, the performance is an independent event, not a tool for other causes.

I feel very much that Koma and I, as well as our presenters, are cultural activists. Or at least we want to be. I participate in designing outreach activities and promotion activities for our events so that people know about the performances. But in the end, I am acutely aware that art itself is the best educational tool for art, and beautiful moments are more important than our intentions.

CP: Have you ever represented a site in ways that the producers or city officials did not agree with or thought was controversial?

EO: Yes, often, I am afraid. Certain people welcome us and accept our work, but not everyone. I don't think we mean to be controversial, but we are aware our work is not for everybody's taste. Our work is sometimes hard for certain people because of our sense of time and aesthetics. Our pieces usually move quietly and slowly. Koma and I like our work to be seen as low-tech and simple, even though it may not be low-key in reality. We are ambitious in reaching out, but we are not ambitious in terms of social acceptance. Our attitude doesn't really jibe well with the American mainstream and their expectations of what art should be.

CP: Have you ever been asked not to do something in a performance?

EO: Well, by the time we are being promoted and produced, producers and local officials pretty much leave us alone, trusting us to not do anything illegal. Art should not be reasonable, but our behavior should be. We hope to create some extraordinary moments without being indecent. We are aware that we can leave town after we perform, but our producers and audience have to live with the consequences.

CP: What makes a site work successful to you?

EO: Can I use the word *satisfactory*? It is a much better word for me. I find a work satisfactory when I feel with my body and soul that I am really enjoying being in a place with a sense of exploration and submission to the place. Second, I feel it is satisfactory when the audience response is not good or bad, but intrigued, even for just five or six minutes. While I enjoy hearing people's feedback, I don't necessarily focus on or judge their feedback, because how they will think about it five years from now may be different from what they think about it today. If the audience is drawn to what happened and I can feel it as a performer, I am humbled by that sensation.

What we particularly like about site work is that we can contribute to the ways that people relate to place. We like people to see place as more of a landscape with its own memories, rather than the usability of the place. It is a pleasure for us to feel our bodies as a part of the landscape and to realize that space and time are never empty.

○

Feeling Wind, Feeling Gaze

By Eiko Otake

When Koma and I perform our site work *River*, we come to the river as guests and are grateful for the beauty and pleasure we are allowed to share. But we are not the only guests. Bats, insects, wind, twilight, moon, mist, children, geese, and fishermen also visit the river, and they do not seem to mind us being with them for a night. It feels wonderful to be included. We breathe in the dream of the river and encourage the audience to join in our dream. If some prefer, they can join the dreams of the geese or of the moon instead. Rowboats drifting by and voices whispering in wonderment do not interrupt these dreams.

Wanting to Do Something Different

When Koma and I first started to work together, we performed where it was free and where there were people. In the 1970s, we performed on rooftops, campus greens, and plazas. It was presenters' invitations that moved us into theaters.

Years later, after we had made many theater pieces, we renewed our interest in site work. So far we have produced six site works: *River* (1995), *Breath* (1998), *Caravan Project* (1999), *Offering* (2002), *Tree Song* (2004), and *Cambodian Stories Revisited* (2007). All of our site pieces, except *Breath*, which was specifically designed for the Whitney Museum, are outdoor works that toured widely. By the mid-1990s, we had developed close working relationships with a group of presenters, and as a result, within several years we revisited many of the same cities and same theaters. Other communities, we were told, did not have the "right" space or an "audience ready for our style of dance." But we did not want to limit ourselves to being in the "right" place or with a "ready" audience. We wanted to do something different or at least differently.

From their own perspective, the presenters we worked with understood this. They cared not only about their subscribers but also about people in their communities. So they would send us out to do outreach activities. Often these outreach projects would act as publicity for our performances in their theaters or create another layer of "encountering" between artists and audience members. But we also visited with people who we knew were not likely to come to our shows. They could be ill, old, young, poor, disinterested, busy, or in prison. We and our presenters wanted to offer an artistic experience to these people as well.

We know from our own lives that experiencing art is the best art education. From our visits to senior citizen homes and elementary schools, we slowly learned that not only could we perform in places that were not theaters, but that we could also give these new or "accidental" audiences something profound. So rather than shying away from these activities, we began taking them on. Being without theatrical gadgets, those outreach activities often made us feel *naked*, poor, bottom-line. We liked these feelings because they reinforced the sense that being professional comes from motivation and commitment rather than from any prepared *looks*.

From our experiences in theaters and in other places, we started to wonder how we could offer fully realized performances in neighborhoods and communities without a proper theater space. By bringing the work to places where people were not expecting to encounter it, Koma and I wished to radically enlarge the definition of the art audience. By performing outdoors and in public places, we thought we could also give our longtime viewers an opportunity to watch our dance from a very different perspective. Thus in 1995 we spent a whole summer in a mountain stream in the Catskill Mountains creating and rehearsing *River*. Villagers watched us float downstream many times that summer. After creating a design for that particular river, we brought the design to different rivers, lakes, and ponds. This training made us able to see the potential beauty of nature where it is not expected, even in an indoor site.

Breath (1998)

Commissioned by the Whitney Museum of American Art, *Breath* was a month-long living installation inside the Whitney. After being outdoors for *River*, it was a bit strange to work so intimately with an indoor site, but it was intriguing to create an installation for a specific public gallery (a video gallery), in a specific location in the museum, and for a specific length of time (four weeks).

First we thought we were commissioned to make an installation without us. But the curator, Matthew Yokobovsky, thought otherwise. He reminded us that we have always inhabited our sets. So we began discussing the idea of our physical appearance: how, when, and how long. If we appeared at certain times in the installation (which was on view all hours the museum was open), were we like animals in a zoo appearing at scheduled feeding/show times? How do we present ourselves to viewers who come in and out throughout a day? Our answer was scary. We decided our bodies would be a part of the installation; we would perform all the hours the museum was open for four weeks!

For *Breath*, we created a cavelike landscape with hand-sewn raw silk that was filled with dead leaves. Three video projectors simultaneously projected close-ups of our bodies onto the black painted wall. We hid many small fans so there was movement of the leaves. This "wind" blew small particles in front of the lighting instruments so that light shimmered as if in a wood. We built the structure to merge ceiling and walls and put the projectors at their lowest intensity so that, in and around the projected area, there were no straight lines.

Movement was not the main factor of the work. The experience was about savoring relationships between different beings: the occupants and the land-

Figure 56. Eiko & Koma in *Breath* (1998) at the Whitney Museum. Photo by Tom Brazil.

scape; gaze and subject; those who pass and those who inhabit the space; the most contemporary of buildings and the most ancient outdoor images.

Performing for an audience whose comings and goings we could not control was a challenge. The very idea of performance work was put into question. We found the experience both liberating and satisfying. In this museum, we felt we were becoming a part of a cultural landscape, literally and metaphorically. During the four weeks, one of us was always in the installation. We took turns doing "solos" and taking breaks. "Duet" sections happened when one joined and before the other left. The four weeks gave us a lot of time to step out of the "stage" and observe both the work itself and the viewers' reaction to it. It was wonderful to notice a few familiar faces who came more than once. A few people sat for hours in the room. A woman brought us a poem. Another brought cookies. Some mornings there were only a few viewers in the room. On the weekends the room was so crowded people could not get in. The most delicious time was after the museum closed, when we walked through galleries to the staff exit. We stopped to see artworks by Georgia O'Keefe and Andrew Wyeth; we were alone with artists and paintings we admire. They were our neighbors! Sculptures and installations, bodies and gaze.

Our Bodies Being Vulnerable and Our Work Being a Verb

Being outdoors or in public spaces, we have fewer tools to make us look special. We cannot, as in theaters, disappear into dressing rooms before or after the performance. We prepare our shows in public, often answering the questions of curious passersby, or we stay to hear an audience's response. Being around and exposed to our audience makes us less protected, more accessible for dialogue, as well as more susceptible to critical assaults and physical disturbances. In the past we created theater works that we performed naked. Those pieces emphasized our vulnerability. When we perform in public spaces, however, not only do we find ourselves already vulnerable, but a law also prohibits us from being literally naked. Thus we had to accept and deepen our metaphorical nakedness. By nakedness I mean being evocative, existential, challenging, and affirmative, the opposite of commercialized nudity. Onstage, Koma and I have never wanted to present bodies that are super-trained or super-healthy. We always wanted our bodies and dances to be something people wanted to touch, sympathize with, feel connection to, and get emotional about.

Working outside of theaters and in many sites that are less than favorable, we can continue to present our bodies as vulnerable and as part of a landscape. This means our intentions, objectives, processes, and our audiences' perceptions of art and environment are more intricately connected and affect each other in surprising ways. The merging of ends and means, as well as a merging of "us and them," is unsettling and curious. We are not presenting a dance work; we are dancing and breathing, using dance as a verb rather than presenting it as a noun. In site work, everything is a work-in-progress.

Caravan Project (premiered in 1999)

We were sad when the Whitney Museum installation ended. We had appreciated being a part of a landscape in public view. So Koma and I created the *Caravan Project*, a portable and totally self-contained theater piece that can also be viewed as a living installation "for delivery." Like a library truck that delivers books to rural areas, or like an old Japanese bicycle man who delivers illustrated stories, we deliver our art. Everything necessary for the performance—the visual installation and the means of lighting it—was installed in a customized 8' × 14' black trailer. Doors on all four sides open up so viewers can see us from all angles as they move around. The landscape is so unlike a theater stage because it is small, asymmetrical, and private. We decorated the interior of the trailer with internal, organlike hangings at one end with a sharply sloped hill descending from these

Figure 57. Eiko Otake performing on the trailer for *Caravan Project* (1999). Photo by Takashi Koma Otake.

hangings. The hangings created a crevice of diagonal space in which we periodically bob and sink. The hangings were made out of tree branches to which thousands of pieces of multicolored, shredded cheesecloth were hand-glued. At night, lit from inside, the detailed interior shines like a magic jewelry or music box. At a quick glance we may look like still figures in the box. One grandmother who saw the entire show still could not believe we were live people! But as they looked closer and spent more time looking, people knew we were conducting our own experiments in our own dance laboratory.

As a site work, the *Caravan Project* is a self-contained, prepared piece, but it recognizes, affects and is affected by the specifics of different sites, landscapes, sounds, and communities. We perform the same basic design, varying the running time from one to three hours. In its shorter manifestation, the dance is theatrical, acknowledging a beginning, middle, and end. But in the longer version our bodies are part of a larger landscape, welcoming any passerby.

On the day of a performance, we drive up, unhitch the trailer from our Jeep, connect to electricity supplied by the host presenter, adjust the lights and the set, and we are ready. We then perform under the night sky for 100 or so people who may have assembled for the event or who just happen by. The site can be anywhere the Jeep can go—a public park, a river bank, a street, a mall parking lot, a beach, a college green, the garden at a senior center, or even someone's backyard.

The piece begins when an assistant opens a door on the longer side of the trailer, revealing the interior. During the piece, the doors are opened one by one until the audience can see us from all four directions. Then at the end of the piece the doors are closed one by one, making the views more limited. When the last door on the narrow side of the trailer is shut, the work is finished, confining us inside.

People can contemplate the installation from whatever perspective they choose. Because of this we can no longer compose our dance for a particular "front" or hide anything in the "back." Given the intimacy of an audience only a few feet away, this confusion of direction is compelling for performers and viewers alike. Viewers see another group of viewers in the background who are looking at us from the opposite direction. In this way, audience members gain other possible viewing experiences that deprive them of the sense of an absolute place. No one sees everything, but everyone can choose their own perspective and what they want to see. Beyond the circle of audience, we all see trees or sky. Wind moves particles of our installation, making our shining jewelry box a part of its outdoor environment.

At the end, viewers inevitably gather in one direction, knowing the last door will soon shut. They crowd together tightly, looking into the narrow opening, as our assistant slowly closes the final door. It is as if people are congregating for a final farewell as a hearse door is shut, sending a coffin away. Sympathetic passersby join the mourners. Following the noise of the last door locking, I hear the audience sigh. We stay motionless while our audience starts to wander into the night.

Free under the Stars

When we perform in prestigious theaters and festivals, Koma and I are well aware that a limited class of people can come to see our work because of the increasing expense of theater tickets. Due to the focus on advertising and spectacle in our society, these people come to a theater expecting their money's worth. This creates a false link between the price of art and the value of art. If a performance does not live up to an audience's expectation of "worth," the audience may be disappointed in the theatrical experience. But Koma and I feel that art is a *gift*, not quantifiable. We want to present our dance as something primal, closer to a prayer or a ritual. Therefore, Koma and I, whenever possible, want to perform free for the unknowable and unknowing public.

When we produce free events, I enjoy the possibility of curiosities and surprises. Free audiences are willing to be puzzled or opinionated, to recommend the event to their friends, or even to help out. Some reactions we have received include "What is this?" "What are they doing?" "Strange!" "Why are they here and for what?" "Free? Why? Great! Then I will come!" "Can I bring children?" "Can we help you clean the river?" "Shall I bring warm soup for you?" "I have never seen this river at night. It looks so ancient. Beautiful!" "Did you know a boat stayed offshore and watched your dance from the opposite direction than us, the audience?" The wide variety of reactions makes me feel that Koma and I are offering unpredictable adventures to people, and by doing so, we are creating a small time and space in which we all are a little more spontaneous.

In this regard, it is always particularly striking for me to see the crowd who ventures to come despite the bad weather that inevitably accompanies some of our free outdoor concerts. People who come for a free concert in difficult conditions have a very different feeling than the easygoing atmosphere of free, comfortable summer events. During our performance in the Delaware River in 1995, the sky broke and treacherous showers started. In a few minutes, we lost half the audience. But people told me that a strong bond was created among the people who stayed and that this bond is often remembered in their family gatherings. For our 1999 *Caravan Project* in Bryant Park, we were encouraged to see more than 100 people show up in heavy rain. Because we perform this piece in a trailer, the performance was announced as proceeding, rain or shine. We were protected by the trailer, but audiences were exposed and wet. I remember reaching out to the rain so I could also get wet. The audience knew my feeling. Our wet eyes met.

Offering (premiered in 2002)

The original idea for *Offering* was to bring what was inside of the trailer of *Caravan Project* to the open air. The trailer in *Caravan Project* was, among many things, a hearse and a womb. Continuing our focus on death, we initially wanted to name the work *Coffin Dance*. However, after 9/11 we felt we had to rename the work *Offering*. Those of us who live in New York saw casket after casket in the weeks and months following 9/11. Death was no longer in a closet. We all grieved, but we also saw the danger of anger. Koma and I wanted to design *Offering* as a ritual that allowed people simultaneously to mourn, remember, share, and face death. Koma and I had a studio in the World Trade Center throughout the year 2000 as a part of the Lower Manhattan Cultural Council space grant program. We remembered details of the buildings and remembered many of the people who worked there. The attack was brutal and merciless, but we did not wish for revenge. Instead, we wanted to mourn.

For this ritual of mourning, we created a 4' × 8' × 4' structure that turns and that was covered by a mound of dirt. Most of the dance was done on this structure surrounded by the audience, who sat in a circle. With our every movement, dirt fell from the structure onto black foil below. Underneath the set we placed a microphone that slightly amplified the sound of the dirt falling. The dirt symbolized a grave when Koma buried me in it, but it also represented a field when I tried to grow or bloom from it. The structure looked at once like a cradle, altar, planter box, and open casket.

In the summer of 2002, Koma and I performed *Offering* in six parks in Manhattan. In planning the piece, we visited the parks and recognized that these were the places, after 9/11, where people gathered to cry or to get information. We met many wonderful people who worked or volunteered to keep their parks clean and beautiful. It was surprising to acknowledge this beauty in wounded Manhattan. Recognizing different neighborhoods and their parks, we wished each performance site—World Financial Center Plaza, Dag Hammarskjold Plaza, Tudor City Green Park, Clinton Community Garden, Bryant Park, and Madison Square Park—could shine as different jewels tied together by our performances.

That summer, each performance of *Offering* was co-produced by a different park committee or a neighborhood organization. These local people and caretakers were our audience. As I was taking off my costume in a janitors' locker room in Madison Park, a woman wearing a park uniform whom we had seen earlier that day hugged me and said, "Thank you for coming." Many park people and neighbors repeated this greeting, reversing the usual performer/audience relationship. In theaters, even in a new town, we welcome our audience, because we regard theaters as our home, our element. But performing in the parks, we became the visitors and the people who live in the neighborhood and play or work in the parks were the ones who welcomed us.

The same lady from the park, who I imagine would not have come to see our show in a theater, gave me her earnest interpretation of the work. She did not need program notes. She did not know us, our origins, or the title of the piece, but her life knowledge responded to our work. She looked happy. When people like art, they congratulate themselves in responding to something they think is good, beautiful, and moving. As this lady taught me again, if there is no intimidation, everyone can be an expert in her understanding.

Figure 58. Eiko & Koma perform *Offering* in Bryant Park (2002). Photo by Tom Brazil.

In 2003, we remade *Offering* for Danspace Project and performed it five times in the graveyard of St. Mark's Church. Koma buried me almost completely with dirt, quietly lay down beside me, and thrashed Japanese ceremonial arrows over and over into the mound of dirt. A war was waging. Dirt became much more than a set. Dirt represented the significance and reality of the earth, the condition and destination of our violated living and dying. The Second Avenue traffic in downtown Manhattan was a significant part of this burial's background music.

On tour and abroad, we had to let go of our *Offering* set, which was too big to carry by air, but we always created a huge mound of dirt as an earthy landscape and a grave. This least exotic, easily attainable, and inexpensive material turned out to speak volumes to many viewers, evoking their memories. Dancing with dirt made us physically dirty, and that enhanced our vulnerability. One Polish woman told me how the dirt in our work reminded her that it "absorbs tears, sweat, and blood." It is this "sensual" reaction we seek in our outdoor site performances.

On September 11, 2003, Koma and I performed *Offering* in Seattle, commemorating the second anniversary of 9/11. Many people surprised me by coming to our performance at a remote beach. It happened to be a very cold and misty day, but more than 300 people dared a long cold walk along the ocean to the performance site. People were bundled up with rain gear and heavy blankets. For 60 minutes they stayed in the coldest wind, giving us their strongest attention. I was deeply moved by their commitment. It was as if they had "invested" in our performance, not with money, but with their willingness to attend.

To Be Continued

We continue to create and perform site work. Our site works connect us with many people in many countries who may never enter a theater. We go to perform in places such as a Cambodian village or a monastery on a Hungarian mountaintop. We continue to love the juxtaposition of our own vision and other factors of life and landscape, for which we can take neither blame nor credit. We hope our audiences will someday tell their grandchildren what they remember about seeing two strange Japanese people dance in the summer air of their towns. Then our dance will become a part of old stories that live in the landscape and in the backdrop of people's lives.

10

Sally Jacques

Sally Jacques and her site-specific aerial dance company, Blue Lapis Light, have been performing in pools, on hotel walls, in airplane hangars, and in government strongholds in Austin, Texas, for two decades. Moving easily from the abstract to the politically motivated, Jacques' work encourages us to see the beauty of our surroundings and to rectify injustice on scales from the global to the local. Among her many awards, including being honored as a lifetime member of the Golden Key National Honor Society and the Susan B. Anthony Award for Peace, Jacques was recently inducted into the Austin Arts Hall of Fame and was nominated for a USA Fellowship 2008. Pavlik and Jacques met up in Austin on December 5, 2004, for a conversation about Jacques' site work.

An Interview with Sally Jacques

CP: What is your definition of site-specific dance?

SJ: In a word: beauty. Site-specific work is an integration of the environment, its elements, and the emotional language suggested by the space. A work is site-specific when it does not impose an idea onto the space. In other words, it does not set a theatrical environment onto the landscape but uses what is inherent in the space to create the dance. The site's environment is itself a collaborator, and it determines what unfolds from myself, the dancers, and the rest of the collaborators.

CP: What motivates you to create work on site as opposed to work in a theater?

SJ: I am motivated by the unknown, the mysterious, and the silence that invites imagination to live and breathe freely. A boxed framed space limits my perceptions; it almost scares me as I feel its limitations, freezing my thinking into its requirements. To enter a site is exciting; the site is alive and ready to engage in a dialogue, demanding that you listen. It speaks volumes in its skeletal form.

I have choreographed in a theater, but even there I was changing the perception of the space by placing structures in it or by working with set and lighting designers to somehow make the space shift into something else.

My attraction to creating site work is rooted in the challenges these works demand of the soul. For me, it is a spiritual journey, an internal weaving of struggle, trust, and listening. All the senses are centered on the physical demands on the body, on finding the courage to experiment, to risk, to defy gravity, and to hang in precarious ways. Also, the collaborative interaction with the dancers emulates the relationships found throughout nature, in that the interdependence of creativity exists for all the elements to thrive and be. This fascinates and intrigues me and informs my life on many levels. I believe if we live without the framework of societal expectations, we live in a world of spontaneous imaginings and endless possibilities.

CP: Have there been any events or experiences in your life that have inspired you to create site works?

SJ: I was certainly inspired the first time I saw the Sankai Juku Dance Company perform. I was mesmerized by their exquisite sense of purpose and beauty, by the stillness, attention, and intention of each movement, which was sometimes barely noticeable, like breathing. I am also inspired by the Japanese film director Akira Kurosawa's work, especially what his movie *Dreams* presented: the flocking behavior and movement patterns of birds. He explored how we are a part of a greater universal system and not an isolated planet.

I have lived in many parts of the world and have a fascination for diverse cultures, art, and architecture, especially places of worship. I have been shaped by these cultures on many levels, especially by East Indian philosophy and meditation.

I also find early experiences crucial to my inspiration; my childhood influenced my worldview, as well as my political and social insights. I was not raised in a small nuclear family. I was brought up in a large institution and developed many instincts at an early age, the most beneficial of which was to dream and imagine. My inner world was strengthened at a very early age. I often listened and prayed and talked to nature for solace and comfort.

CP: Do you find sites, or do they find you?

SJ: This has varied. About two years before I started working on *The Scaffold Trilogy*, I was taking a walk along Town Lake in Austin, Texas, and I saw a scaffold against the edge of the shore. I remember looking up at it and thinking, "What a great space to dance on!" I also loved the natural environment situated in the center of downtown Austin—the water, the surrounding vegetation, and the birds and bats that make their habitat there.

Each of the sites I have chosen is a place with a history or story unto itself. I have created collaborative site performances in an abandoned swimming pool, in empty warehouses, at Barton Springs Pool in Austin, in airplane hangars, at the Texas State Capitol, and even at the Jefferson Memorial in Washington, D.C. Often I find myself looking at buildings, bridges, or overhead passes and wondering if I could persuade the city to let me use them. But insurance and liability are the biggest factors that prevent me from using some fantastic places. For example, buildings that are under construction are hard to obtain for site works.

My work *Where Nothing Falls*, a site-specific dance work about the eternal and the present, was inspired by a partially finished, somewhat futuristic warehouse. Architecturally it was like a church. It is the youngest place I have created a site work. It was empty and new, but not cold. It spoke to me, and over time I found its heartbeat. When I was looking for a site for this piece, I turned down another site—a 1950s gym in which the police force had trained. This was because when I walked in, I could still hear the memories and stories of the gym, and I thought it would interrupt what I wanted to do. It felt busy, although it was empty.

Figure 59. Theresa Hardy and Ishaq Clayton in the warehouse in *Where Nothing Falls* (2003). Photo by José Medina, courtesy of Blue Lapis Light.

CP: Do you attempt to create a relationship to the community nearest your chosen site?

SJ: I look for a space that in the end speaks to me. Instinctively, I want to linger there, to know its smells, its emotions, and its challenges. I try to stay very conscious of the environment, using as much of its voice as I can. The site is already woven into the community; it already speaks the language of the community. Site is not separate from the community. The people in the communities around the sites visit and watch us, ask questions, and are very curious. We always have a free night or pay-what-you-wish, and they usually invite all of their friends to attend.

CP: Is there one piece that you see as instrumental in your development as a site choreographer?

SJ: For many reasons, I consider *Blue Pearl* one of my most significant pieces. The challenges of the site tested all my abilities. We had to build and take down the scaffold twice for electrical and safety reasons. There were environmental hazards created by bugs, mayflies, floods, and droughts. One of the dancers fell from the scaffolding, and it was terrifying. I considered canceling the show, but the other dancers voted to go on. The interaction between the dancers and nature was spectacular. I remember a flock of geese taking off against a full moon rising as dancers, at 35 feet, lined up against the night sky, moving and articulating their bodies throughout the structure. The visual experience created a sense of other-worldliness, an epic poem of wonder and beauty.

CP: Do you find that audiences respond differently to site work when it is outdoors?

SJ: The audience's senses are more engaged in an outdoor environment. They are participants with the natural environment and the elements. They are bitten by bugs and are often hot or cold depending on when the work takes place. Sometimes, they are confronted by a certain level of discomfort, like sitting on bleachers, using outdoor facilities, etc. Also, the work itself differs enormously in an outdoor space because of the ability to expand in height and other dimensions. I love the sense of open spaces and of night skies. That sense of open space allows the audience to view a dance work that is vast, and that changes their perspectives.

CP: In your experience, is it more expensive to do a site performance or a performance in a theater?

SJ: Creating work in unusual settings and environments is far more expensive. One also has the added risk of inclement weather, which often means canceled performances and financial losses. In terms of obtaining funding, I have found that most panels at the local level have not understood what is entailed in developing and creating site works. They tend to view them as similar to a theatrical production. This has been very frustrating for me, because there are so many additional factors to consider in site work. Trying to explain this to granting agencies has often been a real point of contention.

CP: I know that you have spent considerable time as a human rights activist. How does your work as an activist inform your art?

SJ: I cannot separate the two. Once you feel your relationship to humanity in a larger sense of the world, it all links together. Being an activist possibly makes you more articulate and thoughtful in the way you create; your passion is engaged. You feel more of a connection with the world, the earth, animals, etc. It's like the giant redwoods that have root systems that are intertwined; when a tree falls, it nourishes all the other trees and life expands.

Activists and artists make changes where they see stagnation. They both can point out limits in bureaucracy and show that there are other possibilities. As in activism, site work can bring attention and hope to an issue.

CP: In what ways do the political and/or social issues that you address in your activism manifest in your site work?

SJ: It depends. For example, before I began working on my site piece, *64 Beds*, homelessness in America had increased because 75 percent of the affordable housing was cut by the Reagan administration. In Austin, we immediately started seeing more people living on the streets, especially women and children. It happened very quickly. I started thinking about beds as places of nourishment and rejuvenation and as a place where we go for reflection and sanity. I wanted to explore what not having access to a bed meant for people living on the streets.

Also at the time, I was very involved with the Book of I-Ching. The 64 hexagrams used in the I-Ching became the cohesive concept for my site work. I had visual artists create the beds based either on these hexagrams or on the idea of homelessness. But to stay true to the homeless image, the artists were limited to a 6' × 3' foam mattress to design. The idea was that, when all of the beds were put together and the lights were dropped, they would combine to look like beds in a homeless shelter.

I wanted to raise money and awareness about the truth behind the issue of homelessness. So I worked with an organization called HOBO, or Help Our Brother Out, and Caritas, another organization concerned with home-

Figure 60. The decorated beds in *64 Beds* (1988). Photo by Danna Byrom, courtesy of Blue Lapis Light.

lessness. I also went into the business community to raise funds and persuade businesses to sponsor beds.

When I was creating the work, I did not, as an artist, separate myself from the issue of homelessness. Some of us involved in the project went and slept on the street. I also worked within the homeless community. I rode on the bus with them in the morning to go to the church where they had access to facilities. I felt I didn't want to be just an elitist observer. I wanted to feel the connection. You know, I spent my formative years, up to eight years old, in an orphanage. Because of this experience, I realized that just because you are given a bed within an institution does not necessarily mean that you will not feel lonely or isolated or unloved by society.

CP: Where was this work performed?

SJ: The work was first performed in a museum in Austin, then in Houston and Dallas. Later it was re-sited at the Jefferson Memorial in Washington, D.C. In the museum, it struck me as odd that we put art on the walls instead of interacting with it. So, even though we had created "art beds," we also had people sleep in the beds, including several homeless people. The keepers of the sleepers were assigned to eight beds each and were responsible for the complete nurturance of the people who slept in their beds. One of the artistic elements was that we would have to stay awake all night, as homeless people often have to. I also invited eight or nine performers to create dance, music, and poetry. On opening night, the mayor kicked off the event, and the community and all of the TV stations came. People commented that they truly felt an unbelievable community involvement.

CP: What was it like to re-site the piece in Washington, D.C.? Did you have the same level of community involvement?

SJ: When we re-sited it at the Jefferson Memorial, we again worked with the community. We worked with the homeless community there as well as with the parks and recreation department and the police. We even involved people in the House of Representatives. In fact, during the performance, I woke up in my bed next to the bed of Senator John Glenn's aide.

CP: Have you created other site works that address social and political issues?

SJ: In the past, every year I would stage a work called *Body Count* on the Great Walkway of the Texas State Capitol for World AIDS Day and Day Without Art. This was before the time of security considerations due to terrorism in the United States, an issue we now face in site works. Anyway, I had just been with a friend of mine who died of AIDS, and I was struck by how still and how serene his body was; that gave me an image for the piece. The first year of the performance, it was a cold December night, and people started showing up early. I was very surprised that there were hundreds of people. So I invited them into the Capitol Rotunda to sit in silence and hold in their hearts the memory of their loved ones. We then went outside to the Great Walkway, where there were even more people, including city council members. We had everyone lie down side by side by side all the way down to the end of the walkway. I asked people to bring flashlights so that when the lights went down in the Capitol and downtown, the performers/participants could light up their faces. It was a tremendous community coalition and truly inspirational.

My performance piece *Inside the Heart* also took place on the grounds of the Texas State Capitol after the first Gulf war. Being an activist, I have spent many years working toward peaceful solutions to political issues; violence never creates peace. So when the war broke out, I was thinking about how I, as an artist, could bring people together, whether they were for or against the war.

The piece took place in four movements: the banquet, the last supper, the heartbreaking, and the transformation. For the performance, my collaborators and I placed 36 oil drums along the 450-foot long Capitol walkway. We also placed a visual installation at the entrance of the building with banquet tables complete with fake pig heads and oil cans to suggest excess and to metaphorically represent the last supper. At the foot of the installation was a plaza in which 36 performers, each in a black body bag, huddled together breathing to create the image of a huge beating heart.

My idea for this piece was that greed can never fill you and that the violence we inflict upon each other can break apart the strongest of hearts. Most of us feel a spiritual hunger inside, but we end up surrounding ourselves with and fighting for material possessions. During the final transformation, we released doves into the air. One dove remained in the middle of the walkway, and it came onto my finger and stayed for a moment; it seemed very eternal. That can only happen in site works, especially when you are outside and interacting with nature.

o

The Making of *Requiem*

A Site-Specific Dance Opera

By Sally Jacques

Even in the drought of a Texas summer, one cannot count on three consecutive weekends without rain.

On June 15, 2006, our site-specific dance company, Blue Lapis Light, was set to open its fifth performance of *Requiem*, staged at the former Intel Building in downtown Austin. A concrete skeleton since 2001, when construction at the site was abandoned, the building has remained for some a symbol of economic downturn, the end of the dot-com boom; for others, the building is an eyesore that has cost Austin taxpayers millions. Ownership of the property had recently reverted to the government with a planned demolition of the structure to make way for a federal courthouse. I was given the opportunity to create a dance work there prior to its demolition. I was thrilled.

The skies opened early on that June morning with torrents of rain pounding onto the site, winds carrying it across all five floors to form giant puddles, up to four inches in depth.

In my 25 years in Austin, I have produced dance works in a variety of outdoor spaces: on the shores of Town Lake, in an empty swimming pool, on the grounds of the Texas State Capitol, on bridges, and in other urban spaces. I find the four walls of conventional theaters inhibiting and uninspiring to the vision of a work.

As with all site works, the space is a major collaborator. Cooperating with the elements and the unpredictability of them invites mystery and moments of synchronicity and great beauty, such as when a flock of geese passed in front of a full moon at our *Scaffold Trilogy* performance or splashes of purple, burnt gold, and grey skies complemented the score of *Inside the Heart*, our piece at the State Capitol. Conversely, the presence of people or animals that pop up unexpectedly, interruptions by sirens and aircraft, insects, cold fronts or thunderstorms, and other logistical challenges are the occupational hazards of site-specific performance.

The downpour finally stopped around 9:00 A.M., and I then assessed the situation. Pleas for help went out. Crew and volunteers arrived and joined in the effort to dry the floors and cables using towels, brooms, mops, and wet-vacs. By afternoon, with the pace still frantic, the progress not nearly fast enough, and the makeshift crew tiring, an ingenious crew member invented a 12-foot-long super-sized squeegee, using materials found entirely on the property.

Now with our hopes realistically renewed, we relaxed and relished the beauty of the water: the tranquil lakes rippling into rolling waves before cascading over the sides of the building with a thunderous crash.

My cell phone rang constantly that Saturday afternoon, with callers wanting to know if the performance would still take place. My answer? A confident yes.

But two hours before the gates were scheduled to open, lighting designer Jason Amato arrived to do a systems check. He found that although we had dried the wiring adequately, water had gotten into some light fixtures and was still dripping down the shaft, forming puddles in and around the dimmer packs and power systems. To safeguard the dancers and protect the equipment, everything needed to be thoroughly dried and tested, first on low and only gradually juicing the lights to full power, a time-consuming but mandatory safety procedure.

As shadows deepened, the growing ticket line outside the gates snaked down the block and around the corner. The loss of one night's receipts could make the difference in the run breaking even or going into debt. And though the audience might be sent away disappointed, the dancers' safety had to come first. As the clock ticked, a decision had to be made: cancel or open?

Figure 61. Performers in *Requiem* (2006) on the Intel building in Austin, Texas. Photo by Amitava Sarkar, courtesy of Blue Lapis Light.

The Site

From the ground, the building's design resembles an Escher drawing. It has 80-foot columns of cement and steel supporting five stories of empty concrete cells; the columns shoot upward to the sky, tapering to clusters of twisted rebar on top. Although the cells are all 27 feet in width, their heights vary: on the first level, they are 20 feet high; on the second, 14; and on the third and fourth, 12. The fifth level reaches up without a ceiling.

Nestled between the two main columns of the frame is a third, right-angled area, smaller and recessed, reminiscent of the ornate, layered altars of European cathedrals. Soaring central columns surrounding it, this niche felt majestic and ethereal to me. It inspired and evoked powerful images of ascent and descent.

The first time I stood on top of the building with the collaborators, looking down and across the vast distances, I recall feeling both awed by the magnificent, unobstructed vistas of the city and terrified by the precipitous height. A work at this site would certainly be our most ambitious undertaking to date. It was challenging, not only due to its breadth but also to a height more than double the 35 feet we were accustomed to in previous aerial site works.

Our challenge and vision was to explore and respond to the environment. Our intention was to make a piece that integrated the enormity of the space into an intimate, sanctified experience for the audience.

We saw that the logical place for seating was the grassy courtyard below. With our audience embraced by the right-angled arms of the building, the only clearly viewed performance areas would be the edges of the concrete cells and the outsides of the immense columns. In our previous site works, dancers performed on roller skates and bungee cords, with poles and cloth, and in fishing nets and harnesses. Their figures could utilize the three dimensions of height, width, and depth in the spaces we chose. But here, scale played with perspective, and like caverns in towering cliffs, this would make it impossible for dancers to be seen once they stepped away from the edge of the cells. While their disappearance into the void was a challenge, it was also of visual interest, and later it became an integral part of the choreography.

There were also some very practical advantages to this site. The center of the structure held two metal staircases and a 10' × 10' elevator shaft, which could be used for hauling lights, cabling, and other equipment to the upper floors. The crew would be able to drive trucks directly into the basement level and use winches and rope to maneuver heavy equipment up the shaft. The basement also housed our generator, dressing room, and a restroom for the dancers.

The Budget and Fund-raising

Once we occupied the space, I turned my focus to the budget. We had successfully procured grants from the City of Austin Cultural Arts Division, the Texas Commission on the Arts, and the National Endowment for the Arts. But even with these, the projected expenses were four times our total available funds. We would have to launch a major fund-raising campaign, so I turned to the experts for help, including Austin's Economic and Cultural Development Office, the Downtown Austin Alliance, and the Austin City Council. We held a fashion show fund-raiser, a raffle, and silent auction.

The amount of lighting alone, with its sheer volume of wire, cables, and lighting instruments, would be extremely costly. We would need 24-hour security on site as well. Also, no amenities existed at the site. Seating, portable restrooms, washing facilities, generators to power the tools, music, and lighting, and an air-conditioned dressing room all had to be brought in. For the months that we were in the space for rehearsals and performances, expenses for these necessities could not have been covered without generous local support.

The Company

Blue Lapis Light is made up of a number of Austin's visionary artists. For this project, the company's technical designers and collaborators included Jason Amato, lighting designer; William Meadows, sound designer and composer; Laura Cannon, dancer and costume designer; Theresa "Terry" Hardy, dancer; Nicole Whiteside, dancer; and Alan Vance, rigger. All of the principal dancers also collaborated on and developed much of the choreography themselves.

We held auditions to complete the company. Many who auditioned either could not handle the height or were unable to commit to our rigorous schedule of rehearsals and performances. In the end, joining the company were our fourth principal dancer, Mimi Kayl-Vaughn, four rock climbers, and nine ensemble dancers, for a total of 17 performers.

The Conceptualization: Dreams and Visions

We had only eight weeks to conceptualize and create a finished piece. I knew I wanted to do a piece about loss, mourning, and prayer. Ideas about how the work might weave itself began to consume my consciousness and subconsciousness. Day and night, images took shape.

In meditation I often reflect on the world we live in, especially collective tragedies such as the tsunami in Southeast Asia, genocide in Darfur, Hurricanes Katrina and Rita, the Oklahoma City bombing, and 9/11. What happens to the souls when a mass of people die together? And what happens globally to our collective psyche with their departure? Poetic moments of beauty counter the turbulence of these times, connect us to each other, and reveal the universal meaning of our existence. Contemplating this universal meaning permeates both my life and art.

Many of the images that came to me were rooted in dreams: I saw figures rolling like lost souls; in another I saw an angel standing in a void with her arms wide open. I envisioned waterfalls of climbers cascading down the sides of the columns and figures emerging and regressing from the cavernous spaces. Later I named them: the Beatific Angel, a symbol of hope and transcendence; the Angel of Sorrow, symbolizing suffering in the world; the Seeker, escorting souls to the next plane; Archangels, bringing light into the darkness; and Guardian Angels, offering comfort and solace.

I am not a traditionally religious person; my own meditative and spiritual journey is based on compassion, planetary and social responsibility, and respect for all species. Yet these messages and dreams came to me over a period of three or four days. I would wake up in the night, write, and make drawings of the images that I received. I took these to rehearsals to share with the dancers who helped me interpret and integrate them into the piece.

The Site Preparation

Getting the site ready was extremely labor-intensive. Following Jason's lighting design, a crew of electricians drilled holes into concrete, hammered light-bearing squares of wood to columns, and installed more than 180 lights over the entire structure, all while working in 90 degree Texas heat. They also conceived and installed a complex system of pulleys and parcans to create a 10,000 watt light harness that tracked and flexed with the dancers as they moved through the altar area.

Figure 62. At the end of *Requiem*, the Beatific Angel (Laura Cannon) descends to earth. Photo by Amitava Sarkar, courtesy of Blue Lapis Light.

To suspend climbers and dancers from the columns surrounding the indented altar area, Alan Vance, our rigger, anchored climbing ropes with Hilti bolts. To protect all of our ropes from fraying, he attached PVC pipe to the cement edges. As an added safety measure, we used one set of ropes for rehearsals and replaced all of them for the live performances.

For the rappellers' performances, we used Air Traffic Controller belay devices (ATCs), which serve as a braking system allowing them to slow down or stop at will. To create the sense of "walking" down the columns, they wore their harnesses backwards and extra tight and descended face-first. They also had to learn to step lightly so that their feet would keep in contact with the wall. In order for

Figure 63. Nicole Whiteside, the Angel of Sorrow, rehearsing her solo for *Requiem*, which prompted numerous 911 calls from neighboring condo and office residents believing they were witnessing a suicide attempt. Photo by Amitava Sarkar, courtesy of Blue Lapis Light.

the illusion to be complete, their bodies needed to stay perpendicular to the side of the column. Although our climbers were all experienced, these were new skills for them and took a great deal of practice.

Sound designer William Meadows had to use two stereo systems to provide the sound, one for the mains and one for the monitors for the dancers. Because of the size of the building, the monitor system was almost as large as the main system. William also programmed the gain and fade times of the different music tracks, using custom software that he wrote and ran from a laptop computer.

The Creative Process: Collaboration

Because the architecture and spirit of the site inform the development of the work, there is always an experimental period when we actually start rehearsing in a space. We play with movements and with various apparatuses and props. What we learn during this investigation begins to shape the piece.

I ask performers to look into their own souls and then "dance themselves." Each performer and technical designer brings not only his or her individual craft and talent but also his or her presence and center. It is from and through these that the journey progresses. In my role as artistic director and choreographer, I am not one to shout commands or dictate movement; rather, I introduce an idea or vision as a starting point, and we find out what feels natural to the dancer.

Music is intrinsic to the emotional impact of my work. I spend a lot of time looking for music while conceptualizing a piece. Composer William Meadows wrote music specifically for *Requiem* including a piece for the "Cargo Net" section and an ascending arpeggio, layered with lush strings, for the main theme. Occasionally I hear a recording that is perfect for a section of a piece. For instance, I was riding in a car with my longtime friend and collaborator, vocalist Tina Marsh, when she played Eliza Gilkyson's song "Requiem." I knew immediately that I would use it, as the words convey the theme of souls departing to a higher place. She agreed to record and arrange it for the show.

It would have been easy for the performers to be dwarfed by the massive gray concrete floors and pillars of the building. Costume designer Laura Cannon found a way to draw attention to the small human frames with hot coral satin ball gowns that incorporated petticoats to keep the skirts standing out away from the body, giving the dancers more physical presence. The color was a striking contrast to the cool cement building. The designs for the four principals/angels needed to take into consideration technical issues, since the women would be spending most of their time in harnesses on the sides of the building. A light blue tunic with slits that went all the way up to the armpits on both sides and up the front to the sternum allowed the harnesses to be hidden, at least partially, while still allowing the anchor points to be exposed. The three long flaps of fabric were covered with a glittering pattern of swirls that played in the light like the wings of dragonflies.

The Performance

The performance opens with two figures. One is sitting alone on the second level of the altar with her back to the audience, arms crossed over her chest. She is the Seeker, aware that her soul is leaving its body. She stands, leans forward, and gestures in sweeping arm movements to heaven with both longing and apprehension of the unknown.

Above the Seeker, standing on the fifth level of the altar, is the Beatific Angel. Her arms extended in a divine embrace, she welcomes the Seeker's soul as it makes its transition to the next realm. Then she departs.

Still on the second level, the Seeker enters the cell to the right of the altar and dances. With movements to lyrics, she expresses sorrow over tragedies, foresees the comfort in a new divine life, and hopes humankind is led to a higher place.

Meanwhile, the ensemble dancers, representing the souls lost to collective, traumatic death, run forward to the edge, reaching out and grasping at empty space. Standing and sitting, rolling and kneeling, touching and caressing, finally expressing their acceptance, they mirror some of the Seeker's movements.

Depicting the line between heaven and earth, two pieces of long white cloth are ascended by two Angels, the beauty and intention of their movements defying gravity. Climbing up with lyrical ease, they reveal the potential strength and grace in life's journey, the perseverance to overcome travails.

As the lights fade on the Angels, members of the ensemble, like glowing figures rising from stained glass, watch from above the altar. They leave the area to enter the cavernous passageways, the trios on the second and third levels processing in a contemplative prayer toward cells on the left.

Appearing on the fifth level at the columns of the altar, four Archangels (climbers) calmly peer down, imparting tranquility. Then one from each side slowly walks down the building backwards.

Witnessing them descend from heaven, the remaining two step over the edge and walk forward, their bodies perpendicular to the columns, their ropes above their heads.

Two Archangels/Angels of Light step from behind the two innermost columns of the third level and extend their hearts over the precipice. Another two

Angels of Light appear from behind the next nearest columns of the third level, and the quartet, suspended ever more weightlessly, begin to lift and hover, then disappear and reappear as they fly, lightly and serenely, somersaulting through the air.

Ensemble souls walk forward on the second, third, and fourth levels, appearing out of the darkness. Looking out, they turn their backs to the audience and begin a series of movements, rolling in unison at the rim of the abyss.

Archangels appear at the top of the four altar columns and, in unison, jump from one level to the next, floating rhythmically from floor to floor.

The Seeker reappears in the place where she began. She lifts her face upward toward the light, which spans the second to fourth levels across the widths of two cells.

Two Angels bathed in rainbows of color dance across the celestial heavens. Using the momentum of rebounds, they leap, jump, pause, embrace, and then fly again in unison.

The Angel of Sorrow moves in gravity-defying intensity, leaping recklessly off the edge and into the night sky, winding and unwinding, touching only air as she portrays the suffering in the world.

The Beatific Angel hovers in the sky far above the altar. Then she comes down to earth, bringing not only solace but also joy in our remembrance of the infinity of our souls. The spiritual dimension shared with humankind, the other Angels join her above, around and beyond the altar. Streams of cloth interweaving, the Beatific Angel ascends lifting our highest aspirations with her.

The Seeker returns to begin the journey again.

The Community Response

As reviews came out, publicity and word of mouth spread and the crowds grew larger. Plus, many watched from inside and atop the surrounding buildings, captivated by the lights, music, and the lyrical movements. Traffic slowed on busy Fifth Street. Passersby on their way to the Fourth Street Warehouse District stopped in their tracks to peer over the fence. The serendipitous beauty seemed to pull in the whole city.

Comparisons to circus acts were inevitable, and though the company performed up to 80 feet above ground without safety nets, it was my desire to downplay the spectacle aspect.

Requiem reminds us that angels inhabit our lives. Not just otherworldly angels, but those that surround us everywhere we go, inspiring us and bringing splashes of beauty to our daily existence.

So the show did go on that evening of June 15 under clear, starry skies. It continued, miraculously, for eight more performances, including one where the night sky was graced with a shooting star arcing over Laura and Nicole as they climbed the fabric. On another evening, a flock of doves flew over just as the Beatific Angel ascended into the heavenly sky.

11

Sara Pearson and Patrik Widrig

Sara Pearson and Patrik Widrig are the artistic directors of PEARSON-
WIDRIG DANCETHEATER, a company that presents site performances and conducts site workshops all over the globe. Invested in site-
adaptive works that may travel from the grassy expanses of a garden estate
in New York to a bird sanctuary in Maine to the campus of Dartmouth
College, Pearson and Widrig enjoy finding both the universal and specific traits of place. Their work has been produced by Lincoln Center,
the Joyce Theater, the City Center Fall for Dance Festival, DTW, The
Kitchen, Central Park SummerStage, Danspace Project, P.S. 122, the 92nd
Street Y Harkness Dance Project, and Dancing in the Streets, and they
have received foundation support from the NEA, NYSCA, NYFA, NPN,
NCCI, Rockefeller, Jerome, Joyce Mertz-Gilmore, and Arts International, among others. They discussed their work with Kloetzel on August 30,
2006, from their home in New York City.

An Interview with Sara Pearson and Patrik Widrig

MK: While perusing your Web site, I noticed that you use the terms *site-
specific* and *site-adaptive* when you discuss your work. Can you talk about the
difference between those terms?

SP: It all began when presenters would invite us to make a site-specific work
that they couldn't afford on their own. So they would team up with another presenter who was interested in a completely different site and then ask
us to adapt the same choreography for each of them. Our first attempt was
truly unbelievable! Conceived as the brainchild of Elise Bernhardt and co-
produced by Dancing in the Streets, Wave Hill, and Lincoln Center Out-of-
Doors, *Common Ground* was initially created for this bucolic hillside garden
at Wave Hill that invited choreography impossible to do anywhere but there.
And then we translated it to the urban cement landscape of Lincoln Center's Damrosch Park. It was a wonderful, terrible assignment that we resisted

mightily, but we needed the job, and so we said yes. This project underscored the fact that while artistic vision is one thing, dealing well within the limitations of the practical world is another. It was one of the great early challenges of our site choreographic careers; it taught us so much and opened the door to a whole new world of touring site-adaptive works. So, by the time we started the *Curious Invasion* series at an Audubon Sanctuary in Maine in 1997, we had developed the skills needed to plan and organize such a residency.

Figure 64. Jason Akira Somma flips over a hay bale in *A Curious Invasion* (1997). Photo by James Murphy, courtesy of PEARSONWIDRIG DANCETHEATER.

PW: Sometimes a piece that starts out as site-specific can become site-adaptive. One example of this came from a section of *A Curious Invasion/Wave Hill* in 2001. We originally made the section on a two-tiered stone ledge in the middle of this beautiful, secluded garden; it was a luxurious unison quartet to Ethel Waters's 1930s recording of "Moonglow" and was just about everybody's favorite section. A couple of years later, we were invited by the Hopkins Center at Dartmouth College to create a site-adapted version of *A Curious Invasion*, and of course, there was no two-tiered ledge anywhere in the chosen site. But then we found these great old leather art deco couches in the boathouse by the lake, and we asked if we could move the couches out to the terrace in front of the building and perform the dance there. So we adapted that same dance to these four couches. It was completely different, and yet it was the same piece.

MK: So it sounds like making site-adaptive works is more economically viable.

PW: Well, the template we've created with *A Curious Invasion* can really be taken into practically any natural and/or architectural space and adapted to the particulars. This adds to its economic practicality. It's exciting for us to come up with appropriate solutions for each new space, but we don't have to start from scratch every time.

SP: Often, we must make choices based on the economics of a project, although, to be honest, it was economics that drove us to site-specific work in the first place. Economics ended up being responsible for opening up one of the great loves of our lives. Back in 1987, when Patrik and I first started working together, we noticed a one-inch ad in the *Village Voice* that read something like, "Searching for choreographers to create outdoor work for Dancing in the Streets' Coney Island Festival." It was the first grant we had ever written, and we got it—$500! It was the first time we were able to pay our dancers a "fee"; there was just enough money to give them subway tokens for rehearsals and performances. It was also the first time we had choreographed for something other than the proscenium stage. It was traumatizing and amazing and wonderful, and we never stopped.

MK: What is it that continues to draw you back outdoors?

SP: It isn't just the outdoors, it is to *site*, whether that be in a Buddhist temple in Kyoto, or on a rowboat in New York City's Central Park, or in a fourteenth-century village on the Greek island of Tinos. Unlike many choreographers who are drawn to a bare stage and bare bodies, we get inspired by time, by architecture, by our own relationship to space and place.

MK: Do you make a distinction between space and place?

Figure 65. Dancers with heads in the sand on Coney Island in *Graven Images* (1987).
Photo by James Murphy, courtesy of PEARSONWIDRIG DANCETHEATER.

PW: Space is an inherent choreographic element in the way we were trained.
Space was and has always been really important, at the forefront of what we
tap into. For many people, it is so often about movement and steps and choreographic patterns. But spatial awareness, onstage or on site, is a crucial ingredient for us. This spatial awareness became magnified when we started going
to sites outside the theater. For me, place would be the architectural landscape,
the geographic attributes of a site, the physical elements. But space is what
radiates out of that, the atmosphere that we sense when we go into a place.

MK: This is an important distinction. A lot of geographers discuss the difference between space and place, but it seems like it would be a significant issue for site choreographers as well.

SP: I think the distinction is really key. For me, place contains the entire history of the location we are working with, in every sense. The space, however, is the tuning, the key that the place is singing in. For us, that is what we tap into.

A year and a half ago, we were invited to Kyoto for a site-specific workshop and performance in a Buddhist temple with Japanese dancers and community participants. Having come of age in the late 1960s, when there was such pride in disobedience, in breaking with tradition, in disrespect for ritual, I had not really expected to be attracted to the Japanese culture. But before day one of the workshop was over, I had fallen deeply in love with Japan. During this experience, I realized how differently the Japanese experience space and place. What shocked me was that within every tradition—of taking off one's shoes, of putting them in a certain place, of restoring a room or gravel path to its original condition after wildly dancing in it—there was such respect for the space, for the ground. Their treatment of the space was based on a deep awareness and appreciation, not merely on tradition.

MK: What were your initial efforts in transitioning from stage to site?

SP: In the beginning, our first site work began with taking choreography that we had created in the studio, transplanting it to the site, and seeing what would happen. What happened was that everything was off, out of tune! So we discovered that Einstein was right, that space and time are indeed relative, and that each environment has its own unique requirements.

It was with *Ordinary Festivals*, our piece with 300 oranges, two knives, and wonderfully weird Italian folk music, that we first figured out how to adapt a full-evening proscenium work to an outdoor site. We first performed it on an outdoor stage at the Maine Festival, and then we adapted it to the Bates College quad—a huge green space intersected with gorgeous old elm trees. We thought our only job would be to adjust the piece to a space without wings and a "cyc." We had absolutely no idea what changes the space was going to demand of us! It was an incredible experience. In an odd way, it felt as if we were forced to become filmmakers overnight. It took me immediately back to the first foreign film I saw, Truffaut's *Jules et Jim*. His use of space just sang! The camera angles had such power, such emotional and spiritual depth.

PW: The quad at Bates offered a huge canvas that allowed us to work with great depth and a palette that was so much bigger than on a concert stage. It opened up the possibility of expanding our vision in a very filmic way. For example, my solo, which on the stage occurs in the most upstage wing, was done along a 100-foot pathway at the other end of the quad, making me a distant figure. This heightened the illusion of me portraying an ephemeral memory of someone's beloved. This spatial magnifier was incredibly effective in increasing not just the visual but also the emotional impact of the entire work.

MK: Does historical research factor into your creative process?

SP: Doing historical research has never been a formal part of our creative process, but it has certainly inspired us, informed us, and even changed the direction of our work. I'm thinking of our first residency in Lewiston, Maine, where we had planned to make a community/site work that explored pivotal moments of change in one's life, whether that change was by choice or by chance. We had assumed that the project would be based on intensely personal stories, which we would then videotape in locations throughout the city. We had done a pilot project of something similar to this in Lincoln, Nebraska, and thought we were ready to roll. But in Lewiston, *nobody* opened up. How naïve we were! This was no hippie counterculture of individuals waiting for an opportunity for the world to listen to their darkest secrets; this was a French-Canadian community that was not about to reveal itself to these New York artists!

What literally broke the ice that first night was when a 98-year-old retired professor spoke up. "Well, I have a choice of what to think about when I have insomnia at night. Being a lover of mathematics, last night when I couldn't sleep, I decided to calculate the tonnage of ice I delivered as a boy." Then this beautiful old woman who had been the town's librarian interjected, "You might be interested in the documentary footage we have down at the county courthouse of the last ice harvest in Maine. And after you look at it, you should go talk to Chuck, who cuts up chickens in the Bates College cafeteria and who knows all about ice." So we found Chuck, and he told us about how ice from Maine was *the* ice to have in your cocktails back in 1900, whether in Havana or Johannesburg or Calcutta. This got us fascinated, not just with the history of Lewiston, but also with ice, which became a significant choreographic ingredient in the piece.

Then a 95-year-old man shared with us, "The pivotal moment of change in my life came by a choice that was not of my own making. I was manager of the Empire movie theater in town, and after 45 years, they closed it down." And then everyone started telling personal stories about what happened to them at the movie theater. We found out that before the Empire was a movie theater, it was a vaudeville house where Laurel and Hardy, Sarah Bernhardt, and Charlie Chaplin had performed. It turns out that Lewiston, this decaying mill town, had once been part of the theater touring triangle along with New York City and Boston. We learned about the waves of immigrants who built Lewiston and how, during the 1940s when the mill workers went on strike, the owners chose to close their factories down rather than allow the workers to unionize. As a result, the town virtually died, and many of its beautiful buildings were boarded up. But we got access to these incredible sites where Patrik shot a dozen videos with our company and community participants, and these became the heart of the piece.

    None of this had to do with our original intentions, but we always try to allow the piece to be defined by the community itself. What will be the key that unlocks the door for the project? We have to be willing to change. The moment we feel it, like bloodhounds we follow the scent.

MK: What else besides history informs your work?

SP: The space itself. It speaks to us. I think Patrik and I both come from a place where our choreographic process is about allowing the piece to be revealed to us. Our job is to make ourselves open and ready for it. That might entail learning about its history or architecture, or it might mean simply sitting in the space for hours, listening.

    But what is the main thing that ends up affecting our process? Economics. Dancers' schedules. The weather. The presenter. The groundskeepers. The distance between the performance site and the nearest toilet. Tomorrow's grant deadline.

MK: Do you find that part of what attracts you to site work is the potential to create community connections?

SP: Yes and no. Performance projects involving the community are a vital aspect of our work, whether on site or onstage. Out of choreographic necessity, we often desire a lot of people for our site casts. We have a large appetite for being able to work with masses of people at one time for certain images; we also love to work with changes in density. If you are making a piece with multiple spaces, and audience members are walking through them on their own, your images will be occurring simultaneously, and so you'll need a large cast. That usually means getting involved in the community. It might mean collaborating with the highest level of artists in the area, or it might mean creating a spoken word/movement duet for a 70-year-old woman and an "at-risk" teenage girl. Or it might mean experimenting with a group of martial artists and hospice nurses.

    As we have grown through the years, we have learned not just about our own needs but also about the needs of the people in the community. We have to consider how much free time they have for rehearsals and performances. We now offer a four-tiered range of possible involvement for community participants, from three weeks of daily rehearsals to a onetime video session. Having that kind of organizational and artistic wherewithal has taken us years to develop. Site-adaptive work helps in terms of time as well. We know that we've got preexisting dances that we can adapt to age and site that can be taught with a minimum of rehearsals. Twenty years ago, we would rehearse daily with five people for two months. That is what we needed, and everybody had the time. It is different now.

MK: Do you feel there is something about approaching a site through movement and dance that is particularly effective for communicating with a site?

SP: Absolutely. Connecting with site through the choreographic language of space, time, motion, dynamics, density, musicality, and design deepens and expands awareness. It gives me a profoundly richer experience of the space and the place than I would have had otherwise. And the same occurs for the audience.

In our culture, intellect is so separated from feeling, sensation, intuition. Site choreography, I believe, can bring it all together for both performer and audience. History, sociology, art, nature, and architecture all integrate into a unified whole in site work. Somehow it quiets the mind, and an internal expansiveness opens up.

MK: Do you have one piece that you consider your most successful?

PW: Oh, definitely our *A Curious Invasion* series. We built a structure that is easily adaptable to almost any kind of site, natural or architectural. This allows for the restaging of certain sections as well as for the creation of new dances in each site. The elements are all there, and we string them together in different ways, varying the emphasis and embracing tangents made possible by the particular site. Each performance is distinct, yet they all feel like a continuum.

SP: With *A Curious Invasion/Wave Hill*, we came of age by being on top of the organizational aspect of it. It was such a big piece that utilized multiple sites; it was choreographically challenging, spatially magnificent, and it truly worked for the audience both logistically and artistically. It worked for the downtown experimental artists; it worked for people who had never been to a dance performance; it worked for the nature lovers who had gone to Wave Hill that day expecting to look at flowers; it worked for the 10-year-olds and their siblings; it worked for the 80-year-olds in wheelchairs. And it works beautifully as a site-adaptive performance project.

MK: Do you get more feedback from your site work than you do from your proscenium work?

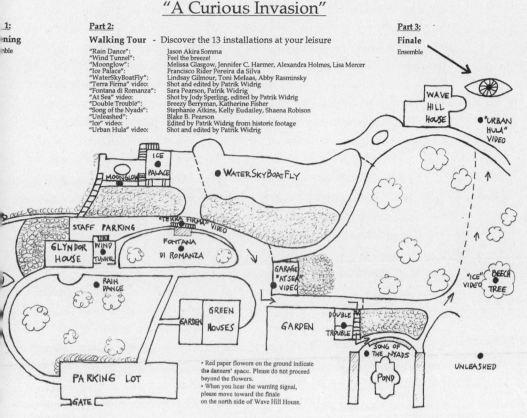

"A Curious Invasion"

1:
ning
nble

Part 2:

Walking Tour - Discover the 13 installations at your leisure

"Rain Dance":   Jason Akira Somma
"Wind Tunnel":   Feel the breeze!
"Moonglow":   Melissa Glasgow, Jennifer C. Harmer, Alexandra Holmes, Lisa Mercer
"Ice Palace":   Francisco Rider Pereira da Silva
"WaterSkyBoatFly":   Lindsay Gilmour, Toni Melaas, Abby Rasminsky
"Terra Firma" video: Shot and edited by Patrik Widrig
"Fontana di Romanza": Sara Pearson, Patrik Widrig
"At Sea" video: Shot by Jody Sperling, edited by Patrik Widrig
"Double Trouble":   Breezy Berryman, Katherine Fisher
"Song of the Nyads": Stephanie Atkins, Kelly Eudailey, Shaena Robison
"Unleashed":   Blake B. Pearson
"Ice" video: Edited by Patrik Widrig from historic footage
"Urban Hula" video: Shot and edited by Patrik Widrig

Part 3:

Finale

Ensemble

Figure 66. Dealing with multiple sites. Patrik Widrig's map for *A Curious Invasion/Wave Hill* (2001). Courtesy of PEARSONWIDRIG DANCETHEATER.

SP: Before yes, now no, as e-mail has extended the avenues for audience response. The phrase "We welcome your feedback" (with our e-mail address) is always in our programs, which has made a big difference. But with site work, it is much easier for an audience member to cross that invisible boundary to approach the performers after a concert. When appropriate with site performances, we'll keep the music going after the bows and invite the audience to join us. They enter the performance space, bring up their friends and family, and everyone dances together. This may not seem like a big deal, but it has a huge impact on people, on their relationship to the arts, their memory of the concert, their experience of the event, and their desire to come again.

Also, in our site work's creative process, we choreograph on location, with rehearsals open to the public. We invite feedback from people who happen to be watching and have learned how to manage such interactions. We have even unexpectedly invited passersby to join our casts—from kids in East Harlem to musicians in Central Park. Old Jewish women sit down and watch our rehearsals outside of Lincoln Center and tell us how we should edit a section we're working on. The Iranian security guard in Bryant Park quietly approaches us as we're running *Ordinary Festivals* and asks us if we're doing a Sufi dance, as it looks very familiar to the kind of dancing from his country. Three teenage bikers silently watch us work and then shout to one another, "I know what this is; it's a race in slow motion!" Having people watch us create and then hearing them tell us what they see is inspiring, enlightening, invigorating, and not always easy to hear!

MK: I am curious about your emphasis on teaching. It seems like you have a particular interest in doing workshops around site work. I was wondering if your facilitating of other's site work also affects your own.

SP: Oh, absolutely. In the last 20 years it has been the people who have taken our workshops who have been our teachers. There is something holy or magical about class. It's a gift. There is this rarified atmosphere that gets created. There is nothing like the energy, thinking, feeling, and artistry of people involved in a collaborative, creative process. I become a student as well when I am teaching; I evaluate my teaching by how much I learn in the workshops. The more I am learning, the better I am teaching. The most beginning-level person can open my eyes and break down my unconscious, habitual patterns of perception.

At Bearnstow, where we teach a one-week site workshop each summer, participants create images in the water, inside their cabins, and throughout a forest that has been untouched for the past 60 years. One of the first assignments this year was to choose a site, decide where the audience would be, and create two images—one still, and one that changes the energy of the space. One participant brought us to a place in the woods, directed us to face the lake, and then asked us to turn around. What we saw was an empty cabin, with no dancers, no movement. Somehow it was breathtaking. He made us see that cabin as if for the first time. I had walked past it every day for the past three summers, yet I hadn't *seen* it until he had me face it with a mind shocked out of its expectations. It never occurred to me to have someone *not* in the space. Having grown up dancing, I assumed someone would be hanging from the rafters or falling into the space. But that simple emptiness—it was brilliant.

MK: Do any of the people who take your workshops go on to make site work elsewhere?

PW: Our Swiss friend Gisa Frank comes to mind. She recently made a beautiful film inspired by our site workshop. There are these giant "holes" in the alpine meadows of the mountainous region where she lives, lending the area a particular mystique. Her colorful play with disappearing into and appearing out of these indentations brilliantly capitalizes on the cultural associations connected to the Appenzell region—a combination of eerie oddity and surprising humor.

MK: Does your site work ever overlap with urban renewal projects?

SP: Funny you should ask. The one time that this was an integral aspect of a project, it got washed away with Hurricane Katrina. We were collaborating on a two-year site project with the Center for Bioenvironmental Research, a cutting-edge science think tank based at Tulane University in New Orleans. They had just purchased a defunct casino at the edge of the river that they were going to gut and turn into an international research institute. Part of their mission statement included a belief in the science/art interface. They wanted us to create a site performance piece in their space before it was developed, a piece that would introduce this new site to the public in a unique, artistic way. For us, it was a dream come true. Half of the space was a Disney-esque faux French Quarter with fake live oaks and a fake river. The other half was raw space the size of an airplane hangar. Part one of the project was to begin the first week of September 2005. We had spent the summer organizing and designing it in minute detail. Over 60 people were going to perform in it—local artists, scientists, engineers, school kids, teachers. Then Katrina hit, and for a few hours we thought the city had been saved. Then the levees broke. We were devastated, heartbroken, in shock. Having fallen in love with New Orleans during two previous guest artist residencies at Tulane University, we had become attached to every street, every tree. It was two months before we could locate most of our cast, and we still don't know where or how some people are.

        A friend who knew us well and was very concerned over the state we were in told us, "You have to go back into the studio, lie down on your stomachs, breathe, and the next project will come." And so it did. The following morning at 4:00 A.M., *Katrina, Katrina: Love Letters to New Orleans* was born. It was realized in February 2006 down in New Orleans with a just re-opened Tulane University as our partner. The site element shifted to videos shot throughout the ravaged city; the subject matter changed completely. We call it a live documentary. It's a full-evening dance/spoken word/video work that continually evolves as it tours from city to city, inviting Gulf Coast evacuees to participate in workshops and video portraits or as members of the performing cast. For the past year, we've been living with our hearts in New Orleans. It is where we are.

MK: So a part of you seems sited at all times?

SP: Yes, yes, yes. And a part of us is sited in India, and another in Japan, along the Kumano coast, where Buddhism met Shintoism centuries ago. So, as we sit in our sixth-floor East Village tenement apartment, where one window looks out at the Empire State Building and the other at where the Twin Towers used to be, we're internally linked to these places that awaken our hearts and call to us to frame them and capture their essence with our art.

o

The Honeymoon Is Over

By Sara Pearson

The middle-class neighborhood in which I grew up sprang into existence shortly after World War II ended. Returning servicemen, armed with their GI bills and new families, quickly built houses that, from my young aesthetic, were utterly lacking in charm or beauty. Framed by a front- and backyard that was 95 percent perfectly green grass (save for the little yellow circles left behind by the family dog's daily business), I found it all perfectly boring and itchy. I considered the grass a representation of what I was so eager to leave behind.

So, 30 years later in New York City, when Patrik Widrig and I were commissioned by Dancing in the Streets to choreograph our first site work for Wave Hill—the bucolic garden estate with endless expanses of green in Riverdale, New York—I was challenged to discover a new relationship to this previously rejected phenomenon.

With old visual associations having faded from my mind—a result of living many years in Manhattan and from touring to developing countries and urban centers around the world—I was suddenly seeing grass as if for the first time. Green! Greenness! It reminded me of Socrates' question, "What is red?" which, during my first years of college, my friends and I pondered nightly—all the while fueled by homegrown marijuana and background music alternating between Bach's Mass in B Minor and the Doors' "Light My Fire."

It would be an exaggeration to say that my choreographic muses were instantly awakened by Wave Hill. As Patrik and I walked through what had previously been Teddy Roosevelt's and later Toscanini's magnificent summer residence (now a public garden and cultural center), we searched for the site we would choose for the new work. I waited for a space, a place to speak to me—nothing happened. We kept walking; I kept waiting—nothing kept happening. This was clearly starting out as an arranged marriage.

We finally came upon a secluded corner of a garden bordered by an old stone wall, which held the possibilities of working with tremendous ranges of spatial perspective. At this point, we had no idea what the dance would be or what it would be "about." But we did know this much: it would be a duet with this particular environment, and we wanted the space and the place to dictate to us both the choreographic vocabulary and structure.

The following week we invited the dancers out for our first exploratory rehearsal. The manicured lawns were unexpectedly smooth and even—it was the equivalent of an outdoor dance floor. With earth in place of wood, the possibilities for running and rolling (yes, we found the one hill on the entire estate) and flying and crashing and being still forever were endless, delicious. And it being a summer project in hot hot hot New York City, we somehow couldn't resist experimenting with water—throwing it, pouring it, choreographing its arcs and visual delights. With the ceiling lifted infinitely upwards and with lighting left

Figure 67. Playing with water in *Common Ground* (1994). Photo by Carlo Adinolfi, courtesy of PEARSONWIDRIG DANCETHEATER.

to the gods, the possibilities for working with perspective and depth became irresistibly and ravishingly appealing.

Via subway and bus, our small group of seven would commute several times a week from our 100-year-old stifling-in-summer-overheated-in-winter apartments in the East Village. It would often take two hours to get there, two hours to return. How or when anyone had time to work at a paying job with that schedule is a mystery to me now.

By the end of the first week of rehearsals, much of the palette for *Common Ground* had been developed. Discovering the ways in which this new environment demanded a new relationship to time, dynamics, space, sound, motion, and stillness, we became infatuated with the creative possibilities and were ready for more.

By the third week of rehearsals, the thermometer had soared and New York City was experiencing its worst drought in years. The soft grass dried up virtually overnight, and in its place appeared a hardened, parched surface no one wanted to lie on, let alone roll in. Subways broke down; dancers forgot to bring long-sleeved shirts and pants for protection; and with temperatures hitting the high nineties, tempers within our company flared. Group unity of focus wavered, and the timing we had set the week before that had seemed so perfect now felt endlessly long, irritating, and boring. The honeymoon was over.

The next month the rains finally came and, along with the return of our newly beloved green grass, there arrived hundreds of bees. Like an audience that attempts not to get distracted when latecomers are seated, we would try to rehearse with the bees. Largely invisible to me—as I was sitting far away with megaphone in hand—the only way I could tell of their presence was from the continual interruptions in the choreography: someone would dash madly off in the wrong direction; another would stand perfectly still when they were supposed to be doing their solo; another would refuse to drop to the ground for that brilliant moment of perfect unison.

John Cage and Merce Cunningham would have loved it: it brought an element of chance and surprise into the working process that opened up new possibilities and challenged patience to the hilt. It just about drove me out of my mind. And while this was perhaps what was needed, at that time I was far from recognizing it, let alone surrendering to it.

○

With every site project, as with every romance, there is a honeymoon. Dwelling perhaps in what Plato terms the "World of Ideas," one can perceive the essence of a place, listen to the space, and see how best it can be framed by color, chore-

Figure 68. Looking for clarity in the water arcs of *Common Ground* (2004).
Photo by Carlo Adinolfi, courtesy of PEARSONWIDRIG DANCETHEATER.

ography, and sound. This opens up a heightened awareness where both performers and audience enter into a rarefied state of aliveness and attunement, where
beauty and humor and musicality and memory and history and sorrow and joy
flow through each other in a contrapuntal fugue of love. This is the gift.

And then one is dropped back to earth, back into this body, back into a world
of deadlines and bad moods and bad backs and talented dancers having to work
three jobs to pay exorbitant rents with $50,000 student loans hovering over
them. What had been so clear in that pristine environment becomes lost in the
dramas and traumas of self-doubt, conflicting needs, physical limitations, and
bad weather.

This is the work. This is the time when all the years of learning to continue
when all one can hear is interference come into play. Give the dancers an unexpected 15-minute break. Lie down on the ground or, if you are in an art museum,
in front of the Hopper painting. Find that hidden corner in the back garden of

the Buddhist temple, when everyone else is smoking a cigarette, breaking up with a boyfriend, or eating a rice triangle. Exhale and remember what Philo of Alexandria said: "Be kind, for everyone you meet is fighting a great battle."

Settle down, settle back, and listen. Soften your face. Relax your wrists. Allow your seeing to become an act of receiving rather than of forward assertion. Let the images come to you. Listen to the rhythms in the architecture, whether it's a New Zealand fern forest, an abandoned mill in rural Maine, or the Eu-In Buddhist temple in Kyoto. Slow down and see the space. Yes, it is invisible, but you *can* see it, feel it, breathe it. Let the site speak to you. It will tell you where to place the dancers and how they can frame the site's soul, so that the audience can tune in to this newness as their habitual patterns of perception and expectation dissolve. Drop by drop it comes, or sometimes, as the tightness defrosts, there is a mighty CRACK! and a huge, frozen chunk breaks away as an entire new section in the dance is revealed and discovered. It may take a long time for it to find its way into this world, let alone for you to teach and communicate it. You will need every skill you ever learned in your life to make it happen. It will take 100 percent of your will, 100 percent of your diplomatic talents, and 100 percent of your surrender. Some days everything will go wrong, when presenters and gardeners and museum directors and dancers will say no when you know the right answer is yes. And some days, everything that had seemed impossible becomes possible. A dancer suddenly illuminates the next unknown moment with transcendent clarity; an elegantly efficient solution to a logistical logjam reveals itself thanks to a passing remark from the presenter; and the storm, once again, actually passes over. And finally, Hafiz's poem that begins with "This place where you are right now, God circled on a map for you" is somehow no longer a threat but a comfort.

This is the work. There is nothing else like it in the world. It will kill you, and in so doing, you will become more alive than ever before. Congratulations. Stop complaining. Get to work. Be grateful. Enjoy. Hallelujah!

4

Civic Interventions

Accessing Community

Figure 69. Martha Bowers's *Safe Harbour/CORK* (2001). Photo courtesy of Dance Theatre Etcetera.

Because of its placement in public spaces, site-specific dance is an accessible art form. People who might never frequent a theater or who do not conceive of dance as part of their daily lives may come across site-specific dances on the side of a building, or in a community garden, or even in a local waterway. Almost all site choreographers interact with the general public in some way; yet certain site choreographers seek such interactions as the fundamental basis for their work. For them, site art is, above all, a means to create and affect communities and their quality of life. The three choreographers included in this section, Jo Kreiter, Tamar Rogoff, and Martha Bowers, are heavily invested in the intersections between site art and the community. For these women, community involvement in key issues is vital and their work attempts to portray the community as an active player, not only in cultural events but also in decisions that affect their lives from politics to real estate to crime.

Jo Kreiter's background in political science sometimes seems as important as her interest in athleticism in dance. The artistic director of San Francisco–based Flyaway Productions, Kreiter has been making aerial site dances since the mid-1990s. These site pieces demonstrate the power of women, as audiences watch her women's-only group flip and spin overhead on billboards, murals, and fire escapes. The company goes further still in championing women's empowerment by hosting and performing for the 10 Women Campaign each year in San Francisco to highlight women in activism and the arts. Kreiter enjoys interacting with community members around all kinds of critical issues from workers' rights to homelessness. When an old industrial crane was going to be torn down, Kreiter joined with neighborhood labor and environmental organizations to draw attention to the crane through a performance. Her piece *How to Be a Citizen* (2004) celebrated the importance of San Francisco's Market Street as a place of peaceful protest, and *Mission Wall Dances* (2002) dealt directly with people who had been displaced in the Mission area of San Francisco due to arson.

For Kreiter, sites that expose a conflict within a community entice her. "[T]he site holds a quandary in its 'hands,'" she explains in her interview in chapter 12. In particular, these controversial spaces inspire her to create works that spark a civic dialogue, one in which she is eager to participate.

In her article, "Making *Sparrow's End*," Kreiter chronicles her difficulties in reclaiming a public space riddled with fear and urban blight. In her account of the creation of *Sparrow's End* (1997), process balances product as drug exchanges, bodily neglect, and community wonder pervade their attempts at creation. At the close of the article, Kreiter contemplates the aftereffects of site work, wrestling with the reactions of the audience and the inevitable ephemerality of what she has made. As Kreiter zeroes in on social and political dilemmas of our time, we can see how site-specific dance can actively intersect with the civic dialogues that develop around place.

While Kreiter was swinging off buildings in San Francisco, Tamar Rogoff was exploring her father's home country of Belarus. In the mid-1990s, for her first major site project, Rogoff decided to examine the effects of the Holocaust on her father's hometown of Ivye. Yet, even as *The Ivye Project* (1994) raised the specter of the Jewish massacre by Nazis in a forest near the town, Rogoff found herself comforted by the love and friendships that developed among the residents of Ivye and the surrounding area. Rogoff incorporated community members including children and Holocaust survivors into the performance, and she was pleased to discover that, just after the piece, the Jews in the town celebrated their first Seder in over fifty years. Rogoff has become even more community-focused in recent years. When her daughter left for college, Rogoff created a piece in her own Lower East Side neighborhood in New York in order to foster a sense of community among her neighbors. Young children, teenagers, and elderly people from the area all had roles in the piece and Rogoff centered the work around an endangered community garden. Rogoff's ethnically diverse neighborhood came together in a way that even Rogoff found surprising.

For Rogoff, the emotional resonance of place stems from the communities on site. In her interview, Rogoff details site work's ability to slice through barriers and bring disparate groups together in an uplifting project. As she notes, "Creating site work gives me a positive way of being in the world, of being able to transcend problems and boundaries and prejudice." In her article, "Carriers of Consciousness: The Role of the Audience in *The Ivye Project*," Rogoff writes of her large-scale project in Belarus. She notes her delight in exploring personal stories, rather than tales of victimization, to connect to a community. As she views her work through her audience's eyes, she displays the impressive agency that site choreographers grant their audiences; only through them is the work complete. In conclusion, Rogoff ponders the lasting impact that site work can have on a deeply involved audience.

Martha Bowers has been making site works since the 1980s. From her earliest pieces, she found herself drawn to community involvement in art. As her work has progressed, Bowers has incorporated local community members—young, old, revered, or marginalized—into a process that underscores empowerment. She believes that it is important to unearth all the stories around a site, and she finds herself pulled again and again to the narratives that are unwritten or unrecognized. A major touchstone for her work continues to be the neighborhood of Red Hook in Brooklyn, where she has produced many site works and where her company, Dance Theatre Etcetera, is based. After creating her first site work in Red Hook in 1993, she wanted to continue her relationship with the community. As such, for the last two decades her company has been conducting workshops, producing performances, and organizing an annual community festival in which people of all ages and socioeconomic backgrounds participate.

In her interview in chapter 14, Bowers notes how she enjoys challenging audiences to see familiar surroundings as potential spaces of civil action. As she details her interactions with community performers as well as audiences, she demonstrates how site work can dovetail with endeavors to foster democratic participation. In her article, "Choreography for Uncontrollable Contexts," Bowers recounts her long-term site efforts in Red Hook. She notes the conflicting role of site work as both a force of gentrification and a mode for encouraging public discussions about place. Yet, in the end, Bowers continues to celebrate site work as a vehicle for collective expression.

As evidenced by their work, Kreiter, Rogoff, and Bowers do not shy away from tackling problematic issues in a community. Further, they have an investment in how these issues continue to be addressed. As choreographers who place a priority on fostering community, these women tend to have ongoing relations with a community after a performance work is complete. Rogoff, for example, created a film in her neighborhood to continue her work with the teenage girl performers and their mothers. Bowers has found new ways of performing and teaching in Red Hook and has crafted connections with a multitude of people in the neighborhood. In addition to the ongoing classes Kreiter teaches in San Francisco,

Kreiter's company offers an annual summer camp for San Francisco youth to—as she says on her Web site—"remedy . . . the ways in which women and girls remain an underserved element in public culture as a whole." This is not always typical for choreographers who often travel far from their homes to satisfy a commission to create a single site piece. Yet, as Bowers, Rogoff, and Kreiter demonstrate, site-specific choreographers are not artists who see their work as existing apart from a community. Indeed, for these three artists, whether they are in their own neighborhoods or across the world, site art acts as the most effective tool for developing and empowering community. As these three choreographers discuss their work, site dance reveals its ability to encourage performers, community members, and audiences alike to participate in a kinesthetic and discursive experience of place. In short, Kreiter, Bowers, and Rogoff demonstrate site dance as a tool for developing and empowering community.

12

Jo Kreiter

Jo Kreiter is the artistic director of Flyaway Productions, a San Francisco–based dance company. Since 1996, Kreiter's site dances have addressed issues of political relevance to the communities of San Francisco and beyond. Using complex apparatus that launches dancers into the space above alleyways, around industrial cranes, and in front of billboards, Kreiter and her company members demonstrate the physical prowess of women through their site-specific aerial dances. Kreiter/Flyaway is a recipient of a 2006 Creative Work Fund grant, a 2006 Meet the Composer's Commissioning Music/USA Program grant, a 2005 Irvine Fellowship, and a 2003 Rockefeller/MAP grant. She conversed with Pavlik from her home in San Francisco on April 20, 2003.

An Interview with Jo Kreiter

CP: How were you introduced to site work, and what about it appealed to you?

JK: I was introduced to site-specific work via a long-term company membership in Zaccho Dance Theatre. Joanna Haigood, the director, integrated me into her process and her point of view. She works with an idea called place memory.

My own love of site work has to do with bringing an audience to the exact place where an issue, conflict, or need lives. For example, in 1999 my company, Flyaway Productions, danced on a five-story crane in the middle of Islais Creek, which pours into the San Francisco Bay. I chose this site for *Copra Dock Dances* in part because I fell in love with the architecture of the crane, but also because the Copra Crane Labor Landmark Committee and a neighborhood environmental organization, the Friends of Islais Creek, were working to preserve the crane as a labor landmark.

CP: It sounds like site work allows you to address issues critical to a community.

Figure 70. Dancers suspended off a crane in *Copra Dock Dances* (1999). Photo by Elizabeth Gorelick.

JK: Yes, I choose to create site-specific dances because I love dance making where the artistic process is in service of a larger political or social goal. I know this is done on the stage as well, because I have done it myself. But there is such power in site work because creating a dance in order to illuminate a place in a new way helps ground artistic ideas. Site work is the most potent artistic expression I know how to make. By that I mean it has such a strong impact because it unfolds at the very place where a conflict lives. The site itself lends validity to the artistic inquiry, because the site holds a quandary in its "hands," or in the bricks or steel I-beams or concrete walls, etc. Sometimes a site holds the possibility of celebration as well.

I believe this was accomplished with *Copra*, but also with *Mission Wall Dances*. For this piece, I commissioned a three-story, block-long mural in the Mission District of San Francisco that used fantasy and realism to portray the Mission's history of displacement and renewal. Now the dance is done, but the mural remains. That corner of the mission is permanently marked—in the best of ways, I think—by the energy and thought and passion of a group of interdisciplinary artists—myself as a choreographer, the dancers, the composer (Pamela Z), the set designer, the rigger, etc.

CP: Have there been any inspirational people or movements that have sparked your interest in site work?

JK: People that have influenced me include Joanna Haigood and Gene Kelly, for his use of site and set in the movies. I've also been influenced by the postmodern dance movement, particularly because it introduced pedestrian simplicity into a complicated world of steps and positions. The tradition of political dance brought to me by the Dance Brigade in San Francisco, as well as the Mural Movement in terms of the presence of large-scale visual art in neighborhoods, have also been quite influential.

CP: Do you feel your background or your worldview have had an effect on your decision to do site-specific works?

JK: Being politically minded and having trained as a political scientist influences my choice to make work that centers on political and feminist themes. I would say that my work is part of a feminist discourse on the body and the transformation of women's images in the public domain, as a means to affect women's self-esteem in their public and private lives. It is part of a hybrid exploration in dance integrating risk, circus skill, rigging, and spectacle.

I would say that my site work is part of a tradition of public art that believes in the beautification of the external environment as an influence on the social fabric of neighborhoods and communities. As I mentioned above, site work introduces a new kind of realism into politically motivated artwork, and this is particularly attractive to me. There is less abstraction on site than if you are dancing on the stage.

CP: Which comes first most of the time, an idea for a dance piece or the discovery of an evocative location?

JK: Either and both. For example, for *Copra Dock Dances*, I saw a picture of the crane and knew I had to dance on it. It was after that that I discovered it was in the midst of being saved as a labor landmark.

Recently, I have been looking at the issue of water scarcity. It astounds me that militarism and greed dominate the way we live as a global community and that we, as citizens of this country and the world, do not choose to honor basic needs above all else. So I developed a piece for the stage called *The Grim Arithmetic of Water*. But I am also looking for a site, ideally a rural site, where I can explore the issue where it is expressed in the world, maybe at a dry riverbed, maybe at the disintegrating Lake Powell, maybe at a dam. I am still searching. So in this case, the broad idea came first, but the specifics of its development will come later when I find the site.

Sometimes I also get commissions to do a piece on a particular site. For instance, the San Francisco Arts Commission wanted artists to respond to the texture and architecture of Market Street. So I proposed a piece called *How to Be a Citizen* to be performed on the Plaza at the foot of Market Street at Embarcadero.

CP: Do you research the history of a site, and does it find its way into your work?

JK: Yes, I do research. For *How to Be a Citizen*, we focused not on the daily hum of Market Street commerce but on its occasional history. We researched the history of a century of peaceful protest down Market Street, including the labor marches of the thirties, the Harvey Milk Candlelight March, and past and current antiwar gatherings. We wanted to show these events as evidence of public political participation that has led to meaningful change, and the piece reflected this century of citizen participation in public policy. I have an avid interest in the workings of democracy as it is embraced beyond the walls of official institutions, and I was excited about the possibilities for this piece exploring such history.

CP: In addition to the site, do you also look for communities with which you'd like to interact? Does a site's surrounding community affect your work?

JK: I do not look for a community, but definitely find one in the process. This happens in different ways. For *Mission Wall Dances*, we made contact with the Mission Single Room Occupancy Collaborative, which documents displacement that occurs due to hotel fires. Through this organization, we found three individuals willing to be interviewed about their experience of arson and displacement. Their stories affected the piece, and their voices were used in the sound score. For *How to Be a Citizen*, we interviewed people who had participated in Market Street marches, including a woman who was pregnant as a teenager and chose to have her baby adopted. Her choice was in the context of illegal abortion, and her interview became the basis of the section on women's rights.

CP: Do you consider one of your site-specific works to be your signature piece?

JK: I guess I would say that *Mission Wall Dances* would be my signature work, partly because it left behind not just the mural but also the dancers painted into the mural. It attracted huge audiences, in part because of news coverage; this included a wonderful feature in the daily paper that was not in the arts section, so more people read it. Most importantly, this piece captured the spirit and imagination of the city. It spoke to a wound in the city's history that is still festering, and people responded to that in ways I never imagined. So many people were thrilled that their own history/pain was being reflected in such a spectacular piece of art. It was truly the best of spectacle, politics, and history that I have manifested yet.

CP: When you are commissioned to do a site piece, as opposed to choosing the site yourself, do you find that this impacts your creative process?

JK: Many years ago I was asked to do a short solo performance in Sparrow Alley in the Mission. I did it as an improvisational solo on a fire escape, accompanied by an accordion artist named Nina Rolley. It was a very low-key community arts event. But then the solo, or I should say the site, got deep inside me, so that I was inspired to make a large-scale work in the Alley called *Sparrow's End*. This became my first major site work, for which I received my first major grant. That was in 1997.

CP: Has your audience expressed their views on your work?

JK: Here is an excerpt from one of the best reaction letters I have ever gotten: "Dear Jo, I made a very special effort to get my lazy tail out of bed yesterday morning to be a fully functioning audience member at yesterday afternoon's 2:00 P.M. performance of *Mission Wall Dances*. Having lived in the 16th and Valencia area for years prior, and years after the terrible fire that had such a devastating effect on so many back in the seventies and the failure of the City to ever really address the injustice of that fire, I was profoundly moved by yesterday's performance.... Your production was unique, beautiful, and moved me to tears."

CP: Do you think being a woman has influenced your choice to create site work?

JK: What I value in my site work is bringing strong, liberated women together in public space. It matters to me to show women at work, at play, and in states of flight and freedom in public spaces. When we rehearse on a site, we inevitably have drive-by and walk-by audiences for rehearsal. I think it impacts people to see us as women doing something creative, difficult, imagi-

Figure 71. Tara Brendell, Aimee Lam, Yayoi Kambera, and Tam Welch performing on the commissioned mural in *Mission Wall Dances* (2002). Photo by Elizabeth Gorelick.

native, and productive. So bringing strong women artists into public space is a choice I make as a woman and as a feminist.

CP: Does creating site-specific work help or hinder your chances of obtaining funding for your work?

JK: I find site work is more fundable than work for the stage. It attracts funders who support both experimental and community-based artwork. It also attracts funders who value accessibility. All of my site pieces have been free of charge and are therefore more accessible.

But site work is more arduous to make. You enter into relationships with public bureaucracies that are difficult to navigate. It takes amazing patience, diplomacy, and persistence. It is difficult to raise the money to pull it off, interface with city/university/civic officials, and deal with the logistical problems that arise. Some of these problems can never be anticipated in advance. The logistical problems are probably the most challenging, because at this point I know the other two are coming.

CP: Do you ever tread contentious ground in your site work?

JK: Yes, there is often controversy. The work makes officials nervous. It makes presenters nervous. It makes landlords nervous. Right now, I am be-

Figure 72. Contesting concepts of beauty. Jessica Swanson, Damara Ganley, and Jo Kreiter in *The Live Billboard Project* (2006). ©Austin Forbord Photography.

ginning production for the creation of a live billboard. With the project, the goal is to encourage civic dialogue about the ownership of public air space, as well as to celebrate the female body in a way where nothing is being bought or sold at women's expense. The project is meant to challenge who controls the flow of media information above our heads. This is an aspect of urban development I am very interested in right now. I think that this piece will be controversial with audiences as well, because we are pointedly challenging the politics of beauty. The billboard has a literal slogan about beauty at a crowded intersection of the city. I am nervous about it, but also thrilled at the possibilities.

CP: Have you found that your site work intersects with economic redevelopment schemes for a given area?

JK: With *Mission Wall Dances*, we were mourning the effects of market-dominated redevelopment, which I believe to be detrimental to the human ecology of a city. We were dancing after the damage had already been done, though.

I would love to have an opportunity to be involved in a redevelopment process while it was unfolding, to have some kind of positive impact for community needs. Unfortunately, I am not on the list of people who are called when the men in back rooms decide what growth happens where. Actually, I am not that cynical. I do think some redevelopment processes are very responsible. Maybe those people will give me a call some day.

○

Making *Sparrow's End*

By Jo Kreiter

Sparrow's End *was a site-specific dance performed for over 800 people in San Francisco's Mission in October 1997. Eleven dancers, including three 10-year-old girls, performed on the rooftop, fire escape, walls, and floor of Sparrow Alley. The performance featured original music composed and performed live by Charming Hostess and Pamela Z. Alongside the performance, one of the company members and I taught "outside dancing" workshops to neighborhood youth who lived across from the Alley.*

As the director, choreographer, and instigator of the project, I hoped to counter the drug-based despair and violence that unfolds in Sparrow Alley on a daily basis. I hoped to give audiences an experience of dance as a whirlwind of virtuosic daring and as a creative effort to reclaim urban space. In making the piece, the company rehearsed on site for two months, developing a committed presence in an alley that is usually home to drug deals, garbage, and sex trade. It was emotionally draining to make work in that context, but also tender, as we were esteemed by shop owners, junkies, mothers, and many of the street regulars for conjuring vibrancy in an environment that commands fear.

The following chronicles my experience of creating and performing the dance.

○

18 Aug 1997 First rehearsal. Kathy and I are dancing in the Alley. A man walks by. Talks with us. Asks us why we are dancing here, in this alley, such a dark place with such dark energy. He describes the Hotel Sunrise as a Pandora's box—the source of this part of the Mission's ugliness, drugs, rampant violence. And yet, he says, when he turned the corner today and saw us dancing, he saw things differently.

22 Aug Midway through the rehearsal, I ask Angela, Kathy, and Rachel to place their hands on the wall of the Hotel Sunrise. I study the shapes of their bodies, not sure what I am looking for. A man walks by the Alley, bursts into a smile, shouts to the women something about working hard to hold up the building so it doesn't fall. He sees with fresh eyes what I have been missing—the women in relationship to the building, three women holding the place up—because it is breaking, rotting out, collapsing under the weight of so many displaced people hovering in its rooms.

25 Aug A man watches most of the second half of rehearsal. When we are done, he comes up to me and tells me his story. He has been a heroin addict for nine years; he is about to go away to a six-month rehab program. "Watching all of you dance," he says, "you dance your joy. It reminds me how I have taken all of my joy and hidden it behind my drug. How the drug becomes joy and then not even that anymore." Over and over he thanked us for our dancing. For crossing into his life that day.

6 Sept I have become acquainted with a woman who lives in the hotel. Her name is Karen, and I believe she is either a prostitute, a dealer, or both, because men are always calling up to her window from the alley. I introduced myself to her on our first day of rehearsal. Today she asked me about my problems with the hotel management, because she has witnessed my struggle to get permission to dance on the hotel roof. I tell her that things have worked out in the end, but if she wanted, it would be great if she told the management that she was enjoying having us around and dancing. "Oh, sure," she says. "This here looks like a woman thing, and I'd support that." It touches me deeply that female solidarity crosses race and class lines.

10 Sept I arrive at the alley early to clean the ground and to gather my thoughts

Figure 73. Rachel Lincoln and Leslie Seiters hang off the roof in Sparrow's Alley. Photo by Elizabeth Gorelick.

for rehearsal. I walk into the alley corridor. The stench is particularly bad today. I walk further and see a man sweeping. His name is Pablo. He lives on the ground floor of the hotel. He is cleaning the whole alley because he thought we might show up today to practice and he wanted it to be clean. I clean with him for a while, a shared silence of sweeping glass, condom wrappers, a rusted hanger, and chicken bones into a cardboard box. After a while I leave to greet the dancers. He finishes cleaning without me.

Late evening I've been thinking about souls. How they become injured and how they, too, seem to break. Making this dance in the alley is hard. It drains me to hold creative focus against the shouts of men to their buddies for drug money, against the yellow stench of dirt and human waste, against the glazed eyes of an old man just released from the hospital with nowhere to go.

13 Sept For the past few rehearsals, three or four children and their mother have walked through the alley on their way to or from home. They live in the hotel. As far as I can tell, they are the only children living there. Today the children appeared with their mother, who left them in the alley for a little while. I imagine that she had some shopping to do and felt that it was safe to leave her daughters playing in the alley near us. Others might judge her for leaving her children to play in the street, but I am struck by her trust. We brought a sense of safety to her neighborhood, to her yard that is not a yard in front of the hotel that is barely her home.

I am watching a line of dancers run down the center of the alley. We are starting to work on a section of movement that I am the most excited about so far. In my excitement I don't see a woman enter the alley. I only notice her once she is there, in the center of the space, in the center of the dance. I ask her name. Fatima. She starts dancing with us, working with the alley wall in the same way that I have instructed the dancers. Except that she is off-kilter somehow. I imagine it is drugs, mental illness, or probably some combination. She stays dancing for a long time, though more and more she starts to be in our way. I am starting to wonder if there is something I should do to get her to leave, but most of my attention is still focused on the dance-making.

Then something horrible happens. Fatima walks toward the dancers. She is more and more incoherent. She foams at the mouth, and she is crying and screaming. The dancing seems to have gotten inside of her and taken her somewhere unbearable. She walks backwards, arms out, screaming fear and pain into the alley. She stops moving suddenly, lifts her arms, and falls backward, hitting the concrete with her full weight, a trust fall with no one to catch her. Her head slams into cement. I run for a phone to get an ambulance. The dancers and others hanging out near the alley gather around her. One of the dancers finds a huge lump on her head, but there is no blood.

Waiting for the ambulance. It feels like forever. Fatima becomes conscious. Refuses ice. Wants to know what happened. We tell her she fell and that an ambulance is on its way to make sure she is OK. She refuses to wait. She gets up. Walks away. It is a miracle to me that she can even move. The drug in her system (a man standing around the alley says that she is on PCP) must be a strong block to the effects of falling onto concrete. I wonder if she will die from a concussion, if someone will find her heavy body dead in another alley, later today or in the middle of the night.

I feel uncomfortable responsibility for her accident. In our rehearsal, we created a strong energy. It was swirling, persuasive. Fatima took that energy and added it to her own. But she didn't have the physical or emotional stability to handle it. As dancers, we become ecstatic from motion, but we never lose a conscious sense of where the tangible world begins and ends. Fatima entered the alley high on drugs. The dancing infected her and accelerated a collision with unkempt demons and despair.

24 Sept Cleaning the alley before rehearsal. Ran into Adolph, who owns a business nearby. He told me that Pablo was in jail. Pablo is the man who cleaned the alley for us. Word has it he went to jail for beating on his wife and pulling a knife on the cops. The spiral of despair is drawn wider.

7 Oct The greatest sorrow I have yet felt. The three girls are rehearsing in the alley. A man in a dirty green sweatshirt walks to the back of the alley. Sits on the steps. Smokes his crack. He doesn't care that there are children present. He doesn't care that I am watching him. I have no compassion for him today; he has brought a poison into a space that I am trying, just a little, to make beautiful. And I hate him for it. My spirit dissolves, and we end rehearsal early. I have no strength to battle with today.

17 Oct Dress rehearsal. It was a thrill to finally put all of the pieces together. The first run was a bit messy; props weren't exactly as they were supposed to be; costume changes were difficult. But by the second run we had smoothed all the edges, and I could feel the power of the whole.

It is midnight now, and I am crying. It's hard to explain to anyone what it is like to work for 11 months, conjuring a vision of a dance that will touch an audience or change someone or resonate like a poem; gathering the artists together, getting to work, and then soaring into that moment when it all comes together. It's exhilarating, explosive, and then lonely. I make dances in part because they keep me company. So here I am. The dance is done. I have handed it over to the performers, gladly and with pride. All that energy is out in the world now and separate from my body. I feel bereft.

18 Oct We premiered the piece today. Three dances, sky to asphalt, comprising a luscious whole. *The Roof*: Rachel, Leslie, and I dangling off the edge of the roof; a trio of blackbirds peering in at the city; a requiem for all that is sorrowful here. *The Fire Escape*: four dancers caged at the outside perimeter of the hotel and wanting to escape; water in buckets, and pouring—an effort to cleanse. *The Alley Floor*: rattling bars on the windows and doors; running up walls to push them away; three little girls in a sing-song circle game—what you would *want* to see when you look down an urban alley; a slow ritual of walking to the end of the alley, leaving, we hoped, some kind of beauty behind.

Afterthoughts

The dance was received with a flurry of praise, support, even awe. I feel proud of the work. I started to sense the poetry of the piece in my limbs and my spine as I performed. The feeling intensified as the run progressed, as if I could feel myself communicating with the audience body to body.

In the middle of the second show, a homeless man walked through. It was simultaneously sad and enchanting to see him out of the corner of my eye. I was afraid he might freak out at being watched by an audience. But he went on his way without incident—a reminder of who really lives here and whose life will remain once the dance is gone.

Figure 74. The audience watches the performance of *Sparrow's End* (1997). Photo by Wayne Campbell.

Some dancers in the audiences commented that they wished the piece had more dancing. This confused me. The piece moved through roof, wall, and alley floor. It was fast, athletic, virtuosic, and yes, also slowly unfolding. The movement used function as a point of departure, and this is an important choreographic element for me. It ties dance to the daily world.

Other people have been critical of the piece because it did not seem to engage the stories of the people who surround the alley. Over the course of the project, I developed relationships with social service and church service organizations, with neighborhood children whom I taught "outdoor dancing," and with merchants, including the management of the SRO Hotel. Yet I did not choose to canvas the neighborhood and interview its varying residents.

As I am not a theater artist, I am not drawn to the use of text-based stories. For me, stories from the neighborhood were contained in the site—the garbage in the alley that I cleaned out before each rehearsal: popsicles smashed into the wall, condoms, soiled diapers, needles, broken bottles, and human waste. Boxes of ammunition on the roof. Stained mattresses piled in hallways of the hotel. Televisions competing at full volume. Candy wrappers and pop cans thrown regularly out windows. Metal bars on all the windows. Steel cage balconies of the fire escape.

Any failure to interpret or transform these stories into dance-based images is a shortfall of my own craft and something I am working on as my work evolves over the long term. At worst I have been accused of cultural imperialism, of dumping my art in someone's backyard without their consent or shared participation. I agree that for five afternoons a week over a two-month period, a group of artists took command of the alley. And in our presence (perhaps because of our presence), there were no drug deals, no one shot anyone, no one pulled a knife, no one fucked anyone in the street in broad daylight.

There is emptiness at the end of performing. The last two weeks of October I gave the world a vulnerable and honest part of myself. Tonight I wander around my house, through the kitchen, the hallway, turning lights on and off, looking out the back porch window. I struggle to settle into myself. Can't find center. Question my worth. There are aspects of making art that are relentlessly cruel.

In the end, though, I know that I did what I set out to do: enliven a mean street with beauty and the power of bodies in motion. Still, it is hard to know how a performance lasts.

○

This article was originally published in *Contact Quarterly* 23, no. 2 (Spring/Fall 1998): 99–103.

13

Tamar Rogoff

Tamar Rogoff has been creating site works in her hometown, New York City, and abroad for over fifteen years. Rogoff often joins professional artists and community members as performers in her work; as such, neighborhood children, elderly townspeople, and artists of all nationalities explore and reveal the particularities of site together. Rogoff brings to light facts and artifacts from the past as her works take audiences on tours of forests and urban spaces. Films of her site work, which she directed with Daisy Wright, have been shown at the Walter Reade Theater, the Hamptons International Film Festival, and most recently in Cape Town, South Africa. She is artistic director of Solar1 and curates the Solar Power Dance Festival. From her home in New York, Rogoff spoke with Pavlik on August 2, 2006.

An Interview with Tamar Rogoff

CP: What initially inspired you to make site work?

TR: In the 1970s, I lived in India for three years where the major venue for performance was outdoors. There was a lot of interaction between spectators and performers. Outdoor performance was not a by-product of inside theater. I lived in Varanasi, and they perform the Ram Lila, or the Festival of Ram, every year and have done so for thousands of years. It is community-based and takes place in and around the grounds of the Maharajas' Palace. It goes on for about a month. During this time the pundits were chanting the *Ramayana* text day and night, and the whole story was acted out in various places across the river and around the palace. Everyone in India was familiar with the story. You could see Sita, a character in the story, braiding her hair in one corner, and then there would be a whole battle scene somewhere else. It depended on where you were walking. It was all around you. When Ram went to marry Sita, the whole audience would follow the marriage procession from one location to another. The Maharaja rode on an elephant with torches all around. Each year they relive and enliven part of their religion and their culture through this reenactment. This was my very first influence, and this is what I hold up as my model for site work.

CP: How wonderful to be a part of such an event.

TR: Yes. I saw it two years in a row. I had my two-year-old son with me in India, and we would walk along the river, and all of a sudden there would be Krishna, all painted blue, diving in the water and fighting with a snake. Life seemed to be one big piece of theater. Every year, the townspeople would participate in the event, so you could see your milkman or your tailor performing roles in it. This was my orientation into site work. It is the least elitist form of art. There are a lot of people who think that the scale of my site work is very large, but compared to the epics that happen in India, mine don't seem that big.

CP: Did you start creating site work when you came back to the United States?

TR: In general, when I came back to the United States after being gone so long, I did not just pick up where I left off; I was looking for new ways to do things. I have to credit Elise Bernhardt and Dancing in the Streets for providing me with the opportunity to do site work. Dancing in the Streets helped fund two of my large-scale works. One of them cost $130,000 and the other $90,000.

CP: Do you consider *The Ivye Project* to be one of the more significant site works that you have created?

TR: Yes, it was one of my first major site works. At the time, I was choreographing on dance companies in Lithuania. I knew that my family, who is Jewish, came from Belarus, so I crossed the neighboring border and found my father's hometown. Growing up, I did not know that my family had anything to do with the Holocaust. It turns out that 29 members of my family were killed on one particular day, and they had been buried in a mass grave in a forest in the small town of Ivye. When I got back to the United States, I decided to make a work at the site of the massacre. I didn't feel I had a right to mourn people without knowing their history, so I started this gigantic project in 1994. Dancing in the Streets helped fund it, as well as Richard Lanier at the Trust for Mutual Understanding.

CP: How did you research the history of your family?

TR: A lot of people who escaped this massacre came to the United States and created an Ivye Society, so there were people in New York who had known my family. I did a lot of research and interviews with people in Brooklyn. I kept asking them, "What were the theater companies in town, and what books did people read?" They would intersperse the positive parts with telling me about the horrors of the Holocaust. I learned a lot through interviewing these people, and I read. I also gathered things from my own family, like photos and stories, which were never previously shared with me.

CP: Can you talk about how you incorporated movement into the work?

TR: Well, the piece included professional dancers from the Aura Dance Company of Lithuania, the Fine Five Company of Estonia, and the National Ballet Company of Lithuania. It also included elderly Holocaust survivors, the people from the community, and 18 children. I did not want movement to stand out. I didn't want people to say, "Oh, now here is the dance portion," so I kept it subtle. I had people in trees, and I had a Sabbath bride performed by this beautiful prima ballerina, slowly lifting her arms as she crossed a huge field toward the audience. It looked as if she were walking through a painting. She did not do a lot of typical dance movements like arabesques. Despite the fact that it was outside, it was minimalist. Russians and other people from Eastern Europe focus a lot on very technical performances and spectacles, and I wanted to undercut this expectation. I would take actors and slow down their movements. I would fracture pedestrian movement and use that distortion to make the audience see in a new way. I would look for how things moved from one place to another. For example, someone riding a bicycle through the scene would add movement to that scene and quickly change the pace. I did a laundry dance where the dancers had clothes pinned to them that they whipped around. I also did one dance for a man on top of a rickety table. I drew a storyboard for each scene; I really wanted to accomplish that image and not do a lot of embellishing.

CP: Did this piece have an impact on the town?

TR: The town has changed in so many ways. At first, there was a wonderful movement forward. They were going to reinstate one of the synagogues as a museum instead of as a storage facility for sports equipment. The year after the performance they had their first Seder since before the war. But now there aren't any Jews left in the town. They have either died or left for Israel or Australia. There is no chance I could ever do the piece again. I could only have done that piece in 1994. As the Soviet Union disbanded, a window of opportunity opened. For that one summer, things seemed freer. But shortly after that it again became bleak, politically and economically.

CP: Have you created any site works inside?

TR: I do other kinds of performance in theaters, but my site work is always outdoors and relates to community. When I do site works outdoors, I feel more connected to the universal, linking myself with other people. I meet communities that I would not ordinarily meet.

For example, I have lived in New York on the Lower East Side for 30 years. In 1997, it was a Hispanic, Puerto Rican neighborhood. For decades, I never knew anybody who would say hello to me on the street. So I decided to immerse myself in the neighborhood and do a site work here. My daughter was leaving for college, and at the time it felt almost mythically significant. I used the myth of Demeter and Persephone as the base for my piece *Demeter's Daughter*. I sited the work in a community garden in my neighborhood that looks like a Greek amphitheatre. Somehow, looking to this myth and making this piece helped me transcend a bit of my own personal chaos. Because I was not known in my neighborhood, and because my daughter was leaving, I felt like I needed to expand my sense of the family, particularly to people her age and to other mothers.

CP: Did you have to get permission to use the garden?

TR: I needed to get permission from the city, but really I had to get permission from one of the elderly neighbors who was the custodian of the keys. I negotiated my way and tried to make allies and friends by including the community and their concerns in the piece.

CP: Did you involve community members as performers in the project as well?

TR: I worked with Loisaida, Inc., a group that counsels teenagers who have various problems. I also worked with new graduates that I had taught at NYU's Experimental Theater Wing and with six-year-old girls from a local Girls Club who performed in white communion dresses. I hired Felicia Norton and Kevin Kortan, who are very esteemed performer/dancers, and some wonderful musicians, Bill Ruyle, Peter Zummo, Jeff Berman, and Jon Gibson.

Often, I feel that there is prejudice against site work due to the involvement of community members as performers. Some people feel that it is amateurish or low-brow or that it is not as high an art form. But for me, my works have to be well rehearsed, and I need to have strong performers. And even if I am using performers from the community, I want them to be working next to people who are of the highest professional standards. For example, in this piece, I set up a mentoring situation where the professionals mentored the emerging NYU graduates, and they in turn mentored the teenagers, and the teenagers took care of the 6-year-olds. This was the way I could handle this gigantic confluence of people, which included performers ages 6 to 76.

CP: How did you use the story of Demeter and Persephone?

Figure 75. Performers exploring the story of Demeter and Persephone in a Lower East Side neighborhood (1997). Photo and costume design by Alyson Pou.

TR: Unlike in India where everybody knows the story, here I needed to familiarize the audience with it. So I asked the notable people in the neighborhood, like the bodega owners and the UPS man, to sit in the community garden before the piece and tell the story of Persephone and Demeter in Spanish and in English. We then took off and went all through the neighborhood following the action. Zeus was on a rooftop, and there were several Persephones. The elders, who told the story at the beginning of the show to groups of 12 or 15 people, held red umbrellas, and their group followed them from scene to scene. These elders started the piece, and at the end they joined in the finale.

     One of my favorite things that happened was that we had blocked off the whole block, but there was still a car parked there. No one knows how it happened. Right before we got to that scene, enough people came and picked up the car and moved it.

CP: They literally picked it up and moved it?

TR: Yes. The neighborhood really got swept up in the project. People got the idea that all of these people from outside the neighborhood were going to be showing up, so between scenes they would put out pies and cakes to sell. While we were walking with Demeter and Persephone toward Hades, somebody was selling sweet potato pie—a true entrepreneur!

CP: Do you feel like the piece impacted your neighborhood?

TR: After the project, there was this really different feeling in the neighborhood, especially between me and the people that I met and interacted with so intimately. The kids that were involved felt good about themselves, and the neighbors loved it. Imagine this happening every night in your neighborhood; it was like being back in India!

I made a film about the piece, and the teenage girls narrated the film. As part of the film, I interviewed their mothers at my house, in my daughter's room, and we talked about mother-daughter stuff. In that way, I got a lot of free advice about kids and heard a new point of view. One of the nicest things was that the mothers would tell me positive things about their daughters that they would not tell the daughters themselves. Then the daughters would hear it on the tape and they would say, "My mother never, ever says that I do anything good." So it was a way for them to talk to each other on a nonhabitual, deeper level using the performance, the myth, and me, as a go-between.

Also, at the time that I did *Demeter's Daughter*, there was a threat that the community gardens were going to be sold by the city. There was an article printed in the *Village Voice* about saving the gardens, and they spoke about my site piece. The article focused on showing how these gardens were useful and not just land that no one needs. It gave credibility to this precious land that developers did not think was being used in an economical way.

CP: Why was it so important for you to incorporate the neighborhood teenagers into the work?

TR: In Persephone the teenagers saw a person their age who had crossed a line, who went where it was forbidden to go. The myth was relevant to them, and they in turn made it relevant to the audience. The teens functioned as part of the site because they were the people of the neighborhood. So their involvement carried an enormous weight because everybody knew who they were. They were part and parcel of the landscape. They were the site. In other words, it was not only about the architecture or what was around them, but it was about them as representatives of this neighborhood.

CP: Why do you create site works?

TR: Creating site work gives me a positive way of being in the world, of being able to transcend problems and boundaries and prejudice. It situates you in a place where, if you band together, all things are possible. That transcending of obstacles is amazing for everybody. None of the teenagers in my

Figure 76. Celebrating site work's accessibility. Kyla Barkin and Brad Ellis in *Night for Day* (2004). Photo by Flash Rosenberg.

neighborhood could believe that we did the performance. It exceeded their expectations of themselves and what they expect from the Lower East Side.

I think of site work as a very ancient, well-honed form of art that has been here longer than dance in theater spaces. I think of it as connecting to those early, early forms. In so many countries around the world, it has been honed for many years for the purpose of having everyone see it; it isn't an elitist thing. It joins community, history, architecture, landscape, and audience, which all interact with the performance in a major way.

CP: What attracts you to specific sites?

TR: Sometimes they just come out at me. I am walking down the block, and all of a sudden a story lands in the space. Other times, I am commissioned to do a piece. Like this summer, with one week of rehearsals, I did my version of *Romeo and Juliet* in Italy. The piece turned into *Romeo and Juliet* because the balconies were so beautiful in the town. I even got an older woman to shake out a wedding dress from a window. I put performers on benches at a scenic lookout and covered them from the waist down with cloth, so it gave the illusion that they were eight feet tall. The town is so gorgeous, and most of the people have been living there all of their lives. I don't know how they see their town, but I am almost sure we reinvented it for them in some ways. I know that the neighbors were surprised, probably shocked, but ultimately pleased.

CP: The site-specific process can be an arduous one. Are there moments that stand out as particularly demanding?

TR: The most demanding thing is getting the money and permission and then dealing with the weather or the elements. Also, you have to rehearse fairly quickly. It is usually seasonal, and depending on the community, you usually do not get much time to create and perform it. You really have to be organized and figure out how you are not going to be a burden but an addition to the community. You have to be very conscious of what you are contributing and what you are disturbing.

Also, communities are never quite ready for what I propose. It's in the very nature of the beast that boundaries are going to be pushed, known quantities redefined, and feathers ruffled. Still, step by step, the art happens. Sometimes it leaves me with my mouth hanging open, wondering how so many disparate forces can actually come into focus.

o

Carriers of Consciousness

The Role of the Audience in *The Ivye Project*

By Tamar Rogoff

Site work is always multi-layered. The performers, the choreography, the music, the text, and, most importantly, the site itself contribute layers of meaning. But, for me, the quintessential part of site work is what the audience brings to the piece and how their presence enhances the work and gives it texture. This became especially clear in the creation of my site piece *The Ivye Project* (1994).

In 1992, while on a choreographic residency with a company in Lithuania, some friends and I borrowed a car and crossed the border into Belarus. We went in search of Ivye, the town where my father's family came from. We found the town and asked an apple seller in the main square where the Jews were. Almost immediately, I was introduced to six of them, all that remained from the more than 4,000 who lived there before World War II. They knew my family and took me to the house where my great-grandfather lived. Then they took me to the forest and showed me the mass graves where he and 28 other members of my family were executed and buried. Shocked by this untold family history (my father never spoke of it), I returned to the United States vowing to find my own way to mourn my relatives.

In 1994, Dancing in the Streets issued a call to artists to do site work around the world. I responded with a proposal that would take me back to Ivye for a project that would set a precedent for my site work in terms of depth of preparations, degree of investigations, and time of involvement. Assembling an international cast and crew of 100 people, I began work on *The Ivye Project*. This project was a deeply personal challenge for me, as it addressed the disappearance of many of my relatives and took place at the actual site where most of the Jewish residents of Ivye, circa 1942, were buried.

In the years since that summer, I repeatedly asked myself: How was it possible to walk into such a completely foreign and chaotic situation? How could I relate to a place where there was so much poverty and political turmoil? What kind of response did I expect to receive, especially as an outsider? I didn't know the language, I was ignorant of recent history, and I knew no one in Ivye. The answer lay in the partnerships I made in the town. Two Ivye residents in particular helped make it happen. One was an elderly Holocaust survivor. The other was the principal of the local school. Both had relatives buried in the mass graves. They were key to giving me "permission" to do the piece, which is something I emphatically believe you need when working with community.

The Ivye Project presented a significant challenge for me. I had to make a piece that would commemorate the lives of the Jews of Ivye, be true to my artistic vision, and still be meaningful to a diverse audience. Very few audience members were Jewish, and fewer still had prior experience with experimental theater. From the onset, I insisted that this was not to be labeled a "Holocaust piece." I knew how loaded that topic was and how it could alienate different factions of an audience. Guilt, pointing fingers, getting revenge, or reenacting the horrors were not on my agenda. I had simply come "home" to where my family had lived, and I wanted to connect to the warmth, intelligence, and culture that were theirs before the war.

Although *The Ivye Project* was simple and minimalist in its approach, the larger context in which we were doing our work was highly controversial. My cast included Lithuanian, Estonian, and American actors, dancers, and musicians, as well as local schoolchildren and five Holocaust survivors who had known my family firsthand. During press conferences, the Belarusan reporters blamed the non-Jewish Lithuanian and Estonian cast members who played Jewish characters for killing the Jews. The Jewish survivor community of Minsk heard rumors that there would be dancing on the graves and initially boycotted the performances.

To combat these misperceptions, our audience development included going into the schools where Soviet revisionism had wiped out all accounts of Jews in the Holocaust. We also had press conferences in the capitol in Minsk and conducted interviews. There were daily accounts of the cast and their doings in the local papers. As the project brought visitors constantly, the KGB was ever more vigilant, skulking around the forest checking on us. Adding so many foreigners to this tiny town turned it on its head.

In order to encourage our audience to come over the border from Vilnius, Lithuania, and from Minsk, some two hours away, we sent buses, helped with visas, and made the performances free. We also set up a big dining hall in the local school to give the audience members dinner before they journeyed back. Our eclectic audiences came from as far away as Moscow and Tallin, Estonia. Walking across the fields were heavy-set women with babushkas and gold teeth. Children mingled with sophisticated theater-goers from Lithuania. Twenty-six Americans, members of my board of directors, and my family joined the group. Many local children and townspeople attended more than once, drawn in by the participation of their peers.

The piece was subtle and surreal, and it needed the peacefulness of the forest as a background. Before the piece officially began, the audience gathered just outside the forest and, with the help of a translator, I was able to speak to them. I asked them to wear green capes that would distinguish them from the performers and also make a visual unity between them. I wanted to prevent their huge numbers from being a distracting presence and to cover up their T-shirts, which advertised Coca-Cola and other products.

Then Kostas Smoriganas, a star of the Lithuanian theater and cinema and a major draw for the Lithuanian audience, took over. He played my Uncle Beryl, a charismatic watchmaker who walked with a cane. My Uncle Beryl was one of the town's leaders and one of the first Jews killed and buried in the mass grave. Kostas functioned both as a guide for the audience and a guardian angel of the dead. He led the audience from scene to scene through the forest. Although the piece was anchored in movement, Kostas was able to speak directly to the audience in five languages—Russian, Yiddish, English, Polish, and Lithuanian—as they toured the forest.

Figure 77. Kostas Smoriganas as Uncle Beryl with a child from the village in *The Ivye Project* (1994). Photo courtesy of Aaron Paley, all rights reserved.

Before they entered the memorial, the audience met Kostas, who told them that they were not yet ready to enter this sacred place. Suddenly, a teenage girl from the audience darted forward, pushed him aside, and ran between the mass graves, jumping over the memorial wall at the far end of the site. Beryl then explained to the audience that jumping back into the past was forbidden and that they must follow this girl and bring her safely back into the present. The search for the girl in the forest is the impetus for going from scene to scene. In following this girl, the audience entered a realm where time has stood still. It was as if the forest held the voices and the spirits of the Jews who died there. If one entered with a certain reverential awareness, those voices could present themselves.

Throughout *The Ivye Project*, the audience members were like invisible voyeurs coming upon intimate love scenes, private jokes, and family occasions. Universal symbols of home were present in the forest: a child's bed, a table for two set with china and a samovar, a card table, an old wooden dining table with seating for 12 and set for a Passover Seder, and a window frame that hung from the boughs of a tree. Some scenes in the piece were designed for the audience to just walk by, while others were designed so that the audience formed a circle and watched for several minutes. In longer scenes, they were seated. In a clearing where two paths crossed, we built a stage to rehearse *The Dybbuk*, our play within a play. Life in prewar Ivye could be glimpsed amid the trees as a child was sung a lullaby, a teacher took attendance, lovers intertwined, a bride crossed a field to meet her groom, a shoemaker surveyed dozens of well-worn shoes, and men played cards. There were sad moments and happy ones, dance, text and music. As the scenes accrued, the audience came to know the characters. They would happen upon private moments such as an elderly Jewish couple sitting beneath the trees, alternately feeding each other raisins and kissing.

I filled the forest with characters, not victims. This helped create an enormous sense of identification for our primarily non-Jewish audience. The Holocaust was represented by the gravesite itself, which shouted its history. As the audience walked from scene to scene, consciously or not, they knew that 2,500 Jews had walked these same paths on May 12, 1942, to their deaths.

As the piece unfolded, I couldn't help but notice the physicality of the audience as they watched the performance. In site work, necks swivel many more degrees than in the theater. Infinity is present in terms of the sky, and the horizon line stretches in all directions. In the forest, audience members were not restricted to a theater seat. They could travel to different vantage points and make choices, signifying their willingness to get close to the performers, both literally and figuratively. The questions for each person became, "How close do I want to get?" "What are my boundaries as an audience member?"

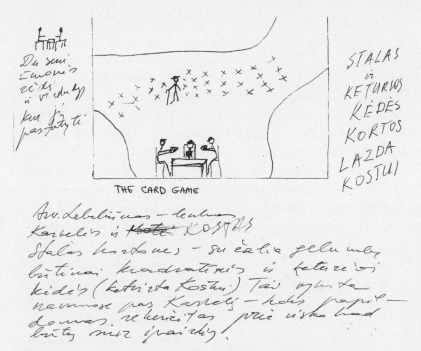

THE CARD GAME

STALAS
ir
KETURIOS
KĖDĖS
KORTOS
LAZDA
KOSTUI

Figure 78. Rogoff's storyboard image for the card game in the forest.

Figure 79. The realization of the storyboard concept of the card game. Photo courtesy of Aaron Paley, all rights reserved.

I observed how present people were by the expressions on their faces and where they chose to place themselves in relation to the action. Sometimes when the group moved on to the next scene, an audience member would linger, as if he or she was unready to leave the previous scene. Some people kept their distance, satisfied to watch the action from farther back, possibly with an obstructed view. I had created opportunities for audience members to observe each other watching. When the audience's architecture dictated that they be in a circle or across from each other, did they take in not just the scene but also each other?

During *The Ivye Project*, the forest was filled with life and musicians were everywhere. After more than an hour of walking through the woods following the action, they came full circle back to the memorial. It was twilight, and the walk to the last scene was long and uncharacteristically quiet. Uncle Beryl, the guide, had his arm around "the girl from the present," lovingly ushering her back from the past. It seemed like the forest had emptied. There was no sign of the shoemakers or the band of amateurs raucously rehearsing *The Dybbuk*. Conspicuously absent were the voices of the schoolchildren. The music had also quietly disappeared. Where there once was life, there now was a gaping absence.

Before the audience could enter the memorial, they were asked to remove their capes. It was in this moment that their status as audience dramatically changed. In researching this piece, I spoke with elderly survivors who knew my family and who also had family buried in Ivye's mass graves. Often they recounted with great difficulty how their loved ones were forced to take off their clothing and whole families, mothers, and teenage sons saw each other naked in their last seconds together in that very same forest. Having worn their capes throughout the piece, taking them off for the last scene became a significant act. The audience now represented themselves; they became visible as individuals. Did that play any part in why a layer of self-consciousness and responsibility descended on my audience as they stepped into this sacred space? Hundreds of people recalling thousands of people. Each of the cast members reappeared for a brief moment, peering out half hidden by the boundary wall. For a moment all were present. And then all were gone. The Jews had truly vanished, and the historical truth resounded. The guide waved one last good-bye and disappeared. The "girl from the present" picked up a trumpet that had been carelessly left behind and walked out of the memorial in the direction she had first come until she could be seen no more.

The audience remained looking at each other for some clue as to what to do next. They stood in two lines, with the mass graves between them, seeing themselves and connecting to the depth of the experience. They seemed immobilized for quite some time. Uncharacteristically, no one clapped. What I wanted and what I think I perceived was the sense that each of them had lost something irreplaceable and precious. That a whole population was gone and that we, Jews and non-Jews, relatives and nonrelatives, were the poorer.

The audience slowly dispersed, some going toward a commemorative stone, others leaving the memorial but milling around just outside. Everyone seemed unsettled. Some wept. After a while, people talked in small groups. One woman believed her reaction was so deep because in a past life she must have been Jewish. Another spoke for the first time about her memories of being a little girl and her family hiding Jews. Elderly residents of Ivye remembered how windy it was the day of May 12, 1942. I remained there until the last person left. This postperformance group processing time was the audience's improvisation of a kind of eulogy; it functioned as an epilogue and a necessary bridge out of the forest.

Inherent in site work is a set of layers beyond and beneath the artistic creation. Site work happens in a real place with real history. Enhancing the site work is the choreographer's and the audience's sense of this reality. This is the crux of site work and why it is essential for the choreographer to take advantage of what the audience brings to a piece. To disregard this unique partnership of audience and place dilutes the power of the site, its history, the hosting community, and the performance. In *The Ivye Project,* the layers were the foundation of the work; these included my history and connection to Ivye, my daughter as a cast member, our relatives buried there, the mass gravesite, the connections between audience members and people buried there, possible links between audience members and perpetrators of the crime, and finally the Holocaust survivors who were cast members. These layers, some of which were consciously acknowledged and others subconsciously present, were essential for the effectiveness of the project. I am hopeful that because of these layers, *The Ivye Project* was able to rekindle an empathy that could stretch not only back to 1942 but also forward to the present and beyond.

I have fundamentally changed as a result of *The Ivye Project.* I am writing this 13 years later, as if the performance were yesterday. In fact, it continues to live with me. The 18 children who participated could now be parents; the Holocaust survivors have all died or moved away. After centuries, there are no Jews left in Ivye. The trees remain, having witnessed *The Ivye Project* in 1994, and perhaps somewhere in their rings having recorded the horror of 1942. But I often wonder if the audiences of 1994 think of that summer and what must have been for them a most singular experience.

14

Martha Bowers

Martha Bowers is the executive director of Dance Theatre Etcetera, based in Brooklyn, New York. Since 1993, DTE has presented major site-specific works on the Red Hook, Brooklyn, waterfront as well as in other national and international locations. From the streets of Cork, Ireland, to a former electronics factory in Massachusetts, Bowers's performance events have brought a multifaceted view to local places and communities. Bowers has worked as a teacher of and advocate for arts in education in universities and public schools across the nation. She is also the recipient of a 2002 BAXten award in arts education as well as numerous choreographic fellowships and commissions for site-specific projects. Bowers has worked as a consultant for the Third Millenium Foundation, designing and implementing the Dance for Tolerance initiative. Bowers and Kloetzel discussed her work at her home in Brooklyn on April 22, 2006.

An Interview with Martha Bowers

MK: What is your definition of site-specific dance?

MB: I'll give you my short answer. Site-specific dance is a conscious, performative response to questions concerning locational identity. However, the range of new technologies available and the addition of virtual space as a locus for art making render this a much more complex question. In fact, new technology has made the whole notion of location a much more complicated concept. There are virtual locations, discursive locations, and also actual material locations. Artists' interactions with, responses to, or interventions in our experience of these many kinds of space are redefining the field at this point. If, in previous decades, at least one impetus for artists to leave galleries and theaters was the urge to engage with the world more directly, to go to the public and private spaces where issues were actually played out, then it makes perfect sense that artists see virtual space as a territory ripe for intervention. The performing arts are coming more slowly into the question of how you meld technology with site-specific work. There are notable exceptions, of course. Perhaps because we, as dancers, carry our traditions literally within our bodies, we are slower or more reluctant to adapt to new strategies of art making that incorporate technology. Or perhaps it's just that it's expensive!

MK: What attracts you to making site-specific work?

MB: When I was a dance student in the 1970s, there was a prevalent notion in the modern dance world that choreographers were solitary geniuses who toiled away in private in their studios, Martha Graham being the preeminent model. I always struggled with that formula, the artist as solitary genius. It was lonely, and what did I really know at that point in my life? A limited amount! I found myself attracted to those artists evolving different models of art making such as Meredith Monk, Allan Kaprow, and Vito Acconci.

I think what really attracted me to site work was the idea that you were making work in the context of everyday life. It displaced the focus of the work from the individual and redirected it to a location, a community, and/ or issues related to that space. Also, site work necessitates collaboration, not just with other artists but with a whole range of individuals and organizations that are linked to the site. The whole process of making site work as a collective enterprise really redefined my thinking about the role I played as a choreographer/director. I was attracted to site work because it was a form of engaged art making.

I had a whole different awareness of what I was doing as an artist when I began. I was much less aware of the history of the field. I knew what excited me: scale, perspective, placing art in non-art contexts, working with a combination of professional artists and community members, operating outside the power construct of the New York downtown dance scene. I was responding to the excitement of working in contexts other than theaters. It took some time to develop a reflective practice, to discover a rationale for creating site works.

MK: Did political and social issues influence your early site works?

MB: Yes, I think I've always been interested in human rights and politics. I was brought up discussing politics at the dinner table. I was just entering my teens at the end of the 1960s, but I was certainly aware of the civil rights movement, the Vietnam War, the student protests, and the struggle against apartheid in South Africa. So it seemed a part of who I was to bring these concerns into my work as an artist. In the 1980s, I was part of a group of dancers who formed Dancers for Disarmament. This organization of dancers, dance presenters, and administrators produced dance concerts that included talks by scientists and policy experts on issues relating to nuclear proliferation. We initiated study groups and in 1982 joined with PAND (Performing Artists for Nuclear Disarmament) in a caravan that toured the Northeast, performing works that reflected on the issue of disarmament. Bread and Puppet, Mabou Mines, Dancers for Disarmament's repertory company, and other solo artists like Paul Zaloom took part in the tour. I remember performing a work I choreographed called *Tango Echo Bravo Romeo November* outdoors on a Native American reservation during that tour. This all took place during the Reagan years.

I have always struggled with the idea of making "political art." But during these years with Dancers for Disarmament, I began to see the relationship between choreography and protest, that there were many strategies for using movement as a form of protest, a vehicle for cross-cultural communication or using the choreographic process as a means of exploring an issue.

MK: Were there any other organizations or programs that stood out as particularly helpful in your early site efforts?

MB: I was introduced to the concept of the public artist early on in my career as an employee of the CETA Artists Project. CETA, which stands for the Comprehensive Employment Training Act, was started here in New York during the Carter administration. It was a government employment program administered by the Cultural Council Foundation from 1979 to 1981. Artists were employed and paid to spend a portion of their time on their own artistic practice and the rest in activities that benefited the general public such as performing at festivals, schools, hospitals, museums, and prisons. That was a really interesting period. Not since the Works Project Administration Artists Project in the 1930s and 1940s had anything like that been attempted in the United States. The dance companies I worked with didn't have to pay me; the government paid me. But the companies had to agree to do free performances in public spaces. Instead of being artists on the extremities of society, we felt we were really serving society. We had a recognized role and were actively participating in the cultural life of our community. That was very different than being an avant-garde artist performing in black boxes in downtown New York for a handful of friends and family. It was very rewarding and, unfortunately, very short-lived.

MK: Is this when you began to incorporate community members into your work?

MB: Yes, soon thereafter. A formative experience occurred when I was hired in the 1980s to create dances for nondancers in Ireland. I was exposed to the

European community arts movement. The concept of the "community artist" was much more developed in Europe. In the United States, the lines between what was considered high art and community art were clearly drawn. Artists whose work involved community members were often devalued as amateur. It was a really interesting challenge to use my artistic skills—whatever kinds of techniques, methodologies, strategies, and training I had—to create valuable aesthetic dance pieces on bodies full of physical expertise from their day-to-day lives, but with no formal dance training. And to make dances that had relevance to the Irish communities in which they were performed. It was during those years that I learned how to work effectively with community performers and create choreography for specific sites. I learned to see what was available, that is, what was already occurring in a site that I could use as part of the choreographic strategy. For example, there happened to be many young mothers with three and four children in the town of Wexford where I primarily worked. So I made dances for mothers and their children in car parks with precision pram-rolling to the Beach Boys "I Get Around."

MK: Could you talk a bit about your site-specific process?

MB: My work seems to lie between the worlds of site-specific performance and community arts. Each project generally involves community members as performers as well as professional artists. In terms of process, there's usually a long development period for each project. Once I land on a site, either through my own curiosity and interest in a place or through a commission for a very specific project, there's a long period of library research as well as field research carried out through interviews, storytelling workshops, and working in dialogue with community members to hear stories from multiple perspectives.

I also like to spend time in a place observing it, feeling it, understanding how it operates on a day-to-day basis, both in the present and in a prismatic way through layers of time. I am often attracted to industrial ruins, places in transition from one thing to another. For example, when I was working on a piece in Lincoln, Nebraska, I could stand in the train yards and smell the prairie. I could imagine the land before and after it was settled—the buffalo, the Native American camps, the steam trains, the hoboes who camped there during the Depression. All those events were still present in the current manifestation of that place and became part of the work we created called *Blue Train*. And there were people who embodied that history who became part of the cast: the drummers from the Omaha tribe, dancers from the Lakota Sioux tribe, retired railroad workers. The railroad men even taught me the language

Figure 80. Dancers and musicians in the train yard in *Blue Train* (1997). Photo by Peter Peirce.

of hand and lantern signals they used to direct the train's engineer before radios were available. So, as each project develops, a team of collaborators is formed that includes professional performers, designers, composers, musicians, and community partners. They become part of the creative process.

Then there's a period of shaping, which I think is my key role: to take the research, the personal histories and reflections, the knowledge I've gained about the site, and the skills of my collaborators to develop a concept, a structure, and specific artistic strategies that will give the work a visual and aural language. In each project, I try to be mindful of the multiple perspectives that arise or resonate in that particular space. Usually the architecture or the predominant media reflects one perspective, but the unwritten ones are those we try to amplify through the work. So it's a process of merging personal storytelling with spectacle.

Equally important is the aftermath, the self-evaluation. Is there anything that comes out of this project? Have any useful networks been formed? Is it going to address anything further? That's the phase where I try to assess the impact of a project, both its aesthetic and social outcomes. In future site works, I would like to include scholars and activists on the creative team who can take part in an ongoing conversation about the project, its goals, and its aftermath.

MK: Do you feel that site-specific performance facilitates an exchange between the site and the community?

MB: Let's talk specifically about Red Hook for a moment. The impetus for my first project there, *On the Waterfront,* was simply the site, this hauntingly beautiful abandoned waterfront. Once I started to do the research, what came to the forefront was the deep, historical connection between the community of Red Hook and its waterfront. I was interested in trying to connect what I saw was going to be the next huge economic resource of the community—the waterfront—to the people who lived in the housing projects. That relationship had been severed basically; nobody went to the waterfront because it was deemed too dangerous. So it was a very conscious decision in this project to locate the performance on the waterfront and to cast people from the local community—kids, and seniors who lived in the housing projects—as performers in the work. I wanted to stimulate an inclusive dialogue about waterfront development, as well as address what voices might have a place at the table in the decision-making process.

That was the very first work. It seeded an annual community arts festival, now called the Red Hook Waterfront Arts Festival, which is produced by my organization, Dance Theatre Etcetera. It's a very inclusive and well-beloved free outdoor event that features both professional performers and local youth groups.

We are now developing a piece that deals with the crisis in affordable housing and gentrification that's happening in Red Hook. We're right at the beginning of working on that piece with an activist organization that does housing advocacy.

MK: What an interesting process to go into a place that has been economically depressed and now be doing a piece about gentrification there!

MB: It is interesting. I've learned a lot about the political process of economic development and the power of developers. These are all things that my site work led me to understand in a more complex way: how a city functions, who holds the reins, who makes the decisions, and what power a community can have if people organize and give voice to their position and their demands.

MK: Did you discover similar concerns when you brought your 1998 Red Hook site work *Safe Harbor* to Europe?

MB: When we were invited to bring that piece to Ireland, in a way we were exploring the theme of the work in reverse. In the original production of *Safe Harbor*, we were looking at Irish immigration to New York. Taking the piece back to Ireland when it was becoming a very popular destination for immigrants, the work focused on the challenges the Irish faced, as they were becoming a multicultural society. Under the auspices of the Institute for Choreography and Dance located in the Shandon section of Cork, composer Tiye Giraud and I went back and forth to do workshops and talk to various constituents of the community for approximately two years. It was a good lesson in flexibility, and the culminating event was definitely not what I had originally envisioned but something that evolved very organically as the community got involved. The point of the project was to build bridges between the traditional Irish Catholic community, a very conservative community that had experienced a lot of discrimination and poverty over the years of British occupation, and the newly arrived immigrants from Africa and Eastern Europe. We explored the community of Shandon's reaction to the influx of people of different colors and races. In the end, it became a huge one-day street fair on the theme of tolerance and multicultural appreciation. Almost every performing group in the town of Cork, from youth theater groups to senior storytellers, all participated in creating work that addressed the theme through their own process.

The fact that the community consented to street performances at all was a minor miracle. They were very fearful of losing control of their streets. So the project's importance lay in the fact that it brought issues of intolerance out into the open, literally into public space. The collaborations that took place across diverse cultural traditions were very significant.

MK: Have there been sites where you were specifically commissioned to address redevelopment issues?

MB: *The Dream Life of Bricks* certainly focused on local economic development. I was commissioned by MASSMoCA, a new contemporary art museum in North Adams, Massachusetts, to make a piece that would reflect the community's responses to the transformation of a local industrial complex into an art museum. Since the 1800s, the site was the primary economic resource of a predominantly blue-collar community. I worked with women in their 60s, 70s, and 80s who had spent most of their lives on the production lines when the site was an electronics factory. They became the primary spokespersons, representing the community's feelings about this urban renewal scheme. The topic might sound rather dry, but the site was so evocative; it consisted of huge empty nineteenth-century industrial brick buildings. I approached it as the repository of the community's collective dreams. We constructed a bed

Figure 81. Bowers with street performers in Cork, Ireland, in *Safe Harbour/CORK* (2001). Photo courtesy of Dance Theatre Etcetera.

for each of the women made of bricks, each with a beautiful silk pillow. The viewer entered into the work through their dreams and memories. There was a river that ran through the site. We floated their words underwater, so you saw their memories shimmering on the riverbed below you as you crossed a bridge.

MK: Are there any main themes that site work brings up for you?

MB: It's something that changes slightly with each work. But I would say the concepts of public space and participatory democracy are key themes—that your work as an artist can foster participation, by engaging people in dialogue and then amplifying that dialogue through some kind of spectacle or performance. Perhaps a discursive space is carved out about a particular location or

Figure 82. Exploring the dreams of a community. Dancers on site in *The Dream Life of Bricks* (2002) at MASSMoCA. Photo by Kevin Kennefick.

performance that reveals an inherent power structure embodied in the site, which can then be acknowledged and addressed. So I think it's largely about the concepts of public space and participatory democracy.

MK: Do you find those themes resonate in each site?

MB: Yes, but as each project gets closer to the ground, the works get much more specific. For example, they might be about economic development and who benefits, or about crime and who's responsible.

MK: What do you think is most advantageous about doing site work, and what is most challenging?

MB: Let's see, advantageous . . . it's really expensive; it's really time-consum- ing; it's really complicated . . . [laughing]

MK: I'm hearing a lot on the challenging end.

MB: But I think those are its advantages, too. I don't think it's for the faint of heart. I like the bridge site work, which can build between artists and people from a lot of different walks of life. It demands that I increase my knowledge base on a number of subjects. I have to learn about social organizations and their goals, the demographics of different communities. I have to understand historical information, work with local police, and communicate with local politicians. I have to wear a lot of hats, and I like that challenge. I like trying to understand what it would take for a particular person to say yes to a project. It's so much easier to say no. I really have to do my homework about why a particular person might be interested or what the project might offer as a reciprocal benefit for their efforts. Taking the position of "The Other" is a really valuable skill.

MK: Do you consider your site work a form of activism?

MB: Again, that's a complicated question. Art can draw on the power of metaphor and on spectacle to get attention. Artists can put a human face on an issue and dig beyond the sound bites for a more complex depiction of a situation. We are barraged daily with images from the dominant media, selling us everything from underwear to fear. Governments, corporations, and major media organizations use imagery and metaphor, mass spectacle, costume, and music. Artists working in public space can offer a counterhistory.

MK: Do you feel that movement plays a large role in activist art?

MB: Absolutely. I mean, look at the choreography of, say, the AIDS organization ACT UP. They very consciously use movement in their demonstrations to create circles, to disrupt time and normal activity in a public place. They choreograph with metaphor—standing up and falling down recalls death and resistance. Their ensemble structure becomes a symbol of solidarity.

Las Madres de la Plaza de Mayo in Argentina still assemble weekly, demanding the return of and information on their disappeared children. The women walk in a circle slowly, costumed in black, in a public place associated with a repressive male regime. Their choreography is powerful, a metaphor for their implacable will to protest the murders of their children. It shifts time, purpose, intention, and meaning in that public space by virtue of how they assemble and move.

MK: Sometimes I feel like we treat movement as if it's implied, but I think it's necessary to be specific about its possibilities.

MB: This is something I thought about a lot when we did our last project, *Angels & Accordions*. We were asked to do an event for an enormous cemetery here in Brooklyn. It was tricky. It's still an active cemetery, so there are people to whom this space is very sacred. They go there to sit by the gravesite of their loved ones. So how a crowd would come in to view a performance and move through the space (in what spirit or what kind of mindfulness) was really key to the success of the project. It was also important because this site is a valuable resource to Brooklyn; it's 500 acres of park space and exquisite funerary monuments that will no longer be an active cemetery soon because there is no more room to bury people. So the question becomes: can it become a cultural center that allows access to the general public, but also mediates public access in a way that is conducive to its ongoing purpose as a cemetery?

MK: Your choreographic process sounds like it has grown and transformed a lot over time.

MB: Well, certainly what my organization does has expanded. In the past few years I have been putting more energy into building an organization that produces a variety of events and conducts extensive arts and media education programs. It has been a way to both extend and sustain our work in Red Hook.

You know, I started off as a young choreographer with a fairly narrow idea of what choreography was and what my life would look like as an artist. Now I have a much more expansive or complex view of my work as an artist or what I consider choreography to be. I like to think of choreography more broadly as social choreography. I remember *Safe Harbor*, which I think was my most successful work, was basically reviewed as a concert piece. The reviewer had lots to say about the site and the community participants, but she singled out the "choreography" for criticism. To me, she completely missed the point. The choreography wasn't solely about the movement choices for the dancers; it was the structure for moving the audience through a place. It began with the audience's efforts simply to get to the performance, as there was no subway in Red Hook and bus service was notably infrequent. It was about our movements as artists through a community, as well as a set of issues: immigration, waterfront access, economic development.

For the field to develop, it's important to have a critical language that understands it for what it is and doesn't try to evaluate it based on previous models of dance-making for proscenium spaces. We need critics and scholars familiar with the whole process of site work: the interrelationship between the art and the community and the multilevel interaction with the site. To me, that's part of the choreography. And that's why writing about site-specific dance is crucial.

o

Choreography for Uncontrollable Contexts

By Martha Bowers

> Knowing what you don't know is the beginning of knowing.
>
> Chinese proverb

Site artists make conscious decisions to situate their work in non-art contexts—in the middle of messy, often chaotic spaces where life takes place as opposed to the controlled conditions of theaters, galleries, or museums.

We exist in a shrinking world, one saturated with information that doesn't seem to make us any wiser. Google Earth lets us climb into God's eye and zoom down through layers of geography to view the details of our own rooftop; Al Gore's *An Inconvenient Truth* gives us graphic evidence of our species' heavy footprint on the earth. We can see the big picture now; we can see the interconnectedness of all things, yet we seem no closer to alleviating deteriorating environmental conditions or solving major conflicts.

Site artists are willing to dive into the middle of the mess—to engage with people, places, and issues in an effort to make sense of the density of contemporary life. For me, this plunge begins by realizing how much I don't know, that teasing meaning out of a body of information is a complicated process. I acknowledge that I will have to excavate the layers of meaning inherent in every site in order to come close to understanding a site's prismatic and multifaceted truth. Second, I have learned to embrace the uncontrollable conditions of public space as a part of my choreographic strategy.

As a young artist arriving in New York City in the late 1970s, I was the product of the aesthetic experimentations Allan Kaprow and his contemporaries had carried out: Kaprow's Happenings; Meredith Monk's large-scale, multi-sited works such as *Juice* and *Vessel*; conceptual artist Vito Acconci's explorations of his own body as a site of conflict; Trisha Brown's choreography that placed dancers on New York City rooftops. The boundaries between artistic disciplines, art, and life were well blurred.

While intent on pursuing a career as a choreographer, I kept stumbling into situations that required creating work outside conventional theaters and with nonprofessional artists: a job with the CETA Arts Project; a commission to create a piece for the grounds of a home for retired sailors; an offer to work in Ireland to choreograph for a largely untrained local community group; an opportunity to choreograph demonstrations as a member of Dancers against Disarmament. I wasn't making conscious choices based on a carefully considered personal manifesto about the kind of art I wanted to create. I was using my wits and my training to respond to opportunities that presented themselves, and I was finding ways to continue working given economic limitations. These experiences provided a very valuable education that helped me acquire a new set of skills. These skills, bundled into a very bulky, much hyphenated resume, add up to "site-specific community artist." It is interesting to look back and realize that all these different forms of art making I did were exactly what Kaprow was talking about when he described the "blurring of art and life." I had separated the above experiences from what I thought was my "real career" as choreographer. But, in fact, they were determining the kind of artist I was becoming.

Staging Red Hook: Site-Specific Projects in Red Hook, Brooklyn

On the Waterfront (1993)

In order to reflect on my site practice, I will focus on a body of work I developed over a period of 14 years (1993–2007) in the waterfront community of Red Hook, a small peninsular portion of South Brooklyn that sticks out into New York Harbor. Red Hook is the crucible in which I forged a methodology for creating site-specific work in community contexts. It is also a place that has undergone a dramatic transformation. During the years I have worked there, I have been consciously adapting my artistic process and the performance strategies of subsequent projects in response to the changing socioeconomic conditions in the area.

My first project in Red Hook, entitled *On the Waterfront,* was, in a way, an effort to reconcile the divide in my head between what I considered my activist and community-based work and my professional choreographic career. I recognized that I liked, even preferred, working on site in community contexts as opposed to rehearsing in studios in preparation for a proscenium theater performance. I realized that I had been contending with a blend of aesthetics, activist agendas, and diverse peoples and situations my whole career. Given the amount of work I had made in public spaces, I had developed a certain amount of expertise in factoring the uncontrollable into the process of choreographing for these locations. I was raising a stepson and wanted to work in the place I lived—Brooklyn.

Walking through Red Hook in the early 1990s was like walking through a ruin. Boarded-up stores, abandoned piers, people hurrying their children through the streets in fear—all drew a vivid picture of a community in decline. But it was also extremely beautiful. The abandoned waterfront was hauntingly peaceful, especially at sunset when the sky over the harbor was awash in color.

The children were full of stories, scratching and beating time on their desktops as they daydreamed of a better future, often in the form of a trip to Disney World. Their formidable grandmothers, who populated the local senior center, sighed tiredly but with an entirely unshakeable faith that this too they could survive. Bush Sr. was in the White House, the economy was in a recession, and we were briefly at war. The Internet as we know it now did not exist.

I began a phase of participatory research by facilitating dance, theater, and storytelling workshops at a local elementary school and senior center. I discovered the chief concern of most community members was safety. Additional historical research including interviews with old timers from the neighborhood, as well as developers and politicians revealed that this blue-collar community had always struggled with violence. The much-beloved local elementary school principal had just been killed in a drug shoot out.

But this was also a neighborhood in transition. The waterfront, historically the heart of the area's economy, but dormant since the demise of the shipping industry in the late 1970s, was now at the center of many commercial plans. There was an official planning process taking place to outline goals for community development, particularly with regard to Red Hook's most valuable resource—its waterfront.

Key questions began to take shape: Could a site-specific performance project both involve the community and encourage broader participation in the dialogue on waterfront development? Could the project be a vehicle for local residents to articulate the meaning of their community? Could they overcome the media manufactured images of Red Hook as one of the most dangerous areas in New York City? These questions framed the creative process of *On the Waterfront*.

The piece was performed in a series of contiguous empty warehouses located on an abandoned pier reaching out into the water. In previous years, the pier would have been teeming with Irish and Italian longshoremen emptying ships of their cargoes of coffee, bananas, and sugarcane. But in November 1993, the warehouses were vast brick caverns echoing with the sound of pigeons nestled in the rafters and of waves washing through at high tide. Billed as a site-specific performance/walking tour, the audience followed a group of musicians from warehouse to warehouse. In each, performances were staged depicting different chapters in Red Hook history as articulated by a specific community group's point of view. For example, one of the first and only warehouses that was in use housed antique trolley cars (precursors of the New York City subway) that were being restored. The fifth-graders I had worked with at the local elementary school had written raps and dances about the neighborhood that we staged in, on, and around the trolley cars. The seniors' section was largely about faith as the source of their strength. In their warehouse, we erected a small stage on which they sat or stood to recite a group poem, sing hymns, and dance to the beat of tambourines. We transformed the vast warehouse into a waterfront cathedral by filling it with hundreds of votive candles. In other warehouses, the dancers performed work dances to the shouted encouragements of "Work harder now!" as sung by composer David Pleasant. The concluding section depicted a violent confrontation between striking dockworkers and management, as cast members hurled rocks at the enormous iron doors of the last warehouse. The children then slowly opened the doors and scrambled into the space chanting, "Translate the rage, translate the rage; turn your hatred into sudden change." Providing a creative platform for diverse sectors of the community to articulate the past and imagine the future provided both a history of violence and also its antidote.

Reciprocity is a critical component of any site-specific project that seeks to engage local community members: what is being exchanged, and is the exchange mutually beneficial? *On the Waterfront* had a cast of local elementary school students and senior citizens, as well as professional dancers, musicians, and designers. It was produced by Dancing in the Streets, a Manhattan-based arts organization that presents site-specific dance. What did the project offer the community? Participating students got to take dance and theater classes, perform in front of their community, and articulate their perspective. The seniors also got free workshops that provided opportunities for them to share memories, reaffirm the important roles they had played in community and family life, and celebrate their faith. The developer on whose property the work took place benefited from positive media attention, which helped him attract tenants. The artists enjoyed working with on-site challenges, playing roles informed by history, increasing their dance vocabulary by learning a variety of movement styles, and getting paid, albeit minimally. It was also important to know that the work was made of, by, and for the community. Outside audience members were welcome, but frankly, we expected very few. It was really made as an event for local people to learn about their own community from various points of view. Very few of the students or their families had ever been to the waterfront, even though it was a short walk from the housing projects where they lived. The project budget was tiny. While Dancing in the Streets did send out press releases, we were surprised and delighted when the ever-adventurous Elizabeth Zimmer, dance critic for the *Village Voice*, came. She described it as "arte povera," made of the simplest materials. She was right. I had to look hard at the limited resources available and make good use of them: the space, the people, a talented team of collaborators, and a lot of goodwill.

Figure 83. Depicting the immigrant experience as one chapter of Red Hook history. Homer Avila, Jessica Roseman, Scot Willingham, and Lisa Bleyer in *On the Waterfront* (1993). Photo by Charles T. Wemple, courtesy of Dance Theatre Etcetera.

Safe Harbor (1998)

On the Waterfront seeded many subsequent events—art festivals, arts education programs, parades, and arts residencies. By 1998 Red Hook was slowly beginning to feel the benefits of many urban renewal initiatives. Bush Sr. was out of the White House, and Clinton was in. The recession and the Gulf War were behind us. Many were exploring the vast new potential of the Internet.

New immigrants were entering the United States in huge numbers, often settling in New York City. I had been teaching at a public high school that opened in 1994 to serve immigrant teens. I was seeing through their eyes the deteriorating conditions globally that drove their families from their native countries. Locally, there was a lot of interest in waterfront property as environmental conditions in the harbor and rivers around New York City were improving.

The next project I initiated in Red Hook, called *Safe Harbor*, explored the impact of immigration on the area. It also called attention to the improved conditions of New York City's waterways and to efforts being made to include public access to Red Hook's waterfront in local development plans. Improved social conditions also encouraged us to try doing *Safe Harbor* at night, both to include the sunset as part of the show and to challenge the audience to experience Red Hook after dark.

Again, the site was the waterfront, but instead of a single pier, there were now the beginnings of a path along a designated stretch of waterfront. The site suggested the structure for the work: two parallel journeys in which the cast played a variety of immigrants from different times and places. They performed entirely in and on the water (on boats, barges, floating stages, or literally in the water), as the audience traveled along the shoreline to view their progress. Along the way, the audience stopped to hear from local residents who came out to tell their family's history or to see Time Warner Cable's massive satellite dishes being used for projections, turning them into cosmic ears listening in on conversations that drifted between present and past generations. For example, an image of a nineteenth-century immigrant's face appears; then the words, "Are you listening?" Then an image of their contemporary descendant, "Yes!" A conversation via projected words continued on the satellite dishes as if they were telephones that crossed time, enabling long dead ancestors to speak to their descendants. It was the only section of the work unaccompanied by live music. The intention was to allow the relative silence of the night to mix in our imaginations with the sounds of these silent voices, letting the past leak into the present. All along the route, as the night grew darker, the Statue of Liberty stood in plain view as a backdrop to the performance. Cast members included the granddaughter of an Italian longshoreman who had worked the Red Hook docks, young African American women from the local housing projects, a woman in the process of becoming an Orisha, an 80-year-old Irish dance teacher, a 50-year-old African American tap dancer, an 11-year-old boy, an undocumented Mexican dancer, an Australian woman here on a student visa, and a British set designer. This very consciously diverse casting brought many points of view on immigration into the mix.

I received more funding for this project, which meant more time for development. I could be more ambitious, and I was, conceiving the work on a much grander scale than any previous project I'd undertaken. My work was getting more support and attention. The tide was also changing for Red Hook. *Safe*

Figure 84. Performing in and out of the water in Red Hook. Scot Willingham, Kim Woodford, and Allison Easter in *Safe Harbor* (1998). Photo courtesy of T. Brittain Stone.

Harbor attracted huge audiences relatively speaking (more than 2000 over a three-night run), much larger than we anticipated. They came from all parts of the City. The piece celebrated the waterfront with Irish dances, tap dances, stevedore's work songs, Ethiopian prayers, mermaids, and eloquent stories related by local barkeeps.

Anna Kisselgoff, dance critic for the *New York Times*, came and wrote a review stating that the real star of the show was Red Hook, along with local barkeep Sonny Balzano. In terms of excavating Red Hook history, meeting Sonny was like hitting the mother lode. He operated a bar on the ground floor of a house that had been home to generations of family members dating back to the 1800s. And Sonny's bar was quickly becoming a hot, new underground nightspot—the first establishment that signified Red Hook was on its way to becoming trendy! The audience visited Sonny's as part of *Safe Harbor*. He emerged from his bar to hold forth on his version of Red Hook history. The audience was asked to thank him by collectively serenading his elderly mother (who poked her head out a top-floor window) with one of her favorite songs from the 1940s (the sheet music for this song was included in the program).

Craft and the Process of Questioning

One of the benefits of continuing to make work in the same locale over a number of years is the almost unlimited amount of both time and access I can have to the site. This long-term project has given me a wonderful opportunity to learn more about the craft of creating site-specific events, and I have discovered that choosing the movement vocabulary and choreographic strategies for site-specific work is a fundamentally different process than choreographing for the stage.

Choreography can be thought of as a map. Generally, in concert dance forms, the map is memorized in the dancer's muscles and brain. It determines their spatial paths, the specific movements—their timing, size, quality, and speed. It determines in minute detail how the space is traversed. This map assumes a rectangular space that defines a specific relationship between the human body and the spatial dimensions of a proscenium space.

Choreography for site-specific performance can also be thought of as cartography, but of larger, more varied locales—architectural, natural, and even virtual. It can map a physical or discursive site, or it can become a time map that gives a prismatic sense of events of the past and present happening simultaneously within a location. It can provide a map to guide the viewers' eyes and senses to experience a place in a fresh way. Scale changes, perspective changes, and sight lines are often not simply frontal. Movement can easily become dwarfed by the enormity of the space or lost among the many types of movement already going on in the site. For example, in *Safe Harbor*, a dancer on a jetty was easily upstaged by enormous ships passing just behind the jetty. Highly technical movement is often not possible given the terrain. To my eye, it often looks out of place and artificial.

A different movement palette is required. A movement phrase that seemed extremely fast and beautifully detailed in the studio can seem like just a lot of flailing around outside. The key is to acknowledge these conditions and make movement choices that work with or in conscious juxtaposition to the site. The human eye reads contrast, so working with speeds that contrast the tempo of the site is often useful. One technique I use is fracturing the timing of natural movement, "pedestrian movement," or movement that occurs in social contexts (folk or social dancing). I also try to be observant of what movement is happening in the site and incorporate that as well.

Once the "frame" is established, everything becomes part of the performance whether you intend it to or not. Making conscious choices to use this to one's advantage often provides for rich and unexpected results. In other words, it's helpful to work with what's out of your control rather than trying to totally control what's happening. As such, we create movement based on the specific limitations of a space. We rehearse on-site so movement is created for existing conditions: we rehearsed *in* the harbor to create the opening movement ritual for *Safe Harbor*; we rehearsed students *on* the trolleys being restored in a warehouse for *On the Waterfront*. At times, the performance frame simply suggests we look at what is naturally occurring as part of the performance—a sunset, a typical night at a local bar, or a boat passing by.

I want the work to echo the culture of the community, so I consciously select a cast that reflects its racial configuration. In *Safe Harbor*, we were able to make a statement about the blending of African American and Irish cultures that occurred over the years by embedding those movement forms in the choreography. I often ask the dancers to learn new movement vocabulary: body percussion taught to us by composer David Pleasant, who was raised in the Gullah culture of the Georgia Sea Islands, or Irish dances coached by Jo McNamara, a marvelous woman now in her eighties who is a walking encyclopedia of Irish dance forms.

My notion of what the choreography of a project entails has expanded exponentially. It is not only what the performers are doing during the final public performances; it also includes the many interactions between artists and community members that have been part of the process of making the work. It includes people from different cultures, races, or socioeconomic backgrounds crossing cultural comfort zones to interact because they are involved in the project. It includes the journey the audience takes to reach the site and to follow the performance through a location.

Present Tense

Red Hook stares straight across the harbor at the soaring monuments of Lower Manhattan. Only a small stretch of water separated it from the events of 9/11. Winds carried eerie bits of paper and dust across the harbor that littered local streets. Many men from the two local firehouses, as some of the first to respond, were killed.

In June 2006, the cover of *Time Out New York* declared "Red Hook Has Arrived." Small buildings in need of gut renovations have started going for over $1 million. There are luxury lofts for sale and a new upscale grocery store. There are fine French restaurants, clothing boutiques, banks, and pharmacies as well as the usual bodegas around the projects. The waterfront is teeming with a variety of businesses and nowhere to park. A water taxi runs to Red Hook now. Ikea is moving in soon.

I believe Red Hook is a microcosm that reflects changes in American culture in general. While it is definitely safer here now for most people and there are more jobs, few jobs pay more than minimum wage or offer much opportunity in the way of career advancement. The young people are still as concerned about their own safety as they were in 1993, but fear of the police is now greater than fear of the drug dealers. The gap is widening, as it is in the rest of the country, between the have's and the have-not's.

I am sure the solitary herons I used to meet late at night on the piers have left.

It's not news that pioneering artists are often the vanguard of gentrification. The primary question now is: who is benefiting from Red Hook's gentrification? The answer is complex. For one, my organization, Dance Theatre Etcetera, is benefiting, but I am aware that the benefits have not reached everyone. We have been given rent-free space in a newly renovated waterfront building, while others suffer eviction. This calls for a certain degree of soul searching.

I have become a lot more cynical and at the same time, to quote the late, great poet Sekou Sundiata, a "prisoner of hope." I have seen what greases the wheels of development, who makes decisions, and whose voices have little impact. Post 9/11, it is so much harder to work in public space. In former years, a casual conversation held in the cab of a local developer's pickup truck sufficed to get permission to use a site. Now there are increased security concerns, insurance issues, and endless negotiations about parking and permits. Large corporate enterprises now have a major stake in communities that often overshadow the needs of local residents. There is a price to pay for this kind of development, a price similar to that which we pay for increased national security: an intensified scrutiny and control of public space.

So the second question becomes: what kind of site-specific project is right for this time in this place? I have a notebook full of ideas for the next piece that takes place aboard the B61 bus—the bus route that runs from downtown Brooklyn to the Red Hook waterfront. It uses Global Positioning Systems (computer software that uses satellites to triangulate the user's location) to trigger a series of projections on buildings at specific bus stops while local speakers narrate the bus route according to their experience of the changing conditions in the community. The projections turn buildings inside out to reveal their histories. The bus line ends at the building that houses our new home, where people are invited to enter and . . . I don't know the rest yet. But the point is to make the new high-income or artist residents aware of the issues of the total community, both past and present, and to make one of our few remaining communal spaces—our public transportation system—the locus for a dialogue on local issues.

My own final concerns center around the following questions: Can site work shed light on our shrinking public space, our shrinking civic discourse, why only 40 percent of Americans vote? Can site work provoke questions that aren't being asked, encouraging us to reawaken our critical analysis of social conditions and move toward action? Can site work provide, if only briefly, an opportunity to build community by actively engaging in a project with diverse participants? Can it encourage us to actively make art as opposed to simply consuming it?

It's still about knowing how much you don't know but being willing to engage in actively seeking multiple truths. It is also about learning that the uncontrollable aspects of public space are exactly what make it valuable, that public space is a place full of ideological complexity where art, especially site-specific art, can play a valuable role. This is the kind of site-specific choreography that interests me—social choreography, spiritual choreography—choreography that navigates the intersections of place, heart, and public interest.

Bibliography

Site-Specific Dance and Related Topics

Adams, D., and A. Goldbard, eds. *Creative Community: The Art of Cultural Development*. New York: Rockefeller Foundation, Creativity and Culture Division, 2001.

————. *Community Culture and Globalization*. New York: Rockefeller Foundation, Creativity and Culture Division, 2002.

Anderson, Jack. *Art without Boundaries: The World of Modern Dance*. Iowa City: University of Iowa Press, 1997.

Banes, Sally. *Terpsichore in Sneakers*. Rev. ed. Middletown, Conn.: Wesleyan University Press, 1987.

————. *Democracy's Body: Judson Dance Theater, 1962–1964*. Durham, N.C.: Duke University Press, 1993.

————. *Greenwich Village 1963: Avant-Garde Performance and the Effervescent Body*. Durham, N.C.: Duke University Press, 1993.

————. "Choreographic Methods of the Judson Dance Theater." In *Moving History/Dancing Cultures: A Dance History Reader*, ed. Ann Dils and Ann Cooper Albright, 350–61. Middletown, Conn.: Wesleyan University Press, 2001.

————. "Gulliver's Hamburger: Defamiliarization and the Ordinary in the 1960s Avant-Garde." In *Reinventing Dance in the 1960s*, ed. Sally Banes, 12–13. Madison: University of Wisconsin Press, 2003.

Barreras del Rio, Petra, and John Perreault, eds. *Ana Mendieta: A Retrospective*. New York: New Museum of Contemporary Art, 1987.

Basso, Keith, and Steven Fields, eds. *Senses of Place*. Santa Fe, N.M.: School of American Research Press, 1996.

Beardsley, John. *Earthworks and Beyond: Contemporary Art in the Landscape*. 4th ed. New York: Abbeville Press, 2006.

Becker, Carol, ed. *The Subversive Imagination: Artists, Society, and Social Responsibility*. New York: Routledge, 1994.

————. *The Artist in Society: Rights, Roles, and Responsibilities*. Chicago: New Art Examiner Press, 1995.

Blau, Eleanor. "Dancing, with Piping, Bouncing, and Barking." *New York Times*, September 8, 1989. <http://query.nytimes.com/gst/fullpage.html?res=950DE2D7163EF93BA3575AC0A96F948260&scp=309&sq=site-specific+dance>, accessed January 25, 2008.

Blocker, Jane. *Where Is Ana Mendieta?* Durham, N.C.: Duke University Press, 1999.

Boettger, Suzaan. *Earthworks: Art and the Landscape of the Sixties*. Berkeley: University of California Press, 2002.

Burnham, Linda Frye, and Steven Durland, eds. *The Citizen Artist: Twenty Years of Art in the Public Arena*. Gardiner, N.Y.: Critical Press, 1998.

Carlisle, Barbara. "Salon Theatre: Homemade Bread." *Drama Review* 40, no. 4 (Winter 1996): 56–69.

Cavazzi, Deidre Marissa. "Partnering with Space: Explorations of Architecture and Environments in Site-Specific Choreography." MFA thesis, University of California, Irvine, 2006.

Cleveland, William. *Art in Other Places: Artists at Work in America's Community and Social Institutions*. Westport, Conn.: Praeger, 1992.

Cohen-Cruz, Jan, ed. *Radical Street Performance: An International Anthology*. London: Routledge, 1998.

———. *Local Acts: Community-Based Performance in the United States*. New Brunswick, N.J.: Rutgers University Press, 2005.

Copeland, Roger. *Merce Cunningham: The Modernizing of Modern Dance*. New York: Routledge, 2004.

Cotter, Holland. "Remembrance of Downtown Past." *New York Times*, September 1, 2006. <http://www.nytimes.com/2006/09/01/arts/design/01city.html?scp=111&sq=eiko+and+koma>, accessed January 25, 2008.

Crawford, Shanti. "Dancing in the Real World." *Brooklyn Rail*, October 2007. <http://www.thebrooklynrail.org/dance/octo3/redhook.html>, accessed July 27, 2008.

Cresswell, T. *In Place/Out of Place: Geography, Ideology, and Transgression*. Minneapolis: University of Minnesota Press, 1996.

de Certeau, Michel. *The Practice of Everyday Life*. Trans. Steven Rendall. Berkeley: University of California Press, 1984.

Dunning, Jennifer. "Dance: 'Art on the Beach.'" *New York Times*, August 6, 1980.

———. "Outdoor Dance in Its Adulthood." *New York Times*, July 31, 1998. <http://query.nytimes.com/gst/fullpage.html?res=9903E0D91238F932A05754C0A96E958260&scp=8&sq=site-specific+dance>, accessed January 23, 2008.

———. "Dance Moves Back to Nature." *New York Times*, July 30, 1999. <http://query.nytimes.com/gst/fullpage.html?res=9C0DE3D91431F933A05754C0A96F958260&scp=21&sq=sara+pearson+patrik+widrig>, accessed January 23, 2008.

———. "A Tradition of Dance That Graced the Shores of Manhattan." *New York Times*, June 1, 2005. <http://query.nytimes.com/gst/fullpage.html?res=9903E0D91238F932A05754C0A96E958260&scp=8&sq=site-specific+dance>, accessed January 23, 2008.

Felshin, Nina, ed. *But Is It Art? The Spirit of Art as Activism*. Seattle: Bay Press, 1995.

Fineberg, Jonathan. *Art since 1940: Strategies of Being*. New York: Harry N. Abrams, 1995.

Foster, Susan. *Reading Dancing: Bodies and Subjects in Contemporary American Dance*. Berkeley: University of California Press, 1986.

Frederick, Meghan. "Quick Takes in an Old Space on the Brooklyn Waterfront." *Village Voice*, September 27, 2005. <http://www.villagevoice.com/dance/0539,frederick,68252,14.html>, accessed January 25, 2008.

Galanter, Margit. "Little Glimmers." *Contact Quarterly* 32, no. 2 (Summer/Fall 2007): 45–46.

Gioia, Smid. *Off the Boards: Site-Specific Performance in the Netherlands*. Amsterdam: Theater Instituut Nederland, 1994.

Godfrey, DeWitt. "Maureen Brennan—Working the System: Red Tape, Bureaucracies, Permits, Insurance, Protocols, Parking, and Port-a-Potties." *Art Journal* 65, no. 1 (Spring 2006): 61–62.

Goldberg, RoseLee. *Performance: Live Art since 1960*. New York: Harry N. Abrams, 1998.

———. *Performance Art: From Futurism to the Present*. Rev. ed. New York: Thames & Hudson, 2001.

Goldsworthy, Andy. *Parkland*. Yorkshire: Yorkshire Sculpture Park, 1988.

Gottschild, Brenda Dixon, "Some Thoughts on Choreographing History." In *Meaning in Motion: New Cultural Studies of Dance*, ed. Jane Desmond, 167–77. Durham, N.C.: Duke University Press, 1987.

Grande, John K. *Art Nature Dialogues: Interviews with Environmental Artists*. Albany: State University of New York Press, 2004.

Halprin, Anna. "Community Art as Life Process." *Drama Review* 17, T-59 (1973): 64–80.

———. *Citydance 1977*. San Francisco: San Francisco Dancers' Workshop, 1977.

———. *Moving toward Life: Five Decades of Transformational Dance*. Edited by Rachel Kaplan. Hanover, N.H.: Wesleyan University Press/University Press of New England, 1995.

Halprin, Lawrence. *The RSVP Cycles: Creative Process in the Human Environment*. New York: George Braziller, 1969.

———. *Taking Part: A Workshop Approach to Collective Creativity*. Cambridge: MIT Press, 1974.

Henri, Adrian. *Total Art: Environments, Happenings, and Performance*. New York: Praeger, 1974.

Hiss, Tony. *The Experience of Place*. New York: Alfred A. Knopf, 1990.

Hobbs, Robert. *Robert Smithson: Retrospective*. Ithaca, N.Y.: Cornell University, Herbert F. Johnson Museum of Art, 1983.

Hobbs, Stuart D. *The End of the American Avant-Garde*. New York: New York University Press, 1997.

Houston, Andrew, ed. *Environmental and Site-Specific Theatre*. Toronto: Playwrights Canada Press, 2007.

Hunter, Victoria. "Embodying the Site: The Here and Now in Site-Specific Dance Performance." *New Theatre Quarterly* 21, no. 4 (November 2005): 367–81.

———. "Getting Lost: Site-Specific Performance and Re-Location (The Library Dances)." *Performance Research* 12, no. 2 (June 2007): 31–34.

Jarret, Sara. "Dance in Unlikely Places." *Dance Spirit* 9, no. 7 (September 2005): 157–59.

Johnson, Pamela, and Kathleen McLean, eds. *Art Performs Life: Cunningham/Monk/Jones*. Minneapolis: Walker Art Center, 1998.

Jowitt, Deborah. "'What Are They Up To?'" *New York Times*, August 29, 1971, D18.

———. "You Can Dance on Roofs, Too." *New York Times*, August 12, 1973, 130.

———. *Meredith Monk*. Baltimore: Johns Hopkins University Press, 1997.

———. "Monk and King: The Sixties Kids." In *Reinventing Dance in the 1960s*, ed. Sally Banes, 113–136. Madison: University of Wisconsin Press, 2003.

Kaprow, Allan. *Assemblage, Environments, and Happenings*. New York: Harry N. Abrams, 1996.

Kaye, Nick. *Postmodernism and Performance*. New York: St. Martin's Press, 1994.

———. *Art into Theatre: Performance Interviews and Documents*. London: Routledge, 1996.

———. *Site-Specific Art: Performance, Place, and Documentation*. London: Routledge, 2000.

Kirby, Michael. *Happenings*. New York: E. P. Dutton, 1965.

Kloetzel, Melanie. "Site Dance: A Deconstruction/Reconstruction of Community and Place." In *Dance & Community: Congress on Research in Dance,* ed. Ninotchka Bennahum and Tresa M. Randall, 130–37. Tallahassee: Florida State University, 2005.

Kloetzel, Melanie, and Carolyn Pavlik. "Reclaiming Place: Female Choreographers on Site." *In Dance* (October 2006): 6–7.

Kochar-Lindgren, Kanta. "Jennifer Monson: Multisensory Exploration of the Multidimensional Environment." *Art Journal* 65, no. 1 (Spring 2006): 71–72.

Kozel, Susan. "Reshaping Space: Focusing Time." *Dance Theatre Journal* 12, no. 2 (Autumn 1995): 3–7.

Kwon, Miwon. *One Place after Another: Site-Specific Art and Locational Identity*. Cambridge: MIT Press, 2002.

La Rocco, Claudia. "Creating a Dance from Scratch, with Even the Site (at First) Unseen." *New York Times*, August 19, 2006. <http://www.nytimes.com/2006/08/19/arts/dance/19spee.html?scp=5&sq=joanna+haigood>, accessed January 12, 2008.

Lacy, Suzanne, ed. *Mapping the Terrain: New Genre Public Art*. Seattle: Bay Press, 1995.

Lavery, Carl. "The Pepys of London E11: Graeme Miller and the Politics of *Linked*." *New Theatre Quarterly* 21, no. 2 (May 2005): 148–60.

LeFevre, Camille. "Site-Specific Dance: Dance as Big as All Outdoors." *Dance Magazine* 70, no. 4 (April 1996): 66–72.

———. "Site-Specific Dance, De-Familiarization, and the Transformation of Place and Community." In *Dance & Community: Congress on Research in Dance,* ed. Ninotchka Bennahum and Tresa M. Randall, 148–53. Tallahassee: Florida State University, 2005.

———. "Visible Fringe: What Is Site-Specific?" www.mnartists.org. (August 15, 2005).

Lippard, Lucy R. *Get the Message? A Decade of Art for Social Change*. New York: E. P. Dutton, 1984.

———. *The Lure of the Local*. New York: New Press, 1997.

———. *On the Beaten Track*. New York: New Press, 1999.

Mackey, Sally. "Performance, Place, and Allotments: 'Feast' or Famine?" *Contemporary Theatre Review* 17, no. 2 (May 2007): 181–91.

Matilsky, Barbara C. "The Survival of Culture and Nature: Perspectives on the History of Environmental Art." *Art & Design* 9 (May/June 1994): 6–15.

McAuley, Gay. "Place in the Performance Experience." *Modern Drama* 46, no. 4 (Winter 2003): 598–601.

———, ed. *Unstable Ground: Performance and the Politics of Place*. Brussels: P.I.E. Peter Lang, 2006.

———, ed. *Local Acts: Site-Based Performance Practices*. Sydney: Department of Performance Studies, University of Sydney, 2007.

McCall, Brendan. "Excursion: NYC (Metal)." *Contact Quarterly* 31, no. 2 (Summer/Fall 2006): 45–54.

McNamara, Brooks. "Vessel: The Scenography of Meredith Monk. An Interview." *Drama Review* 16, no. 1 (March 1972): 87–103.

Meyer, James. "The Functional Site; or, The Transformation of Site Specificity." In *Space, Site, Intervention*, ed. Erika Suderburg, 24–25. Minneapolis: University of Minnesota Press, 2000.

Miller, Graeme, interviewed by Carl Lavery. "Walking the Walk, Talking the Talk: Reimagining the Urban Landscape." *New Theatre Quarterly* 21, no. 2 (May 2005): 161–65.

Palmer, Robert. "Music: Hums and Birdcalls." *New York Times*, July 15, 1980.

Patrick, K. C. "Dancing outside the Frame." *Dance Magazine* 72, no. 9 (September 1998): 94.

Pavlik, Carolyn. "Into the Community: Site-Specific Dance Artists as Activists." In *Dance & Community: Congress on Research in Dance,* ed. Ninotchka Bennahum and Tresa M. Randall, 206–14. Tallahassee: Florida State University, 2005.

Paxton, Steve. "PASTForward Choreographers' Statements." In *Reinventing Dance in the 1960s,* ed. Sally Banes, 206–207. Madison: University of Wisconsin Press, 2003.

Pearson, Mike. *"In Comes I": Performance, Memory, and Landscape*. Exeter: Exeter University Press, 2006.

Pearson, Mike, and Michael Shanks. *Theatre/Archaeology: Disciplinary Dialogues*. London: Routledge, 2001.

Pearson, Mike, and Yang William. "You can't tell by looking . . ." In *On Maps and Mapping. Performance Research* 6, no. 2 (Summer 2001): 31–38.

Poynor, Helen, and Libby Worth. *Anna Halprin*. London: Routledge, 2004.

Rockwell, John. "'Breaking Ground': For Five Artists, an Experiment with Choreography on Deadline." *New York Times*, September 20, 2005. <http://www.nytimes.com/2005/09/20/arts/dance/20brea.html?scp=57&sq=site-specific+dance>, accessed January 15, 2008.

———. "On Governors Island, Holding the Fort with Footwork." *New York Times*, August 21, 2006. <http://www.nytimes.com/2006/08/21/arts/dance/21grou.html?scp=4&sq=joanna+haigood>, accessed January 12, 2008.

Ross, Janice. Introduction to *Moving toward Life*, by Anna Halprin, ed. Rachel Kaplan,

72–74. Hanover, N.H.: Wesleyan University Press/University Press of New England, 1995.

———. "Anna Halprin and the 1960s: Acting in the Gap between the Personal, the Public, and the Political." In *Reinventing Dance in the 1960s*, ed. Sally Banes, 24–50. Madison: University of Wisconsin Press, 2003.

———. *Anna Halprin: Experience as Dance*. Berkeley: University of California Press, 2007.

Rotkin, Joanna. "Under the Hood: Mind/Body/Car." *Contact Quarterly* 32, no. 2 (Summer/Fall 2007): 47–48.

Sanderson, Marcia. "Flying Women." *Dance Magazine* 76, no. 3 (March 2002): 46–52.

Sandford, Mariellen R., ed. *Happenings and Other Acts*. London: Routledge, 1995.

Seidel, Miriam. "Dancing in Place." *Public Art Review* 15, no. 1 (Fall/Winter 2003): 16–22.

Shteir, Rachel B. "Painting the Town." *American Theatre* 9, no. 6 (October 1992): 28.

Siegel, Marcia B. "Dancing on the Outside." *Hudson Review* 60, no. 1 (Spring 2007): 1–8.

Site-Specific, The Quay Thing Documented. Studies in Theatre and Performance, Supplement 5. Exeter: University of Exeter, 2000.

Solnit, Rebecca. *As Eve Said to the Serpent: On Landscape, Gender, and Art*. Athens: University of Georgia Press, 2001.

Steinberg, Janice. "Trolley Dancing." *Dance Magazine* 77, no. 10 (October 2003): 66.

Stephano, Effie. "Moving Structures." *Art & Artists* 8, no. 94 (January 1974): 16–21.

Stoops, Susan L. *More than Minimal*. Waltham, Mass.: Rose Art Museum, Brandeis University, 1996.

Storr, Robert. "No Stage, No Actors, but It's Theater (and Art)." *New York Times*, November 28, 1999. <http://query.nytimes.com/gst/fullpage.html?res=9A0CEEDF1E3CF93BA15752C1A96F958260&scp=257&sq=site-specific+dance>, accessed January 25, 2008.

Suderburg, Erika, ed. *Space, Site, Intervention: Situating Installation Art*. Minneapolis: University of Minnesota Press, 2000.

Swan, James A. *The Power of Place*. Wheaton, Ill.: Quest Books, 1991.

Tanaka, Jennifer. "Theatrics Out of Thin Air." *American Theatre* 16, no. 7 (September 1999): 24.

Teicher, Hendel, ed. *Trisha Brown: Dance and Art in Dialogue, 1961–2001*. Andover, Mass.: Addison Gallery of American Art, 2002.

Tuan, Yi-fu, et al. *Space and Place: The Perspective of Experience*. Minneapolis: University of Minnesota Press, 1977.

Turner, Cathy. "Palimpsest or Potential Space? Finding a Vocabulary for Site-Specific Performance." *New Theatre Quarterly* 80, no. 4 (November 2004): 373–90.

van der Kolk, Hana. "All at Once: Dancing *The Ridge* in New York City Parks." *Contact Quarterly* 32, no 1 (Winter/Spring 2007): 19–25.

Wakin, Daniel J. "Deadline Choreography." *New York Times*, September 14, 2005. <http://www.nytimes.com/2005/09/14/arts/dance/14stre.html?scp=6&sq=site-specific+dance>, accessed January 23, 2008.

Wilkie, Fiona. "Mapping the Terrain: A Survey of Site-Specific Performance in Britain," *New Theatre Quarterly* 18, no. 70 (May 2002): 140–60.

———. "Kinds of Place at Bore Place: Site-Specific Performance and the Rules of Spatial Behavior." *New Theatre Quarterly* 18, no. 71 (August 2002): 243–61.

———. "The Production of Site: Site-Specific Theatre." *A Concise Companion to Contemporary British and Irish Drama*, ed. Nadine Holdworth and Mary Luckhurst. Malden, Mass.: Blackwell, 2007.

Wilson, Meredith Lee. "Artistic Landscapes: Dancing beyond the Stage, an Investigation of 1960s Site-Specific Dance through the Choreography of Anna Halprin, Trisha Brown, and Twyla Tharp." MS thesis, Dominican University of California, 2006.

Wrights & Sites—Stephen Hodge, Simon Persighetti, Phil Smith, and Cathy Turner. *A Mis-Guide to Anywhere*. Exeter: Wrights & Sites, 2006.

Young, Thomas H. N. "Faceted Places: Accounting for Multiple Meanings in Site-Specific Performance." MA thesis, University of California, Riverside, 2002.

Zimmer, Elizabeth. "From the Field to a Garden: The Fascination of What's Difficult." *Village Voice*, August 16–22, 2000. <http://www.villagevoice.com/dance/0033,zimmer,17283,14.html>, accessed February 12, 2008.

———. "Minds of Summer: Old Fort Inspires Quick Sketches by Choreographers." *Village Voice*, August 25, 2006. <http://www.villagevoice.com/dance/0635,zimmer,74296,14.html>, accessed January 15, 2008.

Articles, Previews, and Reviews of Contributors' Work

Olive Bieringa and Otto Ramstad

Law, Kate. "Thinking Outside the Black Box: Site-Specific Artists Speak Their Minds." *In Dance,* September 2006.

LeFevre, Camille. "OnStage: Or, Rather, Not Quite on Stage." *Star Tribune*, September 14, 2007. <http://www.startribune.com/entertainment/onstage/11502391.html>, accessed February 12, 2008.

———. "On Location: The BodyCartography Project Talks about the Importance of Place." <http://www.mnartists.org/article.do?rid=174536>, January 7, 2008.

Morrison, Mandy. "Olive Bieringa of the BodyCartography Project." *New York Arts Magazine,* May 1, 2006.

Nelson, Robb. "Twisting the Night Away: Welcome to 'Holiday House.'" *Minnesota Post*, January 4, 2008. <http://www.minnpost.com/robnelson/2008/01/04/480/twisting_the_night_away_welcome_to_holiday_house>, accessed January 20, 2008.

Palmer, Caroline. "The Body Cartography Project: Artists of the Year." *Minneapolis./St. Paul City Pages*, January 2, 2008. <http://articles.citypages.com/2008–01–02/feature/body-cartography/>, accessed January 30, 2008.

Shapiro, Linda. "The Body Cartography Project." *Minneapolis/St. Paul City Pages,* January 2, 2008. <http://articles.citypages.com/2008–01–02/calendar/the-body-cartography-project/>, accessed January 30, 2008.

Somdahl-Sands, Katrinka. "Triptych: Dancing in Thirdspace." *Cultural Geographies* 13 (2006): 610–16.

Stevenson, Jenny. "Unique Dancing at Harbour Edge." *Dominion Post* (Wellington), March 5, 2001.

———. "BodyCartography Delights." *Dominion Post* (Wellington), March 10, 2003.

Martha Bowers

Anderson, Jack. "The Dance: Martha Bowers." *New York Times*, March 25, 1987. <http://query.nytimes.com/gst/fullpage.html?res=9B0DEFDD1731F936A15750C0A961948260&scp=5&sq=martha+bowers>, accessed January 12, 2008.

———. "Dance in Review: Dances for Wave Hill." *New York Times*, July 20, 1992. <http://query.nytimes.com/gst/fullpage.html?res=9E0CE7DF1738F933A15754C0A964958260&scp=23&sq=martha+bowers>, accessed January 12, 2008.

"Bringing Her Safely into Harbour." *Irish Times*, June 21, 2001.

Dunning, Jennifer. "Dancing, Chatting, Singing on Brooklyn's Waterfront." *New York Times*, September 14, 1998. <http://query.nytimes.com/gst/fullpage.html?res=9403E0D81531F937A2575AC0A96E958260&scp=9&sq=martha+bowers>, accessed January 12, 2008.

"Green-Wood Cemetery Presents 'Angels and Accordions' on Oct. 6." *Brooklyn Daily Eagle*, September 26, 2007.

<http://www.brooklyneagle.com/categories/category.php?category_id=13&id=15659>, accessed February 21, 2008.

Leland, Mary. "Safe Harbour." *Irish Times*, June 28, 2001.

Stenn, Rebecca. "Site-Specific Work Explores Past and Present of Red Hook." *Dance Magazine* 72, no. 9 (September 1998): 41–41.

Stern, Carrie. "When the Audience Is the Dance." *Brooklyn Daily Eagle*, October 20, 2006. <http://www.brooklyneagle.com/categories/category.php?category_id=12&id=9112>, accessed February 21, 2008.

Ann Carlson

Banes, Sally. "Choreographing Community: Dancing in the Kitchen." *Dance Chronicle* 25, no. 1 (2002): 143–61.

Carr, C. "Ghost Muster: Between the Image and the Reality Lies Ann Carlson." *Village Voice*, May 17–23, 2000. <http://www.villagevoice.com/news/0020,carr,14864,1.html>, accessed January 22, 2008.

Hamlin, Jesse. "History Comes to Life: Artist Stages Re-enactments of Old Photos at Yerba Buena Gardens." *San Francisco Chronicle*, July 7, 2002. <http://www.sfgate.com/cgi-bin/article.cgi?f=/c/a/2002/07/07/PK24430.DTL&hw=ann+carlson&sn=002&sc=87>, accessed February 21, 2008.

Lefevre, Camille. "Ann Carlson." *Dance Magazine* 63, no. 11 (December 1989): 78.

Perron, Wendy. "A Performance Piece Runs through It." *New York Times*, August 10, 2003. <http://query.nytimes.com/gst/fullpage.html?res=9F04EFD71E3EF933A2575BC0A9659C8B63&scp=150&sq=site-specific+dance>, accessed January 22, 2008.

Russo, Francine. "Walk This Way." *Village Voice*, May 24–30, 2000. <http://www.village-voice.com/theater/0021,russo2,15059,11.html>, accessed February 13, 2008.

Whitaker, Rick. "'Mirage.'" *Dance Magazine* 68, no. 12 (December 1994): 103–5.

Yung, Susan. "Installation Sites Its Set on a Mythological Montana Prairie." *Village Voice*, September 24–30, 2003. <http://www.villagevoice.com/dance/0339,footnotes,47247,14.html>, accessed February 13, 2008.

Heidi Duckler

Bleiberg, Laura. "Welcome Back to the Hotel California." *New York Times*, May 25, 2003. <http://query.nytimes.com/gst/fullpage.html?res=9807E4DB113EF936A15756C0A9659C8B63&scp=5&sq=heidi+duckler>, accessed January 28, 2008.

Dunning Jennifer. "In 'Laundromatinee,' Heidi Duckler Conjures Life, Loss, and Lint Traps." *New York Times*, July 25, 2006. <http://www.nytimes.com/2006/07/25/arts/25duck.html?scp=2&sq=heidi+duckler>, accessed January 25, 2008.

Farabee, Mindy. "The Perfect Place for the Show." *Los Angeles Times*, February 14, 2008. <http://theguide.latimes.com/performing-arts/latcl-the-perfect-place-for-the-show-article>, accessed February 19, 2008.

Kinetz, Erika. "All Units, We've Got Cops Dancing at the Academy." *New York Times*, February 5, 2006. <http://www.nytimes.com/2006/02/05/arts/dance/05kine.html?scp=4&sq=heidi+duckler>, accessed January 25, 2008.

Landgraf, H. "Location, Location, Location: Collage Dance Theatre Sets Work in the Where and Now." *Dance Magazine* 76, no.12 (December 2002): 74–77.

LeFevre, Camille. "On-Site Inventions: Heidi Duckler's Collage Dance Theatre." *The World and I* (November 1996).

———. "Dancing through Architecture" *LA Architect* (September/October 2005).

Looseleaf, Victoria. "Site Drives the Stories in 'C'opera.'" *Los Angeles Times,* February 11, 2006, E18.

———. "'My Beowulf' in Four Leaps." *Los Angeles Times*, July 28, 2007, E13.

Reynolds, Christopher. "Location . . . Location . . . Location." *Los Angeles Times*, May 8, 2003, E34.

Segal, Lewis. "And for the Next Course, a Dash of Dali." *Los Angeles Times*, April 2, 2004, E26.

———. "As If the Living Move among the Dead." *Los Angeles Times*, October 8, 2005, E6.

———. "An Unlikely Hero: 'Beowulf on Ice.'" *Los Angeles Times*, March 5, 2007, E2.

Joanna Haigood

Dunning, Jennifer. "Hope and Sanctuary on a Torturous Journey." *New York Times*, August 27, 1998. <http://query.nytimes.com/gst/fullpage.html?res=9803E6DD123CF934A1575BC0A96E958260&scp=10&sq=joanna+haigood>, accessed January 15, 2008.

———. "A Little Night Magic for the Past." *New York Times*, August 27, 2002.

<http://query.nytimes.com/gst/fullpage.html?res=9E06E1DD113CF934A1575BC0A96 49C8B63&scp=8&sq=joanna+haigood>, accessed January 15, 2008.

Felciano, Rita. "Hearing the Stories That Buildings Have to Tell." *New York Times*, August 23, 1998. <http://query.nytimes.com/gst/fullpage.html?res=9407E2DB143DF930A1 575BC0A96E958260&scp=9&sq=joanna+haigood>, accessed January 15, 2008.

Guthmann, Edward. "Haigood's Accustomed to Contrast." *San Francisco Chronicle*, May 13, 2007. <http://www.sfgate.com/cgi-bin/article.cgi?f=/c/a/2007/05/13/PKGL-GPMK3B1.DTL&hw=joanna+ haigood&sn=001&sc=1000>, accessed February 22, 2008.

Howard, Rachel. "Dance Takes Flight at S.F. Airport." *San Francisco Chronicle*, May 18, 2007. <http://www.sfgate.com/cgi-bin/article.cgi?f=/c/a/2007/05/18/DDGR-SPSEP01.DTL&hw=joanna+haigood&sn=003&sc=711>, accessed February 23, 2008.

Jowitt, Deborah. "Changing Places." *Village Voice*, September 4, 2007. <http://www.villagevoice.com/dance/0736,jowitt,77681,14.html>, accessed January 23, 2008.

Kisselgoff, Anna. "California Dreaming against Manhattan Backdrop." *New York Times*, August 3, 1993. <http://query.nytimes.com/gst/fullpage.html?res=9F0CE2DF1F3 DF930A3575BC0A965958260&scp=13&sq=joanna+haigood>, accessed January 15, 2008.

Kourlas, Gia. "Freedom Bound in Forest Dance." *New York Times*, August 20, 2007. <http://www.nytimes.com/2007/08/20/arts/dance/20wing.html?scp=1&sq =joanna+haigood>, accessed January 12, 2008.

Murphy, Ann. "Joanna Haigood." *Dance Theatre Journal* 11, no. 2 (Spring/Summer 1994): 18–20.

Perron, Wendy. "Way Up High, Soaring, Floating, Diving, Dancing." *New York Times*, August 18, 2002. <http://query.nytimes.com/gst/fullpage.html?res=9E06E1DE1E3 AF93BA2575BC0A9649C8B63&scp=7&sq=joanna+haigood>, accessed January 15, 2008.

———. "Flight to Freedom." *Dance Magazine* 81, no. 8 (August 2007): 22.

Ritter, Peter. "Since When Has Tumbling Off a 120-Foot Grain Silo Been a Form of Modern Dance? Joanna Haigood's Flying Circus." *Minnesota/St. Paul City Pages*, August 23, 2000. <http://articles.citypages.com/2000-08-23/arts/joanna-haigood-s-flying-circus/>, accessed January 28, 2008.

Sulcas, Roslyn. "'Invisible Wings': Under the Night Sky, a Vivid History Lesson." *New York Times*, August 23, 2007. <http://www.nytimes.com/2007/08/23/arts/dance/23pill. html?scp=2&sq=joanna+haigood>, accessed January 12, 2008.

Scherr, Apollinaire. "Stage: Broken Wings." *San Francisco Weekly*, July 29, 1998. <http://www.sfweekly.com/1998-07-29/culture/stage/full>, accessed January 20, 2008.

Troup, Christina. "SF's International Arts Festival Takes Flight." *San Francisco Examiner*, May 16, 2007.

Marylee Hardenbergh

LeFevre, Camille. "Makers Who Mattered in 1995—Artists of the Year: Mary Lee Hardenbergh." *Minnesota./St.Paul City Pages*, December 27, 1995. <http://articles.citypages.com/1995-12-27/news/artists-of-the-year/>, accessed January 29, 2008.

———. "Celestial Rhythms: Site Dance as Ritual." *Ruminator Review,* Winter 2003–4.

———. "Riverfront Awakening." *Architecture Minnesota* 31, no. 4 (July/August 2005): 44–48.

"Solstice River XI: Honoring Sacred Sites on the Mississippi." *Edge Life,* July 2007. <http://edgelife.net/article.php?id=0755>, accessed February 23, 2008.

Sally Jacques

Buchholz, Brad. "Angels in Our Midst." *Austin American-Statesman*, May 31, 2006, <http://www.austin360.com/arts/content/arts/stories/xl/2006/06/1cover.html>, accessed August 8, 2008.

Davis, Dawn. "Body Count: To Remember and Forget." *Austin Chronicle*, December 10, 1999. <http://www.austinchronicle.com/gyrobase/Issue/review?oid=oid:74960>, accessed January 25, 2008.

———. "The Blue Pearl: A Heartrending, Joyous Affirmation of Life." *Austin Chronicle*, June 30, 2000. <http://www.austinchronicle.com/gyrobase/Issue/review?oid=oid%3A77718>, accessed January 25, 2008.

Faires, Robert. "The Well Inside: Melancholy and Awe 20 Feet Up." *Austin Chronicle*, May 24, 2002. <http://www.austinchronicle.com/gyrobase/Issue/review?oid=oid%3A93175>, accessed January 25, 2008.

———. "Where Nothing Falls II." *Austin Chronicle*, June 25, 2004. <http://www.austinchronicle.com/gyrobase/Issue/review?oid=oid:217523>, accessed January 25, 2008.

———. "Whispers of Heaven." *Austin Chronicle*, June 24, 2005. <http://www.austinchronicle.com/gyrobase/Issue/review?oid=oid:276227>, accessed January 25, 2008.

———. "Requiem." *Austin Chronicle*, June 16, 2006. <http://www.austinchronicle.com/gyrobase/Issue/review?oid=oid:375801>, accessed January 25, 2008.

———. "Risk for Beauty." *Austin Chronicle*, June 15, 2007. <http://www.austinchronicle.com/gyrobase/Issue/story?oid=oid:492025>, accessed January 25, 2008.

———. "Illumination." *Austin Chronicle*, October 19, 2007. <http://www.austinchronicle.com/gyrobase/Issue/review?oid=oi d:551880>, accessed January 25, 2008.

Goldman, Saundra. "Art and the Public." *Art Papers* 16, no. 6 (November/December 1993): 12–15.

Hamilton-Lynne, Deborah. "Requiem Reprise: Urban Eyesore Transformed into Concrete Cathedral." *Austin Woman Magazine,* October 2006, 66–68.

Pineo, Barry. "Requiem: Making Beauty on an Eyesore." *Austin Chronicle*, June 9, 2006. <http://www.austinchronicle.com/gyrobase/Issue/story?oid=oid:373220>, accessed January 25, 2008.

Stephan Koplowitz

Anderson, Jack. "Troupe Performs among the Dinosaurs and Such." *New York Times*, May 20, 1989. <http://query.nytimes.com/gst/fullpage.html?res=950DE4DC113FF933A1 5756C0A96F948260&scp=283&sq=site-specific+dance>, accessed January 22, 2008.

———. "At Lincoln Center, Folk Dance in a Village Square (Sort Of)." *New York Times*, October 17, 2001. <http://query.nytimes.com/gst/fullpage.html?res=980DE6DC16 3EF934A25753C1A9679C8B63&scp=133&sq=site-specific+dance>, accessed January 22, 2008.

Campbell, Karen. "In Choreographer's New Dance, a Tour of the ICA." *Boston Globe*, July 27, 2007, E4.

Dekle, Nicole. "Ground-Controlled Approach." *Dance Magazine* 65, no. 9 (September 1991): 34.

Gilbert, Jenny. "Quiet Please! People Are Dancing." *Independent* (London), November 15, 1998, 6.

Harris, William. "Shaping a Marathon of Dance That Was Inspired by the Web." *New York Times*, September 14, 1997. <http://query.nytimes.com/gst/fullpage.html?res=9B07E 7DC1439F937A2575AC0A961958260&scp=224&sq=site-specific+dance>, accessed January 22, 2008.

Jowitt, Deborah. "Climbing and Cornering." *Village Voice*, June 22, 2004. <http://www. villagevoice.com/dance/0425,jowitt,54464,14.html>, accessed January 22, 2008.

Mackrell, Judith. "Babel Index: Sparkling Ballade of Reading's Goal." *Guardian* (London), November 13, 1998, 2.

Meisner, Nadine. "Off the Shelf." *Sunday Times* (London), November 8, 1998.

Menotti, Andrea. "All Aboard! Stephan Koplowitz Does Windows." *Village Voice*, October 13–19, 1999. <http://www.villagevoice.com/dance/9941,menotti,8965,14.html>, accessed January 22, 2008.

Mickelson, Angela. "Site Lines." *Dance Spirit* 8, no. 10 (2004): 78–81.

Perron, Wendy. "Step by Step." *Dance Magazine* 78, no. 6 (June 2004): 24.

Reardon, Christopher. "Doing Double Duty: Stephan Koplowitz, Teacher/Choreographer." *Dance Magazine* 77, no. 11 (November 2003): 44–49.

Robertson, Allen. "Barefoot in Jurassic Park." *Times* (London), September 25, 1996.

Yarrow, Andrew L. "Adventurous Performers in Unexpected Places." *New York Times*, October 9, 1987. <http://query.nytimes.com/gst/fullpage.html?res=9B0DE2D8133C F 93AA35753C1A961948260&scp=304&sq=site-specific+dance>, accessed January 22, 2008.

Jo Kreiter

Felciano, Rita. "Stage: 'Mission Wall Dances.'" *San Francisco Bay Guardian*, September 11, 2002. <http://www.sfbg.com/36/50/art_stage_dances.html>, accessed January 23, 2008.

———. "Flyaway Productions: Physically Risky and Socially Relevant." *San Francisco Bay Guardian*, September 12, 2007. <http://www.sfbg.com/entry.php?entry_id=4485&catid=85>, accessed February 21, 2008.

Garofoli, Joe. "Remember the Gartland! Wall Dancers Invoke Deadly '75 Fire as Rallying Cry for Affordable Housing." *San Francisco Chronicle*, September 14, 2002. <http://www.sfgate.com/cgi-bin/article.cgi?f=/c/a/2002/09/14/BA221263.DTL&hw=jo+kreiter&sn=003&sc=429>, accessed February 21, 2008.

Howard, Rachel. "Aerial Dance Rising." *San Francisco Chronicle*, January 18, 2004. <http://www.sfgate.com/cgi-bin/article.cgi?f=/c/a/2004/01/18/PKGTA45O4N1.DTL&hw=jo+kreiter&sn=006&sc=324>, accessed February 21, 2008.

———. "Dancers Blandly Animate Feminist Billboard." *San Francisco Chronicle*, October 13, 2006. <*http://www.sfgate.com/cgi-bin/article.cgi?f=/c/a/2006/10/13/DDGV9LNONS1.DTL&hw=jo+kreiter&sn=002&sc=786*>, accessed February 21, 2008.

Knight, Heather. "Flyaway Dance Troupe Simply Off the Wall: Aerial Artists Believe All the Ceiling's a Stage." *San Francisco Chronicle*, March 29, 2002. <http://www.sfgate.com/cgi-bin/article.cgi?f=/c/a/2002/03/29/WB150223.DTL&hw=jo+kreiter&sn=001&sc=1000>, accessed February 21, 2008.

Murphy, Ann. "Flying High: Jo Kreiter Speaks Softly but Swings from a Big Stick." *San Francisco Weekly*, April 4, 2001. <http://www.sfweekly.com/2001-04-04/culture/flying-high/full>, accessed January 15, 2008.

Nataraj, Nirmala. "Pants on Fire." *San Francisco Weekly*, September 12, 2007. <http://www.sfweekly.com/2007-09-12/calendar/pants-on-fire/full>, accessed February 1, 2008.

Vasilyuk, Sasha. "All Aboard for SF Trolley Dances." *San Francisco Examiner*, October 17, 2007. <http://www.examiner.com/a-994924~All_aboard_for_SF_Trolley_Dances.html>, accessed January 23, 2008.

Witherell, Amanda. "Does Beauty Ravish You?" *San Francisco Bay Guardian*, October 9, 2006. <http://www.sfbg.com/blogs/gsf/2006/10/does_beauty_ravish_you.html>, accessed February 21, 2008.

Meredith Monk

Anderson, Jack. "Roosevelt Island as a Stage." *New York Times*, September 26, 1994. <http://query.nytimes.com/gst/fullpage.html?res=9B00E3DB133AF935A1575ACoA962958260&scp=6&sq=meredith+monk+archeology>, accessed January 23, 2008.

———. "Entering a World Only Meredith Monk Can Map." *New York Times*, June 16, 1996. <http://query.nytimes.com/gst/fullpage.html?res=9E03E4DF1439F935A25755CoA960958260&scp=5&sq=meredith+monk+VESSEL>, accessed January 23, 2008.

Banes, Sally. "The Art of Meredith Monk." *Performing Arts Journal* 3, no. 1 (Spring 1978): 3–18.

Dalva, Nancy. "American Archaeology #1." *Dance Magazine* 68, no. 12 (December 1994): 110–11.

Dunning, Jennifer. "Meredith Monk Looks into Roosevelt Island's Past." *New York Times*, September 22, 1994. <http://query.nytimes.com/gst/fullpage.html?res=9F02E5DA17 3AF931A1575AC0A962958260&scp=1&sq=meredith+monk+archeology>, accessed January 23, 2008.

Jowitt, Deborah. "Take a Trip with Monk." *New York Times*, January 13, 1974, 115.

Kisselgoff, Anna. "Events Complement Nonevents in Dance by Meredith Monk." *New York Times*, November 5, 1968, 56.

———. "Song and Dance to Blend at Guggenheim." *New York Times*, November 7, 1969, 36.

———. "Guggenheim Offers a Setting for 'Juice,' Dance by Miss Monk." *New York Times*, November 8, 1969, 37.

———. "Cantata by Monk Unfolds Further." *New York Times*, December 1, 1969, 60.

———. "'Juice,' 3-Part Work by Meredith Monk, Comes to a Finish." *New York Times*, December 9, 1969, 67.

Eiko and Koma Otake

Anderson, Jack. "Images of Devastating Grief And the Courage to Go On." *New York Times*, July 19, 2002. <http://query.nytimes.com/gst/fullpage.html?res=9503E5DA 1039F93AA25754C0A9649C8B63&scp=6&sq=eiko+and+koma+river>, accessed January 25, 2008.

Asantewaa, Eva Yaa. "'Tree Song.'" *Dance Magazine* 78, no. 10 (October 2004): 92–94.

Dunning, Jennifer. "A Nuanced Production with Nature as Co-Star." *New York Times*, September 11, 1995. <http://query.nytimes.com/gst/fullpage.html?res=990CE0D914 3AF932A2575AC0A963958260&scp=5&sq=eiko+and+koma+river>, accessed January 25, 2008.

———. "A Landscape's Darkness Illuminated by a Nude." *New York Times*, June 8, 1998. <http://query.nytimes.com/gst/fullpage.html?res=9507E2DE173AF93BA35755C0A 96E958260&scp=36&sq=eiko+and+koma>, accessed January 25, 2008.

———. "For Primal Duo, the Memories of Trees Hold No Terror." *New York Times*, July 14, 2003. <http://query.nytimes.com/gst/fullpage.html?res=9E0CE2DC163CF937 A25754C0A9659C8B63&scp=1&sq=eiko+and+koma+tree+song>, accessed January 25, 2008.

Gladstone, Valerie. "Like a Painting in Slow Motion." *New York Times*, May 24, 1998. <http://query.nytimes.com/gst/fullpage.html?res=990CEFD61739F937A15756C0 A96E958260&scp=32&sq=eiko+and+koma>, accessed January 25, 2008.

Jowitt, Deborah. "Dancing in Tune with the Earth: Eiko & Koma Take 'Cambodian Stories' on Their Latest Tour." *Dance Magazine* 80, no. 4 (April 2006): 42–45.

———. "Expecting the Expected: For Pilobolus and Eiko & Koma, Bodies Grow Together." *Village Voice*, June 30, 2003. <http://www.villagevoice.com/dance/0327,jowitt,45217,14. html>, accessed January 25, 2008.

———. "Matters of Life and Death." *Village Voice*, June 7, 2004. <http://www.villagevoice.com/dance/0423,jowitt,54115,14.html>, accessed January 25, 2008.

Reiter, Susan. "Slow Dancing in a Portable Universe: 'The Caravan Project.'" *Village Voice*, August 18–24, 1999. <http://www.villagevoice.com/dance/9933,reiter,7663,14.html>, accessed January 25, 2008.

Zimmer, Elizabeth. "Sacred Spaces." *Village Voice*, July 24–30, 2002. <http://www.villagevoice.com/dance/0230,zimmer,36790,14.html>, accessed January 25, 2008.

Sara Pearson and Patrik Widrig

Anderson, Jack. "Stroll around the Grounds, Mindful of the Sprinklers." *New York Times*, July 17, 2001. <http://query.nytimes.com/gst/fullpage.html?res=9403E5DE113BF934A25754C0A9679C8B63&scp=2&sq=sara+pearson+patrik+widrig>, accessed January 28, 2008.

Brozan, Nadine. "Chronicle." *New York Times*, July 29, 1996. <http://query.nytimes.com/gst/fullpage.html?res=9A01E3DD1439F93AA15754C0A960958260&scp=15&sq=sara+pearson+patrik+widrig>, accessed January 28, 2008.

Dolan, Rachel Leigh. "Dancing on Water." *Dance Magazine* 81, no. 8 (August 2007): 93.

Henderson, Heidi. "Nightmare and Romance: Partnering Place: Interview with Sara Pearson and Patrik Widrig." *Contact Quarterly* 31, no. 2 (Summer/Fall 2006): 40–44.

Kourlas, Gia. "Travelers on a Multitude of Ice-Filled Journeys." *New York Times*, March 18, 2005. <http://www.nytimes.com/2005/03/18/arts/dance/18pear.html?_r=1&scp=1&sq=pearsonwidrig&oref=slogin>, accessed by January 28, 2008.

Sperling, Jody. "Sara Pearson/Patrik Widrig and Company—'Under the Rainbow.'" *Dance Magazine* 75, no. 11 (November 2001): 80–81.

Wells, Roseanne. "'To New Orleans, with Love.'" *Dance Magazine* 80, no. 6 (June 2006): 130.

Zimmer, Elizabeth. "Full and Empty." *Village Voice*, August 1–7, 2001. <http://www.villagevoice.com/dance/0131,footnotes,26813,14.html>, accessed January 28, 2008.

Tamar Rogoff

Anderson, Jack. "The City Becomes a Stage, and Part of the Action." *New York Times*, August 3, 1997. <http://query.nytimes.com/gst/fullpage.html?res=9806E0DA103AF930A3575BC0A961958260&scp=24&sq=tamar+rogoff>, accessed January 12, 2008.

Dunning, Jennifer. "'Angle of Ascent,' Creative Time Collage." *New York Times*, August 20, 1989. <http://query.nytimes.com/gst/fullpage.html?res=950DE4D71030F933A1575BC0A96F948260&scp=43&sq=tamar+rogoff>, accessed January 12, 2008.

Gonzalez, David. "Persephone, True Daughter of the City." *New York Times*, July 2, 1997. <http://query.nytimes.com/gst/fullpage.html?res=9404EEDA1430F931A35754C0A961958260&scp=23&sq=tamar+rogoff>, accessed January 12, 2008.

Korey, Sharyn. "On the Streets, in the Forest: Community-Based Site Work with Tamar Rogoff." *Contact Quarterly* 32, no. 1 (Winter/Spring 2007): 26–32.

Sloat, Susanna. "'The Ivye Project'—Tamar Rogoff." *Attitude* 11, no. 1 (Spring 1995): 52–53.

Stein, Bonnie Sue. "Tamar Rogoff: In the Woods of Ivye, Belarus, Near a Memorial to Holocaust Victims." *Dance Magazine* 68, no. 12 (December 1994): 90–91.

Thom, Rose Anne. "New York City: Tamar Rogoff Performance Projects." *Dance Magazine* 71, no. 10 (October 1997): 102.

Zimmer, Elizabeth. "Under the Gun." *Village Voice*, August 11–17, 2004. <http://www.villagevoice.com/dance/0432,zimmer2,55822,14.html>, accessed January 20, 2008.

Leah Stein

Ackerman, Robert. "Critical Mass/Dance: Jamie Avins/Leah Stein & Jeanne Jaffe." *Philadelphia City Paper*, December 7–14, 1995. <http://www.citypaper.net/articles/120795/article014.shtml>, accessed January 28, 2008.

———. "Critic Pick/Dance: Leah Stein Dance Company." *Philadelphia City Paper*, November 30–December 7, 2000. <http://www.citypaper.net/articles/113000/cw.pick.leah.shtml>, accessed February 2, 2008.

Anderson, Janet. "Places, Everyone!" *Philadelphia City Paper*, September 2–8, 2004. <http://www.citypaper.net/articles/2004–09–02/cover4.shtml>, accessed February 1, 2008.

———. "Bigger, Better." *Philadelphia City Paper*, November 21, 2006. <http://www.citypaper.net/articles/2006/11/23/Bigger-Better>, accessed February 1, 2008.

Apter, Kelly. "Dance the Light Fantastic." *Scotsman*, August 8, 2001, 9.

Brennan, Mary. "Dance Base." *Herald* (Glasgow), August 2, 2001, 24.

———. "Dance in Situ Dance Base." *Herald*, August 16, 2001, 16.

Goldner, Nancy. "A Moving Experience for Both Troupe and Its Audience in Fairmount Park." *Philadelphia Inquirer*, May 21, 1993, 14.

Hill, Lori. "The Next Stage." *Philadelphia City Paper*, September 1–7, 2005. <http://www.citypaper.net/articles/2005–09–01/cover.shtml>, accessed January 28, 2008.

Kasdorf, Anne. "Stepping Out of the Theater." *Dance Spirit* 11, no. 10 (December 2007): 82–83.

Kasrel, Deni. "Leah Stein Dance Co." *Philadelphia City Paper*, June 5, 2007. <http://www.citypaper.net/articles/2007/06/07/leah-stein-dance-co>, accessed February 1, 2008.

Shuck Morais, Amy. "Garden Parties—Sneakers in the Grass." *Philadelphia City Paper*, May 17–24, 2001. <http://www.citypaper.net/articles/051701/ae.dance.grass.sht ml>, accessed February 1, 2008.

Warner, David. "Great Leaps." *Philadelphia City Paper*, June 8–15, 2000. <http://www.citypaper.net/articles/060800/cov.dancepreview.shtml>, accessed February 1, 2008.

Wilde, Anastacia. "Dancing in the Rain." *Philadelphia City Paper*, August 1–7, 2002. <http://www.citypaper.net/articles/2002–08–01/art.shtml>, accessed February 1, 2008.

Articles, Previews, and Reviews of Other Notable Site-Specific Dance Choreographers

Noemie Lafrance

Anderson, Jack. "The Parking Attendant Always Rings Twice." *New York Times*, May 2, 2004. <http://query.nytimes.com/gst/fullpage.html?res=9D00E0D6113AF931A357 56C0A9629C8B63&scp=44&sq=site-specific+dance>, accessed January 14, 2008.

Dunning, Jennifer. "Thugs, Molls, and Murder in a Garage." *New York Times*, May 26, 2004. <http://query.nytimes.com/gst/fullpage.html?res=9B07E2D7143EF935A1575 6C0A9629C8B63&scp=8&sq=site-specific+dance>, accessed January 14, 2008.

Jowitt, Deborah. "Take Me Out—Two Choreographers Make the City Their Stage." *Village Voice*, September 26, 2006. <http://www.villagevoice.com/dance/0639,jowitt,74590,14. html >, accessed January 23, 2008.

Kourlas, Gia. "The Shuffles and Strides of Window Dancing." *New York Times*, May 7, 2005. <http://www.nytimes.com/2005/05/07/arts/dance/00noem.html?scp=77&sq=site-specific+dance>, accessed January 14, 2008.

Kurutz, Steve. "Not Quite Nudes Descending a Staircase." *New York Times*, December 7, 2003. <http://query.nytimes.com/gst/fullpage.html?res=9E04E5DC123DF934A357 51C1A9659C8B63&scp=212&sq=site-specific+dance>, accessed January 14, 2008.

Myers, Rebecca. "Choreographing Community." *Time*, October 2, 2006, 71–72.

Rockwell, John. "Going for a Waterless Dip with Roller Skaters, Bikers, and Superstars." *New York Times*, September 15, 2005. <http://www.nytimes.com/2005/09/15/arts/dance/15noem.html?scp=31&sq=site-specific+dance>, accessed January 14, 2008.

Sommer, Sally R. "Everybody into the Pool (and Dance)." *New York Times*, September 4, 2005. <http://www.nytimes.com/2005/09/04/arts/dance/04somm. html?scp=23&sq=site-specific+dance>, accessed January 14, 2008.

Amelia Rudolph

Ermachild, Melody. "Project Bandaloop." *High Performance*, no. 58/59 (Summer/Fall 1992): 44–45.

Foster, Catherine. "Soaring High above the Earth, Bandaloop Knows the Ropes." *Boston Globe*, May 7, 2006, N7.

Solomon, Deborah. "Air Ballet." *New York Times*, August 5, 2001. <http://query.nytimes. com/gst/fullpage.html?res=9502EEDC113DF936A3575BC0A9679C8B63&scp=1&s q=bandaloop>, accessed January 25, 2008.

Yim, Roger. "Dances with Mountains." *San Francisco Chronicle*, May 23, 2001. <http:// www.sfgate.com/cgi-bin/article.cgi?f=/c/a/2001/05/23/DD228682.DTL&hw=band aloop&sn=001&sc=1000>, accessed February 21, 2008.

Web Sites

www.bluelapislight.org (Sally Jacques)
www.bodycartography.org (Olive Bieringa and Otto Ramstad)
www.camillelefevre.com (Camille LeFevre)
www.collagedancetheatre.org (Heidi Duckler)
www.creativetime.org (Creative Time)
www.dancetheatreetcetera.org (Martha Bowers)
www.dancinginthestreets.org (Dancing in the Streets)
www.eikoandkoma.org (Eiko and Koma Otake)
www.flyawayproductions.com (Jo Kreiter)
www.globalsiteperformance.org (Marylee Hardenbergh)
www.koplowitzprojects.com (Stephan Koplowitz)
www.leahsteindancecompany.org (Leah Stein)
www.meredithmonk.org (Meredith Monk)
www.pearsonwidrig.org (Sara Pearson and Patrik Widrig)
www.projectbandaloop.org (Project Bandaloop)
www.sensproduction.org (Noemie Lafrance)
www.zaccho.org (Joanna Haigood)

Index

Page numbers in *italics* indicate photographs and illustrations.